Taxcafe.co.uk Tax Guides

Salary versus Dividends

How to Extract Company Profits and Cut Your Tax Bill By Thousands

By Carl Bayley BSc ACA

Important Legal Notices

Taxcafe®
TAX GUIDE – "Salary versus Dividends"

Published by:
Taxcafe UK Limited
67 Milton Road
Kirkcaldy
KY1 1TL
Tel: (01592) 560081
Email address: team@taxcafe.co.uk

Ninth Edition   July 2008

ISBN 1 904608 83 3

Disclaimer
Before reading or relying on the content of this Tax Guide, please read
carefully the disclaimer on the last page which applies. If you have
queries then please contact the publisher at team@taxcafe.co.uk.

About the Author

Carl Bayley is the author of a series of tax guides designed specifically for the layman. Carl's particular speciality is his ability to take the weird, complex and inexplicable world of taxation and set it out in the kind of clear, straightforward language that taxpayers themselves can understand. As he often says himself, "my job is to translate 'tax' into English".

Carl enjoys his role as a tax author, as he explains: "Writing these guides gives me the opportunity to use the skills and knowledge learned over more than twenty years in the tax profession for the benefit of a wider audience. The most satisfying part of my success as an author is the chance to give the average person the same standard of advice as the 'big guys' at a price which everyone can afford."

Carl takes the same approach when speaking on taxation, a role he frequently undertakes with great enthusiasm, including his highly acclaimed annual 'Budget Breakfast' for the Institute of Chartered Accountants. In addition to being a recognised author and speaker on the subject, Carl has often spoken on taxation on radio and television, including the BBC's 'It's Your Money' programme and BBC Radio 2's Jeremy Vine Show.

Carl began his career as a Chartered Accountant in 1983 with one of the 'Big 4' accountancy firms. After qualifying as a double prize-winner, he immediately began specialising in taxation. After honing his skills with several major international firms, Carl began the new millennium by launching his own tax and accounting practice, Bayley Miller Limited, through which he provides advice on a wide variety of taxation issues; especially tax planning for small and medium-sized businesses, property taxation and Inheritance Tax planning.

Carl is a member of the governing Council of the Institute of Chartered Accountants in England and Wales and a former Chairman of the Institute Members in Scotland group. He has co-organised the annual Peebles Tax Conference for the last six years.

When he isn't working, Carl takes on the equally taxing challenges of hill walking and writing poetry and fiction. Carl lives in Scotland with his partner Isabel and has four children.

Dedication

For the Past,

Firstly, I dedicate this book to the memory of those I have loved and lost:

First of all, to my beloved mother Diana – what would you think if you could see me now? The memory of your love warms me still. Thank you for making it all possible;

To my dear grandfather, Arthur - your wise words still come back to guide me; and to my loving grandmothers, Doris and Winifred; between you, you left me with nothing I could spend, but everything I need.

Also to my beloved friend and companion, Dawson, who waited so patiently for me to come home every night and who left me in the middle of our last walk together. Thank you for all those happy miles; I still miss you son.

For the Present,

Above all, I must dedicate this book to the person who stands, like a shining beacon, at the centre of every part of my life: Isabel, my 'life support system', whose unflinching support has seen me through the best and the worst. Whether anyone will ever call me a 'great man' I do not know, but I do know that I have a great woman behind me.

Without her help, support and encouragement, this book, and the others I have written, could never have been.

For the Future,

Finally, I also dedicate this book to four very special young people: Michelle, Louise, James and Robert. I am so very proud of every one of you and I can only hope that I, in turn, will also be able to leave each of you with everything that you need.

Thanks

First and foremost, I must say an enormous thank you to Isabel: for all her help researching everything from obscure points of tax legislation to popular girls' names in Asia; for reading countless drafts; for making sure I stop to eat and sleep; for putting up with me when I'm under pressure and, most of all, for keeping me company into the 'wee small hours' on many a long and otherwise lonely night. I simply cannot ever thank her enough for everything that she does for me, but I intend to spend the rest of my life trying!

The next biggest thanks have to go to my good friend, colleague and 'comrade-in-arms', Nick, who believed in me long before I did. Thanks for keeping the faith mate.

Thanks to the rest of the Taxcafe team for their help in making these books far more successful than I could ever have dreamed.

I would like to thank my old friend and mentor, Peter Rayney, for his inspiration and for showing me that tax and humour can mix.

And last, but far from least, thanks to Ann for keeping us right!

C.B., Roxburghshire, July 2008

Contents

Contents

Contents

Contents

Contents

Chapter 1

Introduction

1.1 WHY IS THE SALARY OR DIVIDEND QUESTION SO IMPORTANT?

For many years, one of the most frequently asked questions in tax planning has been "Salary or Dividend?"

The question arises whenever the 'shareholder/director' (or 'owner/manager') of a small or medium-sized company wishes to extract funds from their business as tax efficiently as possible.

On the face of it, it may seem like a fairly simple question. Like so many apparently simple questions in the tax world, however, the number of factors which need to be taken into account render the answer quite complex.

In fact, the complexity of this issue is matched only by its importance, as thousands of pounds are often at stake.

Unlike most other people, shareholder/directors are in the fortunate position of wearing two caps. On the one hand, they can reward their efforts as an employee with salary or a bonus; on the other they can reward their entrepreneurship with a dividend.

The good news is that, to a large extent, you can often decide how you would like any distribution of the company's money to its owner to be classified.

Tax savings will be a prime consideration, but there are many other factors which may also influence your decision.

In recent years, the 'Salary versus Dividends' issue has taken on more importance than ever, owing to significant increases in the rates of both Corporation Tax and National Insurance.

Salaries and bonuses are subject to National Insurance, but are usually eligible for Corporation Tax relief. In other words, the company can usually deduct salaries and bonuses in arriving at its taxable profits.

Dividends are not subject to National Insurance, but must be paid out of the profits remaining *after* the company has paid its Corporation Tax bill.

The importance of Corporation Tax relief has increased significantly in recent years with the abolition of the 0% starting rate in 2006 followed by further increases to the small companies rate of Corporation Tax over a three year period from 2007 to 2009.

These latest changes will bring further total increases of up to 16% to small and medium-sized companies' Corporation Tax bills between 2007 and 2009 on top of the increases already faced by many smaller companies in the previous three years.

Worse still, we are now threatened with new legislation aimed at so-called 'income shifting' which may deem the dividends paid to one person to belong to another person for tax purposes. Thankfully, this new legislation will not apply until at least 6th April 2009, so company owners still have a few months to plan their affairs tax efficiently before the Government hammers yet another nail into the coffin labelled 'Small Business in Britain'.

(We will take a closer look at the potential impact of the proposed 'income shifting' legislation in Section 16.2 at the end of the guide.)

Against this background of a seemingly ever-changing taxation regime over the last few years, the 'Salary versus Dividends' question continues to be a vital part of tax planning for the vast majority of company owners.

In fact, what many business owners don't realise is that structuring company distributions carefully by making the optimum split between dividend and salary or bonus can make an enormous difference to their net personal income.

In many cases, a company owner may obtain a significantly higher after-tax income than a regular employee earning a higher before-tax salary.

In this guide, we will examine the complex, but important, 'Salary versus Dividends' question in detail. We will deal with each of the important taxation factors which need to be considered in turn and then proceed to provide an overview of the possible answers.

In short, we will take a journey through all of the complexities involved in the question in order to arrive at a simple summary of the possible answers.

Having dealt with the 'Salary versus Dividend' issue, we will then progress to looking at a third alternative use of company money – reinvestment for capital growth.

Despite the abolition of taper relief on 6th April 2008, we still have a Capital Gains Tax regime in the UK which is potentially extremely generous for small company owners. Firstly, there is the fact that Capital Gains Tax is now charged at a single flat rate of just 18%, no matter how high your income may be. Secondly, most small company owners can sell their company after just one year of trading and be exempt from tax on almost half of their capital growth.

In this sense, selling a company may be regarded as a means of converting taxable income (i.e. your future salary and business profits) into capital gains which are taxed at a considerably lower rate.

Finally, we will look at some additional factors which should be considered before making the all-important 'Salary or Dividend' decision, and also a number of special cases where some recent developments in tax law will need to be addressed.

1.2   WHICH COMPANIES ARE AFFECTED?

The 'Salary or Dividend' question is relevant to every company owner wishing to extract money from their business. In fact, we will even see some situations where additional salary or a dividend may itself be used as a tax planning tool, even when the director has no actual desire to remove funds from the company.

Let's face it though; most company owners are going to have to take some money out of their company in most years – so why not do it tax efficiently?

The vast majority of the principles explored in this guide will be equally valid for trading companies or investment companies. Only the occasional foray into Capital Gains Tax or Inheritance Tax will give rise to any differences.

Most property investment companies, for example, will be subject to the same Corporation Tax rates as a trading company and their directors will be taxed on salary, bonuses or dividends in just the same way as if these had been received from a trading company.

A few investment companies will, however, be classed as a 'Close Investment Holding Company'. This does lead to some important differences, which we will look at in Section 9.7.

1.3 MARGINAL RATES AND THE INEVITABLE TRADE-OFF

What makes the 'Salary or Dividend' question so complicated is the inevitable trade-off between the tax payable by the director and the tax relief being obtained by the company.

As a company owner you are, of course, not only interested in your *personal* tax position but that of the *company* as well.

Logically, therefore, your aim must be to minimise the *total* tax paid both personally and by the company.

When looking at either side of the personal/company tax equation, it is always essential to consider what we call the *marginal* tax rates rather than the *total* tax burdens. A marginal tax rate is the tax due on each *additional* amount of profit or income.

For example, you may be a higher rate taxpayer, but that does not mean that you pay 40% Income Tax on all of your income. No, you only pay the 40% rate on each £1 of income above a certain level.

It is, however, the marginal tax rate which is relevant in calculating the tax that you will pay on any additions to your income.

So it is with companies. For example, the company's total tax bill might amount to 26% of its taxable profits. However, its marginal Corporation Tax rate might be 32.5%. In this case, it is the 32.5% rate which is relevant to our calculations.

The company's marginal tax rate is important because it can be thought of as the tax *saved* by each additional £100 of business expenditure – which includes paying salaries and bonuses. An additional £100 bonus paid to a director might reduce the company's total tax bill by £32.50. However, it will also be added to the director's personal income and taxed at his or her own personal marginal tax rate.

1.4 WHAT'S THE DIFFERENCE?

The major differences between salary or bonuses on the one hand, and a dividend on the other, are:

- Salaries and bonuses usually attract Corporation Tax relief; a dividend does not. In other words, if the company pays you a salary or bonus, its taxable profits will be reduced and it will pay less Corporation Tax. Dividends are simply distributions of company profits after all expenditure and taxes have been accounted for. Paying a dividend does not help the company's tax position because the company's taxable profit is calculated before the dividend is taken into account.

- A salary or bonus is generally subject to National Insurance; a dividend is not. And remember, it's not just the director who pays National Insurance, the company will also have to pay employer's secondary National Insurance as well.

- The rates of Income Tax applying to dividends differ from those applying to salaries or bonuses.

- Income Tax and National Insurance payable on salaries and bonuses is collected through the PAYE system; any higher rate Income Tax due on dividends is collected via Self-Assessment – generally at a much later date (but see Section 2.16).

- A salary or bonus will rank as 'earnings' for the purposes of tax relief on pension contributions. Dividends are not classed as 'earnings'.

- Salaries and bonuses will not be subject to the 'income shifting' legislation expected to come into force on 6th April 2009 (see Section 16.2); dividends may be.

1.5 SALARY OR BONUS?

In this guide, I may refer to a 'salary', to a 'bonus' or to both.

As readers will know, a salary is generally paid on a regular basis whereas a bonus is usually a 'one-off' payment.

For taxation purposes, there is no real difference between a salary and a bonus. Both are treated the same way for Income Tax and National Insurance and both are capable of providing the same Corporation Tax relief to the payee company.

Generally speaking, therefore, as far as this guide is concerned, the terms 'salary' and 'bonus' are more or less interchangeable.

In a number of circumstances, however, the payment of some regular salary will be sensible. We will explore this further in Chapter 12.

Bonuses are useful in enabling director/shareholders to 'top-up' their income. Here we will often be comparing a bonus with a dividend against a background where the director already has some regular salary.

The other major benefit of a bonus, as opposed to regular salary, is the ability to influence the timing of Corporation Tax relief on the payment. This does represent one very important difference between a 'salary' and a 'bonus' and we will take a closer look at this idea in Section 6.1.

1.6 SCOPE OF THIS GUIDE

This edition of 'Salary versus Dividends' deals primarily with payments to director/shareholders made, or deemed to be made, during the year ending 5th April 2009; although some reference will also be made to payments made in other years.

Over the course of nine editions, this guide has grown from a simple comparison of the overall net tax burden on bonus or dividend payments to a detailed and comprehensive analysis of the many factors affecting company shareholder/directors wishing to extract funds from their company.

This book has now been expanded to cover older directors, pension contributions, child tax credits and dividends or bonuses paid in kind. Although most of the calculations in the guide are based on a single company, it does also include a detailed analysis of the impact of any associated companies.

Going further, the guide now also includes an examination of the benefits of retaining company funds to enhance capital growth, as well as a look at some of the non-tax factors to be considered when extracting company funds.

It remains important, however, to remember that it is impossible for a general guide of this nature to cover every possible situation. In particular, please note that this guide is aimed only at UK resident shareholder/directors owning and working for UK resident companies.

The reader must also bear in mind the general nature of this guide. Individual circumstances vary and the tax implications of an individual's actions will vary with them. For this reason, it is always vital to get professional advice before undertaking any tax planning or other transactions which may have tax implications. The author cannot accept any responsibility for any loss which may arise as a consequence of any action taken, or any decision to refrain from action taken, as a result of reading this guide.

1.7 ABOUT THE EXAMPLES

This guide is illustrated throughout by a number of examples.

Unless specifically stated to the contrary, all persons described in the examples in this guide are UK resident, ordinarily resident and domiciled for tax purposes.

In preparing the examples in this guide, we have assumed that the UK tax regime will remain unchanged in the future except to the extent of any announcements already made at the time of publication, including the 2008 Budget on 12th March 2008 and the so-called 'Mini-Budget' on 13th May 2008.

However, if there is one thing which we can predict with any certainty it is the fact that change **will** occur. The reader must bear this in mind when reviewing the results of our examples.

All persons described in the examples in this guide are entirely fictional characters created specifically for the purposes of this guide. Any similarities to actual persons, living or dead, or to fictional characters created by any other author, are entirely coincidental. Likewise, the companies described in the examples in this guide are similarly fictional corporations created specifically for the purposes of this guide and any similarities to actual companies, past or present, is again entirely coincidental.

Chapter 2

How are Companies and Directors Taxed?

2.1 CORPORATION TAX RELIEF

As explained in Section 1.3, it is the marginal rate of Corporation Tax payable by a company which will determine the value of any tax relief obtained for the payment of salary or bonuses. Over the next two sections, we are going to explore in detail how these marginal Corporation Tax rates are derived.

One unfortunate side-effect of the changes proposed in Gordon Brown's last Budget as Chancellor in March 2007 is the fact that we now face a staggering 3,958 different possible marginal Corporation Tax rates over the next few years.

Nevertheless, by concentrating on the most likely scenarios, we will be able to produce a picture of the marginal Corporation Tax rates which will apply to the vast majority of companies over the next couple of years. Some of this will be quite complex and the resultant numbers are not exactly 'pretty', but the principles explored in the next few sections lay the foundation for the results which we shall see in the next chapter when, hopefully, things should become a lot clearer.

As we proceed through the various calculations in this chapter, remember that it is the marginal Corporation Tax rate applying to the company for the accounting period in which the director's salary or bonus is accounted for which determines the amount of Corporation Tax saved by the payment of that salary or bonus. In most cases, the relevant accounting period is the period in which the salary or bonus is paid. This is not always the case, however, and we will return to this issue in Section 6.1.

Corporation Tax Rates

Officially, there are just two rates of Corporation Tax: the Small Companies Rate and the Main Rate. For the year commencing 1st April 2008, these are 21% and 28% respectively.

However, the Corporation Tax system does not operate in the same way as the Income Tax system. A large company, paying tax at the main rate, does not benefit at all from the Small Companies Rate and will pay Corporation Tax at the main rate on all of its profits.

This is because the benefit of the Small Companies Rate is progressively withdrawn through a system known as 'marginal relief'.

Whilst there are only two official Corporation Tax rates, the practical effect of the marginal relief system is that there are, in fact, actually three effective Corporation Tax rate bands. More importantly, for our purposes, there are also three marginal Corporation Tax rates.

For the year commencing 1st April 2008, the marginal Corporation Tax rates are as follows:

Profits up to £300,000:   21%
Profits from £300,000 to £1,500,000: 29.75%
Profits over £1,500,000:   28%

What this means, for example, is that a company with profits of £400,000 for the year ended 31st March 2009 will pay 21% on the first £300,000 and 29.75% on the remaining £100,000. The all-important *marginal* Corporation Tax rate for such a company would therefore be 29.75%.

Remember always that the company's marginal tax rate is the rate at which a salary or bonus paid to the company's director saves Corporation Tax.

Many owner-managed companies are subject to the highest marginal Corporation Tax rate, which is currently 29.75%. The only good news to be gleaned from this is the fact that these companies therefore also have the greatest scope for making tax savings.

Note that the £300,000 and £1,500,000 limits set out above must be applied on an annual basis.

Furthermore, where there are any associated companies, the limits must be divided equally over these. For this purpose, we must count all associated companies, including any located overseas. We may, however, ignore any dormant associated companies.

Example

Bosworth Limited draws up accounts for a period of nine months ending 31st December 2008, during which it has four associated companies. Two of these companies are, however, dormant throughout this period.

When applying the Corporation Tax 'bands' set out above, we must first reduce the relevant limits to take account of Bosworth Limited's shorter accounting period. Hence, the £300,000 to £1,500,000 band becomes a £225,000 to £1,125,000 band (i.e. reduced by a factor of 9/12ths).

Next, we must allocate this band equally between Bosworth Limited and all of its 'active' associated companies. Bosworth Limited has four associated companies, although two of them are dormant, leaving only two 'active' associated companies. Hence, counting Bosworth Limited itself and its two associates gives us three companies to take into account and a further reduction in the relevant Corporation Tax band limits by a factor of one third is therefore required.

So, the band which started life as £300,000 to £1,500,000 and became £225,000 to £1,125,000 due to the shorter (nine month) accounting period involved, now reduces further to a band of £75,000 to £375,000 in order to allow for the company's associates. [£300,000 x 9/12 x 1/3 = £75,000; £1,500,000 x 9/12 x 1/3 = £375,000.]

Now, let us suppose that Bosworth Limited has taxable profits of £100,000 for this accounting period. At first glance one might have thought that its marginal rate of Corporation Tax would therefore be 21% (the Small Companies Rate), as its profits lie in the 'up to £300,000' band. However, having followed the steps set out above, we can now see that the correct marginal Corporation Tax rate band is, in fact, the 29.75% band, because its profits lie in the range £75,000 to £375,000.

In the above example, I calculated the reduction in the Corporation Tax profit band limits by reference to the number of months in Bosworth Limited's accounting period. In practice, however, this calculation should be done on a more accurate basis, by reference to the number of days in the accounting period.

Throughout most of this guide, I will be concentrating on the position for a single company, with no active associated companies, drawing up accounts for a period of twelve months. It remains vital, however, to remember that the position will be altered in any case where any active associated companies are in existence, or accounts are drawn up for a period of any different length. We will take a further look at the impact of these factors in Chapter 9.

It is also worth noting that company accounting periods may end on any chosen date. It is unusual, however, for a company to draw up accounts ending on a date which is not a calendar month end. We will therefore stick to accounting periods which end at the end of a calendar month throughout this guide.

2.2   CORPORATION TAX RATE CHANGES

For several years prior to April 2007, the Small Companies rate of Corporation Tax stood at 19%.

In his last Budget statement in March 2007, however, former Chancellor Gordon Brown announced a series of increases to the small companies rate to take place over a three year period.

At the same time, the former Chancellor also announced the reduction in the main rate of Corporation Tax to 28% which applies with effect from 1st April 2008.

So, on the one hand, we face rising tax rates for small and medium-sized companies but, on the other hand, we have a 2% reduction in the main Corporation Tax rate paid by large companies.

Sadly, for the vast majority of UK companies, the changes announced in March 2007 mean significant increases in their Corporation Tax bills. In fact, by March 2010, when all of the proposed changes have come into force, any company with annual profits below £576,924 will be paying more Corporation Tax than it did before April 2007.

Financial Years

Corporation Tax operates by reference to 'Financial Years'. Just to make life even more confusing than it already undoubtedly is, the Financial Year is slightly different to the tax year ending on 5th April which applies to income received by individuals.

A Financial Year is the year ending on 31st March in any calendar year but is officially described by reference to the calendar year in which it began. Hence, the 2008 Financial Year is the year commencing on 1st April 2008 and ending on 31st March 2009.

It is important to be aware of this official terminology, as this is what is used on the Corporation Tax Return. As a consequence of the Corporation Tax rate changes over the next few years, I will also need to refer to it quite extensively in this guide.

Corporation Tax Rates

The 2007 Budget included proposed changes to the Corporation Tax rates for the 2007, 2008 and 2009 Financial Years.

The changes to the small companies rate and the main rate of Corporation Tax will also affect the marginal rate applying to companies with annual profits between £300,000 and £1,500,000.

The full range of marginal Corporation Tax rates applying in the previous, current and next Financial Years, are as follows

Company Profits:	Year Commencing 1st April:		
	2007	2008	2009
Up to £300,000	20.00%	21.00%	22.00%
£300,000 - £1.5M	32.50%	29.75%	29.50%
Over £1.5M	30.00%	28.00%	28.00%

2.3 EFFECTIVE CORPORATION TAX RATES

The table shown at the end of the previous section is fine if your company happens to have a 31st March year end. For the rest of us, however, we have to look at the 'split year' treatment. In other words, the company's profits need to be split across two Financial Years.

The element of profit falling into each Financial Year will then be taxed separately using the applicable rates for each of the two relevant Financial Years, as shown in the previous section.

What matters as far as the 'Salary versus Dividends' question is concerned, of course, is the impact that this has on marginal Corporation Tax rates. This becomes quite a complex issue but we will begin by looking at a simple example.

Example

Stamford Bridge Limited draws up accounts to 31st December each year. For the year ending 31st December 2008, the company's taxable profits are £100,000.

The first part of this accounting period, from 1st January to 31st March 2008, falls into the 2007 Financial Year (i.e. the year ended 31st March 2008). This part of the accounting period is 91 days in duration, so the portion of Stamford Bridge Limited's 2008 taxable profits falling into the 2007 Financial Year is therefore 91/366 x £100,000 = £24,863.

The remaining £75,137 of Stamford Bridge Limited's profits for the year ending 31st December 2008 fall into the 2008 Financial Year. This equates to the profit arising for the 275 day period from 1st April to 31st December 2008, i.e. 275/366 x £100,000 = £75,137.

Stamford Bridge Limited's Corporation Tax bill for the year ended 31st December 2008 is therefore as follows:

2007 Financial Year: £24,863 @ 20% = £4,972
2008 Financial Year: £75,137 @ 21% = £15,779
Total: £20,751

This equates to an effective Corporation Tax rate of 20.751% for the year ended 31st December 2008.

The rate of 20.751% is therefore the effective small companies rate applying for the year ending 31st December 2008.

Using similar principles, we can derive the effective marginal Corporation Tax rates for any company with any accounting period and any level of profit. These work out as follows:

Effective Marginal Corporation Tax Rates March 2007 to March 2010

	Company Profits:		
Year Ending:	**Up to £300,000**	**£300,000 to £1.5M**	**Over £1.5M**
31-Mar-2007	19.000%	32.750%	30.000%
30-Apr-2007	19.082%	32.729%	30.000%
31-May-2007	19.167%	32.708%	30.000%
30-Jun-2007	19.249%	32.688%	30.000%
31-Jul-2007	19.334%	32.666%	30.000%
31-Aug-2007	19.419%	32.645%	30.000%
30-Sep-2007	19.501%	32.625%	30.000%
31-Oct-2007	19.586%	32.603%	30.000%
30-Nov-2007	19.668%	32.583%	30.000%
31-Dec-2007	19.753%	32.562%	30.000%
31-Jan-2008	19.838%	32.540%	30.000%
29-Feb-2008	19.915%	32.521%	30.000%
31-Mar-2008	20.000%	32.500%	30.000%
30-Apr-2008	20.082%	32.275%	29.836%
31-May-2008	20.167%	32.042%	29.667%
30-Jun-2008	20.249%	31.816%	29.503%
31-Jul-2008	20.333%	31.583%	29.333%
31-Aug-2008	20.418%	31.350%	29.164%
30-Sep-2008	20.500%	31.125%	29.000%
31-Oct-2008	20.585%	30.892%	28.831%
30-Nov-2008	20.667%	30.667%	28.667%
31-Dec-2008	20.751%	30.434%	28.497%
31-Jan-2009	20.836%	30.201%	28.328%
28-Feb-2009	20.915%	29.984%	28.170%
31-Mar-2009	21.000%	29.750%	28.000%
30-Apr-2009	21.082%	29.729%	28.000%
31-May-2009	21.167%	29.708%	28.000%
30-Jun-2009	21.249%	29.688%	28.000%
31-Jul-2009	21.334%	29.666%	28.000%

31-Aug-2009	21.419%	29.645%	28.000%
30-Sep-2009	21.501%	29.625%	28.000%
31-Oct-2009	21.586%	29.603%	28.000%
30-Nov-2009	21.668%	29.583%	28.000%
31-Dec-2009	21.753%	29.562%	28.000%
31-Jan-2010	21.838%	29.540%	28.000%
28-Feb-2010	21.915%	29.521%	28.000%
31-Mar-2010	22.000%	29.500%	28.000%

As we can see, every different accounting period over a three year period is subject to a different set of marginal Corporation Tax rates.

Naturally, this will make our whole 'Salary versus Dividends' question more complex than ever. However, as we shall see in the next chapter, it is still possible to draw out the fundamental principles which we need in order to determine the optimum mix of salary and dividends on a practical basis.

Look Before You 'Leap'

I must confess that I cheated slightly in order to keep the above table as 'simple' as possible.

An added complication is created by the fact that 2008 is a leap year. In effect, this makes the 2007 Financial Year a 'Leap Financial Year' of 366 days duration.

The result of this little quirk is that for any period which falls partly, but not wholly, into the 2007 Financial Year, we have two extra small 'transitional' profit bands with their own unique effective marginal Corporation Tax rates.

However, as the maximum effect on any company's Corporation Tax bill is just £72 we will ignore these 'transitional' profit bands in the rest of our deliberations.

This may mean that some of our 'ideal' solutions could be out by as much as £72, but it does save me from having to quadruple the size of the book!

16

2.4 MARGINAL TAX RATES FOR DIRECTORS

The director receiving payments from the company also has a number of possible marginal tax rates. These rates vary according to whether the director is receiving salary or a bonus on the one hand or dividends on the other.

Furthermore, in the case of salary or bonus payments, we need to consider both Income Tax *and* National Insurance. National Insurance may not be called a tax but that is essentially what it is. Call it what you like; in my book any compulsory payment to the Government is a tax.

Furthermore, as most readers will already appreciate, National Insurance effectively hits the shareholder/director twice, for when it comes to his or her own pay, he or she is effectively both employer and employee.

We will return to the issue of employer's National Insurance in Section 2.10. For the moment, however, let's concentrate on the director's own personal tax burden.

2.5 TAX YEARS

The Income Tax payable by the director (and National Insurance where applicable) will be determined according to the tax year in which they are deemed to receive the salary, bonus or dividend payment. Usually a payment is deemed to be received when it is actually paid; although there are a few exceptions (see Section 6.1).

The tax year for Income Tax and National Insurance purposes is the year commencing on 6th April in one calendar year and ending on 5th April in the next.

The tax year ending on 5th April is all that is relevant to the calculation of the amount of Income Tax and National Insurance payable on a director's salary, bonus or dividend. For the purposes of the director's own personal tax, it does not matter which company accounting period the payment is coming out of, nor which Financial Year's Corporation Tax bill is affected.

In this guide, we will mostly be concentrating on payments to directors falling to be taxed in the tax year ending on 5th April 2009. This tax year is also referred to as 2008/9.

When I refer to 2008/9 in this guide, I am referring to the personal tax year ending on 5th April 2009. This is not to be confused with the 2008 Financial Year ending on 31st March 2009. They are nearly the same, but not quite, and that 'not quite' can make a big difference to the final outcome!

2.6 TAX PAYABLE ON SALARIES AND BONUSES

Following the changes announced in the so-called 'Mini-Budget' of 13th May 2008, the marginal rates of combined Income Tax and National Insurance applying to director's salaries and bonuses taxable in the 2008/9 tax year are now as follows:

Income up to £5,435:	0%	(earnings threshold)
Income from £5,435 to £6,035	11%	(Tax-Nil + NI-11%)
Income from £6,035 to £40,040:	31%	(Tax-20% + NI-11%)
Income from £40,040 to £40,835:	21%	(Tax-20% + NI-1%)
Income over £40,835:	41%	(Tax-40% + NI-1%)

Full details of the current personal tax rates and allowances are set out in Appendix C.

Readers may recall that the original tax bands applying for 2008/9, as announced in the Budget on 12th March, were slightly different.

In a completely unprecedented move, and in response to the extreme criticism levelled at the Government from all quarters over the abolition of the 10% starting rate of Income Tax on earned income and pensions, two changes to the Income Tax system were announced on 13th May 2008, with back-dated effect from 6th April 2008.

Firstly, the personal allowance for people aged under 65 was increased by £600 from the £5,435, as originally announced, to £6,035. Note, however, that the earnings threshold for National Insurance remains £5,435 and has not been increased.

Secondly, the basic rate band was reduced by £1,200 from the £36,000 originally announced to £34,800.

Taken together, these changes mean that the higher rate Income Tax threshold for 2008/9 is now £40,835, rather than £41,435, as under the original proposals.

For the first time in many years, we now have a difference between the Income Tax personal allowance (£6,035) and the National Insurance earnings threshold (£5,435). Salary and bonus income falling between these two figures will therefore be subject to National Insurance but free from Income Tax.

This is likely to be the cause of much confusion as many people find themselves paying National Insurance on income below the Income Tax personal allowance.

The difference at the bottom end of the pay scale is echoed by another pathetic little difference between the new higher rate Income Tax threshold (£40,835) and the upper earnings limit for National Insurance (£40,040).

The additional complexity caused by these small differences will create significant additional costs for Government and business alike and could so easily have been avoided if two of the residents of Downing Street had given a little more thought to the consequences of their actions!

The initial figures announced for the personal allowance and the basic rate band will be used for PAYE purposes until around September or October 2008, at which point all employed earners and pensioners will be subject to a tax adjustment to bring the revised figures announced on 13th May into force. We will look at the impact of the delay in implementing the new figures for PAYE purposes in Section 2.14.

The revised figures for the personal allowance and the basic rate band will be used for Self Assessment purposes in the normal way.

Fundamental Figures

The combined Income Tax and National Insurance rates set out in the table above are quite fundamental to the whole 'Salary versus Dividends' question and we will therefore be referring to them throughout this guide. You will see the numbers £5,435, £6,035, £40,040 and £40,835 pop up in a number of places in this guide.

Hopefully, once you have reviewed the tables in Chapter 3, you will understand why!

The application of these marginal rates is reasonably simple. The rate of combined Income Tax and National Insurance applying to any additional salary or bonus income received by a director is determined according to which of the above bands their existing income for the tax year lies in.

For example, a director who is already receiving an annual salary of £30,000, and who then also receives a bonus of £1,000, will suffer an additional 31% (£310) in combined Income Tax and National Insurance on that bonus.

The rates given above are based on the assumption that the recipient director has no other income besides salary from the company.

Where other income is also present, the whole situation is altered. Different effective marginal rates will arise and the limits at which the rates change will differ. Higher effective marginal rates of 42.5%, 51% or even 53.5% are also possible!

In Section 2.18 we will take a brief look at some of the many complications caused by the presence of other income.

However, it would be impossible for us to cover every conceivable combination of other income which a director might have. Furthermore, in most cases, the impact of the other income on the tax planning discussed in this guide is minimal. Nevertheless, where significant amounts of other income are present, I would recommend that directors seek professional advice when planning to extract funds from their company.

2.7 TAX PAYABLE ON DIVIDENDS

No National Insurance is payable on dividends and the recipient's marginal Income Tax rate on receipt of a dividend is much simpler.

The marginal Income Tax rates applying to dividends received during the tax year 2008/9 are as follows:

Income up to £40,835:   0%
Income over £40,835:   25%

In this case, these marginal rates remain equally valid regardless of what other types of income the director has received during the tax year.

For example, a director with a salary of £30,000 and interest income of £5,000 may also receive a dividend of £1,000 without suffering any Income Tax on that dividend.

Another director with a salary of £45,000 would suffer Income Tax at 25% on any dividend received. The position would be exactly the same if the director had a salary of £35,000 and interest income of £10,000.

In other words, any person with total income which already exceeds £40,835 will suffer Income Tax at 25% on any dividend income.

Any person with existing income of less than £40,835 may receive dividends free of Income Tax. However, when we come to the question of how much dividend income may be received tax free, the situation becomes a little more complicated. To answer this question, we need to understand the concept of 'dividend tax credits'.

2.8   DIVIDEND TAX CREDITS

As explained in Section 1.4, dividends are paid out of a company's remaining profits after tax. Another way of looking at this is to say that tax has already been paid on the dividends.

For this reason, a dividend carries a notional tax credit to represent the tax which has already been suffered by the company.

Well, at least that was what I was taught when I first learned about the UK tax system over twenty years ago. In those days, it made some sense as the rate of the tax credit did bear some correlation to the rate of Corporation Tax.

Today, however, the rate of the dividend tax credit is just one ninth and it must be accepted that this is a purely notional gesture towards the original concept of a credit for the tax suffered by the company.

Nevertheless, whilst the dividend tax credit is now a purely notional item, it still has some important consequences for a company director's own personal taxation.

How Do Dividend Tax Credits Work?

Whenever a dividend is paid by a UK company, there is a notional tax credit equal to one ninth of the amount actually paid.

Hence, for example, when a dividend of £90 is paid, the notional tax credit is £10.

The individual receiving the dividend is treated as if they have received a dividend of £100 but with tax of £10 deducted at source. The deemed dividend of £100 which includes the tax credit is often referred to as the 'gross dividend'.

For 2008/9, the rates of Income Tax applying to this deemed 'gross dividend' are as follows:

Income up to £40,835:   10%
Income over £40,835:   32.5%

There is no 0% rate for the personal allowance because the notional tax credit is not repayable.

For those with taxable income totalling less than £40,835, the tax due on the deemed 'gross dividend' is equalled by the tax credit, with the result that there is no further tax to pay. In other words, basic rate taxpayers may receive dividends tax free.

Higher rate taxpayers, whose income already exceeds £40,835, have an Income Tax liability equal to 32.5% of the deemed 'gross dividend' but may deduct the notional tax credit. This leaves an amount of tax actually due equal to 22.5% of the deemed 'gross dividend' which equates to 25% of the real amount of the dividend actually received.

Example

Charlie and Flora are the shareholder/directors of Prestonpans Limited. Charlie takes a salary of £45,000 out of the company but Flora's salary for 2008/9 is just £5,435. On 1ˢᵗ April 2009, the company pays a dividend of £1,800. Charlie and Flora own the company's shares equally between them so they each receive a dividend of £900.

Flora's Income Tax liability on this dividend is as follows:

	£
Dividend received	*900*
Tax Credit (£900 x 1/9)	*100*

Deemed 'gross dividend'	*1,000*
	====
Income Tax on deemed 'gross dividend' at 10%	*100*
Less Tax Credit	*100*

Tax due	*NIL*
	====

Charlie's Income Tax liability on his £900 dividend is as follows:

	£
Dividend received	*900*
Tax Credit (£900 x 1/9)	*100*

Deemed 'gross dividend'	*1,000*
	====
Income Tax on deemed 'gross dividend' at 32.5%	*325*
Less Tax Credit	*100*

Tax due	*225*
	====

Charlie's Income Tax liability of £225 works out at 25% of his actual dividend of £900.

So, as the example shows, in many cases we can simply say that a basic rate taxpayer (with income under £40,835) receives a dividend tax free and a higher rate taxpayer (with income over £40,835) suffers Income Tax at an effective rate of 25% on any dividends received. This is the simplified version of the Income Tax payable on dividends received which we saw in the previous section.

The simplified version where dividends received are taxed at either 0% or 25% will suffice for our purposes much of the time and it will often be unnecessary to pay any attention to the notional tax credit or the deemed 'gross dividend'.

However, it is when we must look at the question of when a director's total income will breach the £40,835 limit that the notional tax credit takes on more importance. This is because when it comes to totalling up all of a director's taxable income it is the deemed 'gross dividend' which must be counted rather than the amount actually received.

Example

During the tax year 2008/9 Bonnie receives a salary of £30,000 from her company Culloden Limited.

On 31st March 2009 she also pays herself a dividend of £11,000 thinking that £10,835 of this will be tax free and she will pay Income Tax at 25% on only £165, giving her an Income Tax bill of just £41.25.

Sadly, however, when Bonnie gets her 2009 Tax Return back from her accountants, Cumberland & Co., she sees that the tax on her dividend is calculated as follows:

	£
Personal allowance	*6,035*
Basic rate band	*34,800*

	40,835
Less Salary	*30,000*

Remaining basic rate band available:	*10,835*
	=====
Dividend received	*11,000.00*
Tax Credit (£11,000 x 1/9)	*1,222.22*

Deemed 'gross dividend'	*12,222.22*
	========

Income Tax on deemed 'gross dividend':
£10,835.00 (remaining basic rate band) @ 10%	*1,083.50*
£1,387.22 (£12,222.22 - £10,835.00) @ 32.5%	*450.85*

	1,534.35
Less Tax Credit	*1,222.22*

Income Tax due:	*312.13*
	=======

Poor Bonnie fell into a common trap: she mistakenly believed that the amount of tax free dividend which she could take was equal to the remaining unused amount of her basic rate Income Tax band.

In fact, the amount of tax free dividend which a director can take out of their company is actually only 9/10ths of the remaining unused amount of their basic rate Income Tax band. This is because of the notional tax credit which is added to the dividend.

Foreign Dividends

Prior to 6th April 2008, dividends received from a foreign company (i.e. a company which is not resident in the UK for tax purposes) were not eligible for dividend tax credits.

From 6th April 2008 onwards, however, most foreign dividends are now eligible for the same dividend tax credit as a UK dividend.

Unfortunately, however, there is one major exception. Where the recipient owns 10% or more of the share capital in the paying company, the dividend tax credit is not available on foreign dividends.

From 6th April 2009, however, foreign dividends received by a taxpayer owning 10% or more of the share capital in the paying company **will** be eligible for the same dividend tax credit as other dividends, provided that the paying company is subject to local Corporation Tax in its home country.

Tax Tip

Whilst we are not primarily concerned with foreign dividends in this guide, anyone with a shareholding of 10% or more in a foreign company should give serious consideration to delaying any dividend payments by that company until 6th April 2009 or later whenever possible.

See the Taxcafe.co.uk guide *'How to Save Tax 2008/2009'* for further details.

2.9 MAXIMUM TAX-FREE PAYMENTS

The table below shows how much tax free dividend can be taken out of a company in 2008/9 by a director with total other taxable income for the tax year at various different levels.

The director's other taxable income will include any salary or bonuses received from their company, any other employment or self-employment income, interest, pension or rental income, any foreign dividends from a company in which they own 10% or more of the share capital and 10/9ths of any other dividend income.

Tax-Free Dividends 2008/9

Director's Total Other Income	Maximum Tax-Free Dividend
None	£36,752
£5,435	£31,860
£6,035	£31,320
£10,000	£27,752
£15,000	£23,252
£20,000	£18,752
£25,000	£14,252
£30,000	£9,752
£35,000	£5,252
£40,000	£752

As can readily be seen from the table, the maximum amount of tax free dividends which a director may receive in 2008/9 is actually only £36,752 and not the £40,835 which one might otherwise have thought!

As we shall see later in the guide, however, it is seldom wise for a director to take nothing but dividends out of their company.

Tax Tip

In a great many cases, in fact, the best payment strategy for a director/shareholder to adopt is that given by the second row of the above table, i.e. a salary of £5,435 and a dividend of £31,860. This strategy provides the director with the maximum tax-free sum which can be extracted from the company in 2008/9: £37,295.

We will see the benefits of this strategy in action in Section 7.3.

2.10 EMPLOYER'S NATIONAL INSURANCE CONTRIBUTIONS

Another factor which must be taken into account is that the company generally also has to pay employer's secondary National Insurance at 12.8% on any salary or bonus paid to directors (but not on dividends).

Many people often assume that this naturally means that dividends will always be preferable. This, however, is not always the case, as we will demonstrate in the next chapter.

Employer's National Insurance must be paid at the rate of 12.8% on all remuneration paid to any employee, including directors, in excess of the 'earnings threshold'.

For most employees, the earnings threshold is applied on a weekly or monthly basis.

For directors, however, it must be applied to all of the directors' earnings from the company for each tax year on an annual basis.

The earnings threshold for 2008/9 is £5,435, slightly less than the revised Income Tax personal allowance announced on 13th May 2008.

Any secondary National Insurance paid by the company forms part of the cost of the director's remuneration and hence should generally be an allowable cost for Corporation Tax purposes.

Hence, whilst a director's bonus will usually cost the company an extra 12.8% in National Insurance, Corporation Tax relief should usually be available on the full 112.8% cost.

2.11 WHAT DO SALARIES AND BONUSES COST?

At this stage, I think it is worth summarising what we have learned so far in order to demonstrate what it actually costs to pay salary or a bonus to a director.

The net cost of a director's salary or bonus may be summarised as follows:

Costs:

Income Tax payable by the director	X
National Insurance payable by the director	X
Secondary National Insurance payable by the company	X

	X

Less:
Corporation Tax relief on the salary or bonus
and on the secondary National Insurance

payable by the company	(X)

Net cost of salary or bonus	X
	===

Example

Oliver is the sole director and shareholder of Edgehill Limited. For the tax year 2008/9 he is paying himself a salary of £50,000.

Oliver anticipates that Edgehill Limited will make a profit of £100,000 for the year ending 31st March 2009 after accounting for his salary but before taking account of any bonus payment.

On 25th March 2009, Oliver pays himself a bonus of £10,000. The cost of this bonus is as follows:

	£
Income Tax payable by Oliver at 40%	4,000
National Insurance payable by Oliver at 1%	100
Secondary National Insurance payable by Edgehill Limited at 12.8%	1,280

	5,380
Less:	
Corporation Tax relief at 21% on £11,280	
(£10,000 + £1,280)	2,369

Net cost of Oliver's bonus	3,011
	====

As we can see, the total net cost of Oliver's £10,000 bonus was £3,011. However, the net amount received by Oliver was only £5,900 (after deduction of Income Tax at 40% and National Insurance at 1%). Hence, in this case, the tax cost of a bonus is just over 51% of the amount received by the director.

Expressed another way, it costs £51.04 for every £100 put into Oliver's hands net of tax. This is the basis for the tables which we will see in the next chapter.

2.12   WHAT DO DIVIDENDS COST?

Even with the extra complication of the dividend tax credit, it remains a lot easier to work out the net tax cost of a dividend than the net tax cost of salary or bonus payments.

The total net tax cost of a dividend consists solely of the Income Tax payable by the director. There is no National Insurance to pay and no Corporation Tax relief to worry about.

Hence, if the director is a basic rate taxpayer, the cost of a dividend is zero (but see Sections 2.8 and 2.9 above regarding the question of how big this dividend can be).

Once the director is a higher rate taxpayer with total taxable income over £40,835 (at 2008/9 rates), the cost of the dividend is a straightforward 25%.

Example Revisited

Taking the same facts as the example in Section 2.11 above, let us now assume that Oliver pays himself a dividend of £10,000 on 25th March 2009 instead of a bonus.

Since Oliver is already a higher rate taxpayer, we do not need to concern ourselves with the notional tax credit or the deemed 'gross dividend'; we know that he will suffer Income Tax at 25% on the actual amount of dividend received.

Hence, the tax cost of this dividend is simply £2,500.

After paying his Income Tax bill, Oliver will be left with a net sum of £7,500. Hence, the tax cost of the dividend is 33.33% of the net amount received by the director.

To put this in the same terms as we used in Section 2.11, it costs £33.33 for every £100 put into Oliver's hands net of tax by way of dividend.

As we can now see, for a director in Oliver's position, a dividend costs £33.33 per £100 received net of tax, whereas a bonus costs £51.04.

Subject to any other considerations which may apply therefore (and there are plenty, as we shall see throughout the rest of this guide), a director with other taxable income for 2008/9 in excess of £40,835, whose company has annual profits not exceeding £300,000, will be better off paying themselves a dividend rather than a bonus.

The tables which we will see in the next chapter provide the same comparison for directors and companies with other levels of income and profits.

2.13 CASHFLOW CONSIDERATIONS

Another important difference in the tax treatment of salaries, bonuses and dividends is the way in which the tax is collected. The different tax collection methods applying give rise to significant differences in the cashflow consequences of the payments.

In the next few sections we will explore the cashflow consequences of salary, bonus and dividend payments in detail. There are a few quirks to watch out for but the general position may be summarised as follows:

- The Income Tax and National Insurance payable on salaries is due almost immediately.
- It can take up to 21 months to obtain Corporation Tax relief for salary and bonus payments. On average, relief is obtained after 15 months but, in some circumstances, Corporation Tax relief on bonus payments can be obtained almost immediately.
- The Income Tax due on dividends received by directors may not be payable for up to 22 months. Normally, however, for directors receiving regular dividends, the tax payment will be due an average of around seven months after the receipt of the dividend (subject to the further points raised in Section 2.16).

Subject to the more detailed points in the next few sections, therefore, we can see that from a pure cashflow perspective, dividends are generally preferable to salary or bonuses.

When the overall net tax costs of a dividend or bonus are not significantly different, these cashflow considerations may be enough to clinch your decision whether to pay a bonus or a dividend.

2.14 CASHFLOW IMPACT OF SALARIES AND BONUSES

When a salary or bonus is paid, the Income Tax and National Insurance due (both employee's and employer's) is collected through the PAYE system. This means that the tax will be payable somewhere between 14 and 44 days after the salary or bonus itself is paid.

Tax Tip

Income Tax and National Insurance collected through the PAYE system is generally due for payment on the 19th of the month following the 'tax month' in which the salary or bonus has been paid.

A 'tax month' runs from the 6th day of one calendar month to the 5th day of the next calendar month.

Most people pay themselves at or near to the end of a calendar month, meaning that the relevant Income Tax and National Insurance is due around 20 days later.

But why not pay your salary on the 6th of each month?

That way, the Income Tax and National Insurance won't be due for up to 44 days, keeping valuable cash in your business for almost an extra month!

In the case of large bonuses, delaying payment until the 6th of the month may have significant cashflow advantages. (Just be careful to remember that payments made on 6th April will fall into a later tax year – this may not always fit in with the rest of your tax planning.)

Whilst Corporation Tax relief will generally be available for directors' salaries and bonuses, the effective date of this relief is when the company's Corporation Tax is due. For most companies, this is not until nine months and one day after the end of the accounting period. (Large companies paying Corporation Tax at the main rate must pay their Corporation Tax in quarterly instalments.)

In the worst case, a company paying its director a bonus within the first five days of a twelve month accounting period will have to pay over the relevant Income Tax and National Insurance under PAYE on the 19th of that month and may then have to wait almost 21 months for the resultant Corporation Tax relief.

However, as we shall see in Section 6.1, it is not always necessary to wait quite so long for your Corporation Tax relief.

Cashflow Complications

Further complications arise because of the way in which the PAYE system works. As far as payments to directors are concerned, however, the PAYE system merely has a cashflow impact and cannot alter the ultimate cost of any salary or bonus payments. Hence, whilst the issues described below are important and should be borne in mind when planning payments to directors, they will not alter any of the conclusions drawn in the rest of this guide regarding the overall cost of those payments.

When it comes to salary or bonus payments to non-director employees, however, the position is very different. This includes payments to any such employees who, whilst not a director, are owners or part owners of the company. We will therefore take a look at this topic in more detail in Section 2.17.

Pay Periods

Each employer has to operate PAYE by reference to 'pay periods'. A 'pay period' may be either a week or a month, depending on how the employer operates their payroll, although most payments to directors or other company owners will tend to be made under monthly pay periods.

For PAYE purposes, the personal allowance and the basic rate tax band are divided over all of the pay periods in the tax year. When a payment is made to any employee, including a director, only the cumulative proportion of the personal allowance and basic rate tax band for the tax year to date can be taken into account.

Example

(We will ignore National Insurance in this example for the sake of illustration.)

On 20th December 2008, Nelson decides to pay himself a salary of £6,035 from his company, Nile Limited. Nelson has not taken any other money out of the company since 5th April 2008 and has no other taxable income for 2008/9. His salary payment should therefore be covered by his 2008/9 personal allowance and should thus be free from Income Tax.

Unfortunately, however, as Nelson has made the payment during 'Month 9' of 2008/9 (i.e. the month from 6th December 2008 to 5th January 2009), he is only entitled to 9/12ths of the 2008/9 personal allowance for PAYE purposes, i.e. £4,526 (£6,035 x 9/12).

Nile Limited will therefore have to deduct Income Tax at 20% on part of Nelson's salary, giving rise to a PAYE tax liability of £301.80 (£6,035 - £4,526 x 20%).

Still, when it comes to Income Tax, it does all 'come out in the wash' and if the pay period system results in an overpayment, the excess can always be reclaimed subsequently when another salary or bonus payment is made or via the employee's tax return.

Tax Tip

The quickest way to obtain repayment of excess tax paid under PAYE is to make another small payment before the end of the tax year. This is most effective when the company has other employees.

Example Continued

If Nelson were to pay himself £1 during PAYE 'Month 12' for 2008/9 (i.e. between 6th March and 5th April 2009), he would then have cumulative pay for the year of £6,036 but would be entitled to claim his full personal allowance of £6,035.

This would leave him with a cumulative Income Tax liability under PAYE of just 20 pence, and he would therefore receive a repayment of £301.60 via the PAYE system.

The repayment would be made by Nile Limited in the first instance (when Nelson took his £1 of additional salary). If the company has other employees, the repayment would then effectively be set off against the PAYE payment due on 19th April 2009. Otherwise the company will need to make a claim for the repayment due.

In either case, the refund due will almost certainly be received far quicker than under the Self Assessment system, although it may take a little while for the refund to be processed where the company has no other employees and has to make a repayment claim.

Where the employee has other income for the same tax year and thus has a tax liability under Self Assessment, relief for any net overpayment under the PAYE system which is still outstanding at the end of the tax year will only effectively be obtained on the following 31st January, up to 21 months after payment of the tax.

To avoid the potential cashflow disadvantages inherent in the pay period system, directors whose companies have no other employees will need to either pay themselves on a regular basis throughout the year or pay themselves by way of a single lump sum bonus during PAYE 'Month 12' (i.e. between 6th March and 5th April).

Those whose companies have other employees, however, can usually obtain an effective refund more quickly, using the method described in the example above.

Naturally, these cashflow considerations need to be considered in the context of other planning issues, especially the timing of Corporation Tax relief (see Section 6.1).

Pay Periods and National Insurance

In principle, the position regarding National Insurance on salary or bonus payments to directors is much simpler than the Income Tax position described above.

As explained in Section 2.10, for payments to directors, the National Insurance earnings threshold is operated on an annual cumulative basis. This means that the same amount of National Insurance will ultimately be payable in respect of salary and bonus payments made to directors regardless of when those payments are made during the course of the tax year. The pay period system does not apply to National Insurance on payments made to directors and no overpayments of National Insurance can therefore arise.

Sometimes, however, directors may initially choose to pay the National Insurance on their own salary and bonus payments under the same pay period system which applies to everyone else (see Section 2.17). This facility is merely provided as an aid to cashflow and an adjustment to the strict cumulative annual basis must be made at the end of the tax year.

Nevertheless, in some cases, the pay period system can be used to provide a National Insurance cashflow advantage, especially where the director takes a large salary or bonus payment early in the tax year. This is because the National Insurance upper earnings limit (£40,040 for 2008/9) is also divided across all of the pay periods in the year where the pay period system is being used.

Example

Emma is a director of her own company, Copenhagen Limited, from which she takes a salary of £50,000 each year. In 2008, she decides to take her entire salary for the year by way of a single bonus payment on 6th April. Emma also elects to pay the National Insurance on this payment using the pay period system.

The primary threshold for a monthly pay period in 2008/9 is £453 (see Section 2.17), so £49,547 of Emma's payment is subject to National Insurance. However, the monthly upper earnings limit for 2008/9 is £3,337 (£40,040 x 1/12), meaning that £46,663 of Emma's payment attracts primary National Insurance at just 1% and only £2,884 (£3,337 - £453) is subject to the main rate of 11%.

This gives Emma a total National Insurance liability of £784 (£2,884 x 11% + £46,663 x 1%). If she had used the strict annual cumulative basis, her National Insurance liability on this payment would have been:

First £5,435 (earnings threshold) at 0%:	*£Nil*
Next £34,605 (£40,040 - £5,435) at 11%:	*£3,806*
Last £9,960 (£50,000 - £40,040) at 1%:	*£100*
Total:	*£3,906*

Using the pay period system has therefore given Emma a personal National Insurance cashflow saving of £3,122 (£3,906 - £784). Emma will be able to retain this additional sum until the adjustment to the strict annual cumulative basis is made at the end of the tax year in April 2009.

Emma's cashflow advantage does come at a price, however.

Firstly, the company must also initially operate the pay period system when calculating the secondary employer's National Insurance due on Emma's payment. This means that the company must pay National Insurance at 12.8% on the entire sum of £49,547 which is subject to National Insurance. Under the strict annual cumulative basis, only £44,565 (£50,000 - £5,435) would have been subject to National Insurance. The company therefore pays National Insurance on an additional £4,982 (£49,547 - £44,565), giving rise to an additional cost of £638 (£4,982 x 12.8%).

This, again, is only a cashflow difference and the company will recover the additional cost when the adjustment to the strict annual cumulative basis is made at the end of the tax year. Furthermore, there is still an overall net National Insurance cashflow advantage of £2,484 (£3,122 - £638).

The main problem with Emma's strategy, however, is the Income Tax cashflow disadvantage which we have already discussed above.

As her bonus payment takes place in 'Month 1', she will only be entitled to one twelfth of her personal allowance and basic rate band for PAYE purposes. She will therefore suffer an Income Tax deduction under PAYE of £19,219 when, in fact, her actual Income Tax liability for a salary of £50,000 should only be £10,626.

Her strategy therefore creates an Income Tax cashflow **disadvantage** of £8,593 (£19,219 - £10,626) which far outweighs the National Insurance cashflow advantage.

In summary, therefore, using the pay period system to create a National Insurance cashflow advantage on salary or bonus payments to a director is only worthwhile if you are making those payments anyway, regardless of the tax position.

If, in our example, Emma had some personal, non-tax, reason for taking a large bonus payment out of the company early in the tax year then using the pay period system to calculate her National Insurance will have been worthwhile.

As a cashflow saving strategy in itself, however, it is a total failure because of the much greater Income Tax cashflow disadvantage.

The Revised Personal Allowance

As explained in Section 2.6, the personal allowance for 2008/9 has been increased from £5,435 to £6,035 but this increase will not take effect for PAYE purposes until September or October 2008.

This will add to the Income Tax cashflow disadvantage on any salary or bonus payments made to directors before then in excess of the appropriate proportion of the original proposed personal allowance of £5,435.

Maximum Tax-Free Payments 2008/9

Taking all of the above factors into account, the maximum **cumulative** salary and bonus payments which may be made during 2008/9 without giving rise to any Income Tax liability under PAYE are as follows:

Month	Ending	Cumulative Maximum	Notes
1	05-May-2008	£452	
2	05-Jun-2008	£905	
3	05-Jul-2008	£1,358	
4	05-Aug-2008	£1,811	
5	05-Sep-2008	£2,264	
6	05-Oct-2008	£2,717	(1)
7	05-Nov-2008	£3,520	
8	05-Dec-2008	£4,023	
9	05-Jan-2009	£4,526	
10	05-Feb-2009	£5,029	
11	05-Mar-2009	£5,532	(2)
12	05-Apr-2009	£6,035	(2)

Notes

1. This figure will be increased to £3,017 if new PAYE coding notices incorporating the revised personal allowance of £6,035 have been issued by the time of the payment.
2. Cumulative payments to directors in excess of the earnings threshold of £5,435 will be subject to National Insurance.
3. See Section 2.17 regarding National Insurance on payments to non-directors.

2.15 CASHFLOW IMPACT OF DIVIDENDS

When a dividend is paid, there is no Corporation Tax relief to wait for.

When Income Tax arises on a dividend paid to a director or any other company owner, the basic rule under the Self-Assessment system is that this tax is due for payment by 31st January following the tax year in which the dividend is paid.

Where the Income Tax due under Self-Assessment exceeds both £1,000 and 20% of the director's total tax liability for the year, the director will also be liable to make payments on account in respect of the following year's estimated Self-Assessment tax liability. (The £1,000 limit was increased from £500 for 2008/9 onwards.)

Where applicable, two payments on account are due, one on 31st January (i.e. at the same time that the previous year's tax bill must be paid) and one six months later, on 31st July. Each payment on account is usually equal to half of the previous year's Self-Assessment tax liability.

Example

Hadrian has no other sources of income besides his company, Pictwall Limited, from which he takes an annual salary of £50,000. During 2008/9, he also takes a dividend of £20,000 out of the company. This gives rise to a Self-Assessment tax liability of £5,000 due on 31st January 2010.

Hadrian will also have to make Self-Assessment payments on account of £2,500 on both 31st January and 31st July 2010 in respect of his estimated Self-Assessment tax liability for 2009/10.

As we can see, in cashflow terms, Hadrian effectively pays a total of 37.5% in Income Tax (£7,500) on his 2008/9 dividend on 31st January 2010, plus a further 12.5% (£2,500) six months later. This is what I often call the 'Double Whammy' effect of Self-Assessment.

Of course, the 'Double Whammy' effect is only a matter of cashflow, as the 2009/10 payments on account can eventually be deducted from the final 2009/10 Self-Assessment tax liability due on 31st January 2011. This is small comfort to someone like Hadrian, however, who has to pay out half of his dividend in Income Tax in the space of just six months.

Payments on account can be avoided by ensuring that the Self-Assessment tax liability does not exceed the greater of £1,000 or 20% of the director's total Income Tax liability for the year. The following table indicates the maximum dividends which can be paid in 2008/9 to a director with no other income besides the salary they receive from their company without having to make payments on account under Self-Assessment.

Maximum Dividends without Payments on Account

Salary	Maximum Dividend
£0	£40,752
£5,435	£35,860
£6,035	£35,320
£20,000	£22,752
£30,000	£14,545
£40,000	£6,793
£40,835	£6,960
£50,000	£10,626
£60,000	£14,626
£80,000	£22,626
£100,000	£30,626

A close inspection of the above table will reveal that once the director's salary exceeds £40,835, this 'maximum dividend' increases at the rate of 40% of the excess.

If dividends in excess of the amount given by the above table are paid to the director on a regular basis, year in, year out, the Self-Assessment payments on account system will effectively mean that half of the Income Tax arising is paid on 31st January *during* the relevant tax year and the other half on 31st July following the tax year.

The result of this is to accelerate the payment of tax on the dividends by an average of nine months.

However, when there are reasonable grounds to believe that the following year's Self-Assessment tax liability will be at a lower level than the current year, the director may apply to reduce his or her payments on account to half of the following year's estimated Self-Assessment liability.

Note that if it later transpires that the actual liability for the following year is greater than the reduced payments on account made by the director, interest will be charged on the difference.

Nevertheless, this does provide the scope to avoid payments on account by arranging to receive dividends on a bi-annual basis.

Example Revisited

After taking his £20,000 dividend out of Pictwall Limited in 2008/9, Hadrian decides that he will not take any further dividends out of the company during 2009/10.

Hadrian will therefore have no Self-Assessment tax liability for the tax year 2009/10 and hence, when he submits his 2009 Tax Return (his Tax Return for the tax year 2008/9), he can apply to reduce his payments on account in respect of 2009/10 (due on 31st January and 31st July 2010) to nil.

As Hadrian has no Self-Assessment tax liability for 2009/10 to pay on 31st January 2011, he also avoids having to make any payments on account on 31st January or 31st July 2011, regardless of what his actual Self-Assessment liability for 2010/11 might eventually be.

In 2010/11, therefore, Hadrian will be able to take dividends out of Pictwall Limited once more without having had to make any payments on account in respect of this income. Naturally, he will still have an Income Tax bill to pay on 31st January 2012, but the full cashflow advantage of taking dividend income will have been restored.

To maintain his cashflow advantage and continue to avoid payments on account, Hadrian should again refrain from taking any dividends out of Pictwall Limited during 2011/12, 2013/14, 2015/16, etc, whilst he does pay himself dividends in 2012/13, 2014/15, 2016/17, etc. In this way, he should never have to make any payments on account.

As we can see, bi-annual dividend payments are a useful way to optimise the cashflow position by avoiding Self-Assessment payments on account. (The bi-annual payment strategy has even greater tax-saving potential for some directors with children, as we shall see in Section 11.6.)

The more obvious general point, of course, is that the payment of Income Tax on dividends can also be deferred by a year if the payment of the dividends is delayed until after the end of the tax year.

Tax Tip

Combining these points, the best possible cashflow position is achieved by paying dividends on 6th April every alternate year.

This delays the payment of Income Tax on the dividends by almost 22 months, to 31st January two calendar years after the dividend is paid.

Cashflow isn't everything, however, and the issues covered in this section should always be considered in the context of your overall tax planning strategy.

2.16 DIVIDENDS AND PAYE

Directors who are receiving both salary and dividends may apply to have Self-Assessment tax liabilities of up to £2,000 collected through their PAYE codes for the next tax year after the normal due date for the tax. This can produce a considerable cashflow advantage.

Hence, for a director paying higher rate Income Tax, annual dividends of up to £8,000 may be paid and the tax arising can be deferred by an average of up to two and a half years!

For example, a dividend of £8,000 paid on 6th April 2008 would give rise to a Self-Assessment tax liability of £2,000 which would normally be due by 31st January 2010, but which can instead be collected through the director's PAYE code for 2010/11.

Furthermore, where the director's Self-Assessment tax liability is collected through their PAYE code, they will also avoid having to make any payments on account.

Wealth Warning

HM Revenue and Customs is now attempting to collect Income Tax on up to £10,000 of estimated annual investment income through the PAYE system whenever possible. This includes cases where directors are receiving dividends from their own company.

This results in the tax on such dividends being paid on a 'current year' basis as it arises, just like the tax on salaries or bonuses. Even when HM Revenue and Customs gets its estimates right, this accelerates the payment of tax on this income by an average of more than six months.

Furthermore, where HM Revenue and Customs overestimates the dividend income, the excess tax paid will need to be reclaimed through the Self-Assessment system and interest will only run on the repayment from 31st January, almost nine months after the end of the tax year, or an average of almost sixteen months after payment of the excess tax.

Worse still, where the taxpayer might otherwise have been able to apply to have up to £2,000 of tax collected through a later year's PAYE coding, as explained above, this new approach by HM Revenue and Customs would result in tax payments being accelerated by two years!

HM Revenue and Customs dresses this approach up as being 'for your benefit' and 'to help you plan your finances'. Clearly, the Treasury has been infected by New Labour's fondness for spin!

The collection of tax on dividend income through PAYE is **not** for your benefit, it is merely a way for the Government to accelerate the collection of tax. I would urge all readers who are in the PAYE system to check their coding notices and, if estimated dividend income has been included, exercise your right to have this removed from your PAYE code. HM Revenue and Customs **must** comply with this request if you object to your PAYE code being used in this way and the instructions on how to do this are included on your PAYE coding notice.

Naturally, once dividend income has been removed from your PAYE coding, you will need to ensure that you are able to pay the tax arising when it falls due under the Self-Assessment system. As explained in the previous section, this can be especially painful when the 'double-whammy' effect comes into play.

Nevertheless, the PAYE system is most certainly not the way to save up for your tax liabilities! Instead, I would generally recommend an ISA, a high-interest bearing deposit account or an offset mortgage. Alternatively, as we shall see in Chapter 7, you may even want to lend the funds back to the company until they are needed to pay your own tax bill.

2.17 SALARY AND BONUS PAYMENTS TO NON-DIRECTORS

The main purpose of this guide is to explore how company owners can extract funds from their own companies as tax efficiently as possible.

In most cases, the owners of private companies will also be directors of that company.

In some cases, however, one or more of the owners of the company may be an employee but not a director of the company. This may occur, for example, where a couple own a company but one of them is not appointed as a director.

For most tax purposes this makes little difference and such owner/employees are in the same position as a director/shareholder.

This includes the Income Tax payable under the PAYE system on any bonus or salary payments to the employee, with all of the cashflow consequences set out in Section 2.14.

The major difference which does arise, however, and which potentially may have far more impact than mere cashflow, is the fact that National Insurance on payments of salary or bonuses to non-directors is calculated under the pay period system, with no adjustment to the annual cumulative basis at the end of the tax year.

This represents a significant potential pitfall where small salaries are being paid to non-directors, but can be turned to advantage where larger salaries are involved.

For non-director employees, the National Insurance earnings threshold is divided across all of the pay periods in the tax year to produce a 'primary threshold' for each pay period. National

Insurance is then due on any amount paid in excess of the 'primary threshold' which, for 2008/9, amounts to £105 for weekly pay periods, or £453 for monthly pay periods.

Any National Insurance paid under the pay period system on salary or bonus payments to a non-director cannot be recovered, regardless of the eventual total level of salary and bonus which the employee receives for the year. This applies to both the primary National Insurance suffered by the employee and the secondary employer's National Insurance paid by the company, giving rise to a total non-refundable cost of up to 23.8%.

It is essential, therefore, that lump sum payments are not made to non-director owner/employees when it is intended to only pay them a small salary during the tax year, such as £5,435 (the earnings threshold), £6,035 (the personal allowance) or an amount equivalent to the national minimum wage (see Section 12.7).

Example

Warren is a part-owner of Spion Kop Limited but not a director. He does not take a regular salary from the company but, in March 2009, he is paid a lump sum bonus of £5,435.

If Warren had been paid a salary of £5,435 in regular sums of £452.92 per month, these would have been under the primary threshold and no National Insurance would have arisen.

Instead, however, Warren's single payment of £5,435 exceeds the primary threshold for a monthly pay period by £4,982 (£5,435 - £453). Fortunately, it also exceeds the monthly upper earnings limit of £3,337. Nevertheless, Warren will still be subject to National Insurance at 11% on £2,884 (£3,337 - £453) and at 1% on £2,098 (£5,435 - £3,337), whilst the company will be subject to secondary National Insurance at 12.8% on the full amount of the excess over the primary threshold: £4,982.

The lump sum payment therefore gives rise to National Insurance liabilities of £338 (£2,884 x 11% + £2,098 x 1%) for Warren and £638 (£4,982 x 12.8%) for Spion Kop Limited.

What an unmitigated disaster! That's a total cost of £976 (£338 + £638) which has been incurred quite unnecessarily, simply due to the fact that Warren was paid in a lump sum rather than by way of a regular monthly salary.

As we can see from the example, it is essential that non-director owner/employees who are to receive small salaries from the company are paid on a regular basis over the course of the tax year.

Alternatively, an easy way to avoid these problems is to make them a director. There are, however, many non-tax reasons why this may not always be possible, or desirable.

Furthermore, when it comes to larger salaries, not being a director can be turned to advantage!

Larger Salaries

Where a non-director is receiving a more substantial level of salary, it is possible to make significant National Insurance savings by paying them in a single lump sum.

If you refer back to the example of Emma given in Section 2.14, you will see that she achieved an overall National Insurance cashflow saving of £2,484 by paying herself in a single lump sum. If Emma had not been a director, this cashflow saving would have become an absolute, permanent saving!

The Income Tax cashflow disadvantage of the lump sum payment would then be less important, or could be avoided by making the lump sum payment in 'Month 12' rather than 'Month 1'.

The lump sum payment strategy becomes advantageous whenever the non-director's total salary for the tax year exceeds £15,195 (at 2008/9 rates).

However, for companies with annual profits not exceeding £317,000 or companies with accounting periods ending after 31st January 2009, it can never become advantageous enough for the salary to be better than a dividend. (In other words, the lump sum payment is better than a regular salary but not better than a dividend.)

2.18 DIRECTORS WITH OTHER INCOME

As explained in Section 2.6, the presence of any other income has an impact on the effective marginal rate of tax suffered by a director on any salary or bonus payments.

Where the other income is further employment income from another source, or self-employment or partnership trading income, the Income Tax rates remain the same but the effective National Insurance rates can become rather complicated. Overpayments of National Insurance frequently arise in this situation and I would recommend taking professional advice to see if a reclaim is available.

This leaves us with pensions, rental profits, dividends, interest and other investment income. Interest and most other forms of investment income other than dividends are referred to as 'savings income' for Income Tax purposes.

These types of income are all exempt from National Insurance and suffer Income Tax at the following effective rates:

Income	Pensions or Rental Profits	Savings Income	Dividends	Large Foreign Dividends*
Up to £6,035	0%	0%	0%	0%
£6,035 to £8,355	20%	10%	0%	10%
£8,355 to £40,835	20%	20%	0%	10%
Over £40,835	40%	40%	25%	32.5%

* - See Section 2.8

The band from £6,035 to £8,355 arises because savings income is still eligible for the 10% starting rate of Income Tax which was abolished in respect of all other types of income with effect from 6th April 2008.

There is, however, a set 'pecking order' for the use of Income Tax rate bands as follows:

    i)   Employment income
    ii) Self employment or partnership trading income
    iii) Pensions or rental profits
    iv) Savings income
    v)   Dividends

Hence, for example, where the total income under headings (i) to (iii) already exceeds £8,355, none of the 10% band will be available for any savings income.

It does not matter what order the income is actually received in during the tax year, the 'pecking order' will always take precedence. (For example, a bonus received in March 2009 will take precedence over dividends or interest received in May 2008.)

Where a director has pension income, rental profits, dividends or savings income and also receives a salary or bonus, the marginal tax rate bands explained in Section 2.6 will continue to apply to the salary or bonus itself. In other words, the existence of the other income will not affect the amount of Income Tax and National Insurance paid on the salary or bonus.

So why am I making such a fuss about 'other income'?

The problem is not that the other income affects the tax paid on the salary or bonus; the problem is that the salary or bonus affects the tax paid on the other income!

This happens because employment income always uses up the Income Tax bands set out above in priority to other income. Paying salary or a bonus may therefore effectively push this other income up into a higher Income Tax rate band.

The effect of all this is to alter the overall effective marginal tax rate arising on the payment of the salary or bonus.

Example

Hal takes a basic salary of £30,000 each year from his company, Crecy Limited. In 2008/9, he also receives rental profits of £12,000.

His total Income Tax and National Insurance burden is therefore as follows:

	£
Salary:	
£5,435 @ 0%	0
£600 (£6,035 - £5,435) @ 11%	66
£23,965 (£30,000 - £6,035) @ 31%	7,429
Rental Profits:	
£10,835 (£40,835 - £30,000) @ 20%	2,167
£1,165 (£12,000 - £10,835) @ 40%	466

	10,128
	====

Let us suppose that Hal now pays himself a bonus of £10,000. As his taxable income is already over £40,835, the table in Section 2.6 tells us that that he should suffer a marginal rate of 41% on this additional income. However, the existence of his rental income will alter this position:

	£
Salary and Bonus (total £40,000):	
£5,435 @ 0%	0
£600 (£6,035 - £5,435) @ 11%	66
£33,965 (£40,000 - £6,035) @ 31%	10,529
Rental Profits:	
£835 (£40,835 - £40,000) @ 20%	167
£11,165 (£12,000 - £835) @ 40%	4,466

	15,228
	====

Hal's £10,000 bonus has increased his total tax burden by £5,100 (£15,228 - £10,128). His effective marginal tax rate on the bonus was therefore 51%!

In effect, the existence of Hal's £12,000 of rental profits has created an effective marginal tax rate band of 51% applying to salary and bonuses where his total income lies between £40,835 and £52,040. This is because, in this band of income, he is paying Income Tax at 40% on any additional income and also paying National Insurance at 11% on any additional employment income.

This interaction of tax bands and different types of income creates an infinite variety of possible effective marginal tax rate bands. To give you a flavour of the possible outcomes, however, let's just look at a few examples.

Pensions or Rental Income

Where the director has £1,000 of pension income or rental profits in 2008/9, the effective marginal tax rates applying to any payments of salary or bonus will be as follows:

Up to £5,035:	0%	(£5,035 = £6,035 - £1,000)
£5,035 to £5,435:	20%	
£5,435 to £39,835:	31%	(£39,835 = £40,835 - £1,000)
£39,835 to £40,040:	51%	
Over £40,040:	41%	

Where the director has £10,000 of pension income or rental profits in 2008/9, the effective marginal tax rates applying to any payments of salary or bonus will be as follows:

Up to £5,435:	20%	
£5,435 to £30,835:	31%	(£30,835 = £40,835 - £10,000)
£30,835 to £40,040:	51%	
Over £40,040:	41%	

Savings Income

Where the director has £1,000 of interest or other savings income in 2008/9, the effective marginal tax rates applying to any payments of salary or bonus will be as follows:

Up to £5,035:	0%	(£5,035 = £6,035 - £1,000)
£5,035 to £5,435:	10%	
£5,435 to £6,035:	21%	
£6,035 to £7,355:	31%	(£7,355 = £8,355 - £1,000)
£7,355 to £8,355:	41%	
£8,355 to £39,835:	31%	(£39,835 = £40,835 - £1,000)
£39,835 to £40,040:	51%	
Over £40,040:	41%	

Where the director has £10,000 of interest or other savings income in 2008/9, the effective marginal tax rates applying to any payments of salary or bonus will be as follows:

Up to £5,435:   20%
£5,435 to £6,035:   31%
£6,035 to £8,355:   41%
£8,355 to £30,835:   31%   (£30,835 = £40,835 - £10,000)
£30,835 to £40,040:   51%
Over £40,040:   41%

Dividends

Where the director has £1,000 of dividends which qualify for tax credits (see Section 2.8) in 2008/9, the effective marginal tax rates applying to any payments of salary or bonus will be as follows:

Up to £5,435:   0%
£5,435 to £6,035:   11%
£6,035 to £39,724:   31%   (£39,724 = £40,835-£1,000x10/9)
£39,724 to £40,040:   53.5%
£40,040 to £40,835:   43.5%
Over £40,835:   41%

Where the director has £10,000 of dividends which qualify for tax credits (see Section 2.8) in 2008/9, the effective marginal tax rates applying to any payments of salary or bonus will be as follows:

Up to £5,435:   0%
£5,435 to £6,035:   11%
£6,035 to £29,724:   31%   (£29,724 = £40,835-£10,000x10/9)
£29,724 to £40,040:   53.5%
£40,040 to £40,835:   43.5%
Over £40,835:   41%

See the Taxcafe.co.uk guide 'How to Save Tax 2008/2009' for more information on the interaction between dividends and other income.

Implications for the 'Salary versus Dividends' Question

As we saw in Section 2.7, the effective marginal rate of tax suffered on a dividend is dependent only on the director's total taxable income for the tax year and is unaffected by the type of that income.

From the examples given above, however, we can see that the existence of other income can give rise to several different effective marginal tax rates on bonuses and salary which were not present in our table in Section 2.6. The bands of income in which these different rates apply will differ from one individual to another.

Where one of the 'normal' effective marginal rates of 0%, 11%, 31%, 21% or 41% applies, the position will be just as it is for an individual with no other income and this is what we will be examining in depth in the next few chapters. ('Normal' does not, however, include where the 41% rate arises on income between £6,035 and £8,355.)

In Section 16.4 at the end of the guide, we will return to take a look at the position where one of the other effective marginal rates applies.

2.19 OTHER FACTORS AFFECTING TAX ON A SALARY OR DIVIDEND

The tax position of any director receiving either salary or a dividend will be altered by the effect of any applicable reliefs and allowances to which they may be entitled, such as relief for personal pension contributions or gift aid payments.

National Insurance costs will also be significantly altered if the director is a member of a contracted out company pension scheme.

We will look at the impact of pension contributions in Chapter 13.

The existence of any taxable benefits in kind will also have an impact on the director's tax position. In Section 14.3, however, we will look at how a company car might be used as a tax efficient alternative to the payment of a dividend or bonus.

Yet more complications arise in the shape of Working Tax Credits and Child Tax Credits. The impact of any bonus or dividend payments on these should also be taken into account and we will look at some of the more common scenarios to be considered in Chapter 11.

Another set of 'special' circumstances which we are going to cover later in the guide is that of 'older director/shareholders'. In this context, I mean the following groups of people:

- Women aged 60 or more.
- Men who will be aged 65 or more on 5th April 2009.
- People who are married or in a civil partnership and whose spouse or partner was born before 6th April 1935.

Turn to Chapter 10 to see how your tax position on salaries, bonuses or dividends is affected if you fall within one of these groups.

Those directors within a few years of state retirement age would also be well advised to take a look at Section 10.4.

As explained in Section 1.6, it will very often be essential to obtain professional advice on the impact of the factors set out above, and others, before deciding on the optimum strategy for the extraction of company funds.

However, whilst in reality there are a great many further complications which may arise, we are going to start in the next chapter by concentrating on the position where the director has no other income and no applicable reliefs or credits beyond the personal allowance. We will also begin by assuming that the company has no associated companies.

Chapter 3

The Taxcafe Computer Model

3.1 INTRODUCTION TO THE MODEL

As we have already seen in the first two chapters, the Salary versus Dividends question is highly complicated. The position is dependent not only on the director's own personal situation, but also the company's profit level and accounting period. On top of these factors, we also have to consider the impact of both primary and secondary National Insurance as well.

In order to provide a guide through this maze of conflicting tax rates, reliefs and allowances, we have developed a computer model which takes account of all of the applicable taxes:

- Income Tax paid by the director/shareholder

- Corporation Tax on company profits

- Employee's primary National Insurance

- Employer's secondary National Insurance

Using our computer model, we have been able to analyse the overall tax position for each relevant band of personal income and company profit and hence calculate the **net total extra tax** payable whenever additional salary or bonus is paid or a dividend is declared.

As the proprietors of their companies, director/shareholders are not merely concerned solely with their own personal tax position but also with that of their companies as well.

Hence, our program weighs up the marginal personal tax rate of the director, the marginal tax rate of the company and the impact of the additional National Insurance payable by both the director and the company when additional salary is paid or a bonus is awarded, as well as the Corporation Tax relief obtained.

The model then provides us with the overall net tax cost suffered by both the company and director taken together in order to get a net £100 of additional income into the director's hands after all tax liabilities and tax reliefs have been taken into account.

Our results are published in the tables which follow in the next section. These tables apply to bonuses and dividends treated as income of the director/shareholder for the 2008/9 tax year. In the context of these tables, any payment of additional salary over and above the director's existing salary may also be regarded as being effectively the same as a bonus.

In the case of bonuses, the rate of Corporation Tax relief available will depend on the company accounting period in which these payments are accounted for. Later, in Section 6.1, we will cover the principles involved in determining which accounting period this should be.

Payments of bonuses to directors falling to be taxed in the 2008/9 tax year might be accounted for in a company accounting period ending anywhere between July 2007 and March 2010. (Assuming that we have a twelve month accounting period ending at the end of a calendar month.)

As we saw in Section 2.3, the marginal rates of Corporation Tax applying will vary according to the company's accounting period and it is not therefore possible for us to reproduce in one single table the precise net cost of all salaries or bonuses which fall to be taxed on the recipient director in 2008/9.

What we have done in the tables in the next section, therefore, is to produce the range of possible answers for each relevant band of company profit and director's income. The tables provided in the next section are intended to cover the most basic situation and the notes to the tables explain the assumptions made. As explained in Sections 2.18 and 2.19, there are many reasons why personal circumstances will vary from the results given in our basic tables. These tables will nevertheless provide a reasonable guide to your position in most cases.

Later in the guide, we will explore a number of variations on the basic model.

3.2 MODEL RESULTS 2008/2009

The total net tax suffered on an additional *net* £100 of bonus or dividend at different levels of company profit and director's income is as follows:

Annual company profits up to £300,000

Director's Income	Total Tax on £100 (net) of:		Dividend
	Bonus		
	From	To	
Up to £5,435	£19.33	£22.00	£0.00
£5,435 to £6,035	£2.24	-£1.14	£0.00
£6,035 to £40,040	£31.87	£27.51	£0.00
£40,040 to £40,835	£15.18	£11.37	£0.00
Over £40,835	£54.22	£49.13	£33.33

Annual company profits £300,000 to £1,500,000

Director's Income	Total Tax on £100 (net) of:		Dividend
	Bonus		
	From	To	
Up to £5,435	£32.67	£29.50	£0.00
£5,435 to £6,035	£14.66	£10.65	£0.00
£6,035 to £40,040	£10.08	£15.25	£0.00
£40,040 to £40,835	-£3.86	£0.66	£0.00
Over £40,835	£28.73	£34.79	£33.33

Annual company profits over £1,500,000

Director's Income	Total Tax on £100 (net) of:		Dividend
	Bonus		
	From	To	
Up to £5,435	£30.00	£28.00	£0.00
£5,435 to £6,035	£11.28	-£8.75	£0.00
£6,035 to £40,040	£14.43	£17.70	£0.00
£40,040 to £40,835	-£0.05	£2.81	£0.00
Over £40,835	£33.83	£37.65	£33.33

Notes to the Tables

1. 'Total Tax' means the total Income Tax and National Insurance suffered by both the company and the director, less the Corporation Tax relief obtained by the company.
2. In each case, the £100 referred to above is the <u>net</u> sum left in the shareholder/director's hands after payment of all applicable taxes (see Sections 2.11 and 2.12 for example calculations).
3. 'Director's Income' represents the salary and bonuses already being received by the director during 2008/9 prior to payment of the additional salary, bonus or dividend under consideration. It is assumed that the director has no other sources of income and has not yet taken any other dividends out of the company during 2008/9.
4. It is also assumed that the director has no applicable tax reliefs or credits beyond the personal allowance and is of normal working age.
5. The company is assumed to be paying the bonus out of a twelve month accounting period and to have no associated companies.
6. The total net tax cost of a bonus will vary according to the company accounting period for which Corporation Tax relief is being obtained. The costs given in the 'From' column represent those applying for an accounting period ending on 31st July 2007. The costs given in the 'To' column represent those applying for an accounting period ending on 31st March 2010. The costs applying for an accounting period ending between 1st August 2007 and 30th March 2010 will lie somewhere between those given in the 'From' column and those given in the 'To' column.
7. Negative numbers (such as -£22.00, for example) indicate that the payment will result in an overall tax **saving**. We will see how such payments can be put to good use later in the guide.
8. In these tables, we are assuming that the payment under consideration will not itself push the director's total income into a higher marginal tax rate band. In Chapter 4 we will look at the consequences of payments which do result in the director's income exceeding one of the key marginal rate thresholds outlined in Sections 2.6 and 2.7.

9. We are also assuming that any payment of additional salary or bonus will not alter the company's marginal Corporation Tax rate by reducing its taxable profits below either £300,000 or £1,500,000 as the case may be. We will again consider the consequences of salary and bonus payments which alter the company's marginal Corporation Tax rate in Chapter 4.

We will be referring to the tables shown above throughout the rest of the guide. For ease of reference, they are therefore reproduced again in Appendix A as Tables A, B and C.

3.3 INTERPRETING THE MODEL

To explain how the tables in the previous section work, let's examine a few of the model's figures in detail.

In the first row of the first table, we see that a company with profits of less than £300,000 paying a £100 bonus to a director with existing income of less than £5,435 will result in an overall tax *saving* of between £19.33 and £22.00.

The £100 payment has no Income Tax or National Insurance consequences (because the director's income is less than the £5,435 National Insurance earnings threshold) but *is* an allowable expense for the company.

As the company's profits are under £300,000, its marginal Corporation Tax rate will be between 19.33% and 22.00%. Hence, by not having to pay Corporation Tax on £100 of profits, the company will save between £19.33 and £22.00, as indicated in the table.

What if a dividend of £100 was taken instead?

This would have no effect on the company's Corporation Tax because dividends are paid out of after-tax profits. There is also no National Insurance to concern us because dividends are not subject to National Insurance.

Dividends may sometimes have Income Tax consequences of course, but, as we saw in Section 2.7, the effective tax rate on dividends is 0% unless the recipient is a higher rate Income Tax payer.

Putting all of this together, we can see that no tax is payable when a dividend is paid to a director/shareholder under these circumstances and no Corporation Tax relief is due. This is indicated by the value of £0.00 shown in the above table.

Another Example

Taking a slightly more complex example, the third row of the first table shows us that a net tax cost of between £27.51 and £31.87 will be incurred to get £100 of net bonus into the director's hands when the company has profits of less than £300,000 and the director already has existing income of between £6,035 and £40,040. To simplify the position, let's assume that the company is paying the bonus out of accounts for the year ended 31st March 2010, so that the net tax cost indicated by the table is £27.51.

From the table of Income Tax and National Insurance rates in Section 2.6 we know that a director with income between £6,035 and £40,040 has a marginal rate of combined Income Tax and National Insurance of 31%. To get £100 *net of tax* into the director's hands requires a total bonus payment of £144.93.

Applying the combined Income Tax and National Insurance rate of 31% to the gross bonus of £144.93 gives a combined tax charge of £44.93. Deducting this charge from the gross bonus of £144.93 brings us back to the required net figure of £100. For the mathematically inclined amongst you, the amount of £144.93 is arrived at by way of the formula: £100 x 100/(100-31).

The employer's National Insurance payable at 12.8% on the total bonus of £144.93 amounts to £18.55. This extra charge is added to the company's costs in paying the bonus, giving us a total of £163.48. The company then enjoys Corporation Tax relief on its total cost of £163.48. The company in this scenario has a marginal tax rate of 22%, so the tax relief amounts to £35.97.

Taking all this together, the total tax paid in getting a net sum of £100 into the director's hands is as follows:

	£
Income Tax and National Insurance paid by director	44.93
Plus	
National Insurance paid by company	18.55

60

Total tax paid	63.48
Less	
Corporation Tax relief obtained by company	35.97

Total net tax cost of bonus (as shown by table)	27.51
	=====

Another way of looking at this is to say that the company has to pay out a total of £163.48 but gets tax relief of £35.97. The total net cost of the bonus to the company is therefore £127.51. As it costs the company £127.51 to get a net £100 into the director's hands, the overall net tax cost is thus £27.51.

3.4   STRATEGY CHANGES

Looking at the model results in Section 3.2, we can see that there is a general trend for bonuses (or additional salary) to become less expensive for companies with profits under £300,000, but more expensive for companies with annual profits above that level, as we move towards later accounting periods.

This is a direct result of the changes in Corporation Tax rates over the next few years which we discussed in Section 2.2. Where Corporation Tax rates are increasing, the amount of tax saved through the payment of a bonus increases, thus making the bonus option more attractive.

Conversely, where Corporation Tax rates are reducing, the amount of tax saved by paying a bonus will reduce, thus making the bonus option less attractive.

The tax impact of dividends is unaffected by the changes in Corporation Tax rates, so the 'dividend' figures in our tables remain static whilst the 'bonus' figures are moving. In a number of cases, this results in a change in the strategy suggested by our model from bonus to dividend as we move towards later accounting periods.

In these cases, we need to look a little closer at the position in order to determine when the change in the recommended strategy per our model occurs.

In fact, to be more precise, it is a question of which company accounting periods fall either side of the change in recommended strategy.

The recommended strategy for the bands of director's income and company profit affected by this change can be summarised as follows:

Company profits up to £300,000

Director's income:	Dividend preferable for accounting periods ending up to:
£5,435 to £6,035	30th April 2009

Company profits £300,000 to £1,500,000

Director's income:	Bonus preferable for accounting periods ending up to:
£40,040 to £40,835	28th February 2009
Over £40,835	31st December 2008

Company profits over £1,500,000

Director's income:	Bonus preferable for accounting periods ending up to:
£40,040 to £40,835	31st March 2008 (but see note below)

In each case above, the other payment method becomes preferable for all later accounting periods. (Note, however, that we have restricted our analysis to accounting periods ending at calendar month ends. Remember also that the notes given to the tables in Section 3.2 continue to apply.)

Let's Be Realistic!

The saving generated by paying a bonus when the director's income is between £40,040 and £40,835, the company's profits are over £1,500,000 and the accounting period ends on or before 31st March 2008 is just five pence per £100 of net income. In fact, the maximum total saving generated by paying a bonus for this income bracket is just 31 pence!

The complications caused by taking this potential saving into account will therefore almost always cost you more than the tax you theoretically save. Cashflow considerations alone will almost certainly wipe out this miniscule saving.

Hence, whilst theoretically a bonus is the best solution in these circumstances, a dividend is actually almost always going to be more beneficial in practice.

For the rest of this guide, I am therefore going to recommend a dividend payment under these circumstances.

3.5 MODEL CONCLUSIONS

Having now covered all of the possible permutations of accounting period, company profitability and director's income, what conclusions can be drawn from our computer model results?

Summarising our model results for the 'Salary versus Dividends' question, we can now establish the following guiding principles:

i) Sufficient salary or bonus to bring the director's income up to the level of the National Insurance earnings threshold (£5,435) should always be paid.

ii) Sufficient further salary or bonus to bring the director's income up to the level of the Income Tax personal allowance (£6,035) should also be paid **unless** the company has profits not exceeding £300,000 **and** the company's accounting period ends on or before 30th April 2009.

iii) Thereafter, dividends are always preferable where the company's profits do not exceed £300,000.

iv) Where company profits are between £300,000 and £1,500,000 then, depending on the company's accounting date (see Section 3.4), bonuses may be preferable where the director has any level of income in excess of £40,040. Dividends become preferable in all other cases where the director's income exceeds his or her personal allowance.

v) Where company profits exceed £1,500,000, dividends are always preferable where the director's income exceeds his or her personal allowance.

vi) For companies of all sizes with accounting periods ending on or after 31st March 2009, dividends will always be preferable when the director's income exceeds their personal allowance.

For directors over State Retirement Age, bonuses generally become a more attractive proposition, as primary National Insurance is not due. This and many other differences which arise in the case of older directors are dealt with in Chapter 10.

It is important to remember that the £300,000 and £1,500,000 limits must be reduced whenever the company has any active associated companies or draws up accounts for a period of less than twelve months (see Chapter 9 for more details).

Other limitations to the general conclusions drawn above are covered in the notes to the tables in Section 3.2.

Despite these limitations, however, the general principles outlined above provide a sound basis for answering the 'Salary versus Dividends' question in many cases.

Nevertheless, a key point to bear in mind is the fact that the conclusions set out above represent a 'snapshot' of the position at a given level of company profit and director's income.

Payments to director/shareholders will, of course, themselves alter the level of the director's income and possibly also the company's profit.

In the next chapter, therefore, we will explore how the conclusions set out above can be applied to the 'moving picture' created when we actually start making payments to director/shareholders with existing income of varying levels.

In Chapter 12 we will also deal with some of the practical issues which may need to be considered in reality and which may sometimes need to take precedence over the optimum results recommended by our model.

In the meantime, however, let's look at a definitive overview of our model's recommendations.

3.6 OVERVIEW OF MODEL RECOMMENDATIONS

On the basis of the assumptions set out in Section 3.2, our model recommends that payments to directors made, or deemed to be made, in 2008/9 should be structured as follows:

Director's Income	Company Profit		
	Up to £300,000	£300,000 to £1.5M	Over £1.5M
Up to £5,435	Bonus	Bonus	Bonus
£5,435 to £6,035	Dividend for APs ending by 30/4/2009	Bonus	Bonus
£6,035 to £40,040	Dividend	Dividend	Dividend
£40,040 to £40,835	Dividend	Bonus for APs ending by 28/2/2009	Dividend*
Over £40,835	Dividend	Bonus for APs ending by 31/12/2008	Dividend

'AP' = Accounting Period
* - see note in Section 3.4

The model recommends that payments out of accounting periods ending after the dates shown above should be structured in the opposite way.

This table is central to the whole 'Salary versus Dividends' strategy. It is therefore reproduced again as Table D in Appendix A at the end of the guide for ease of reference.

Chapter 4

Planning Dividend or Bonus Payments

4.1 STEP BY STEP

When a payment of salary, bonus or dividend is made to a director, there is one thing which *will* definitely happen and one thing which *may* happen:

i) The director's taxable income *will* increase.

ii) The company's taxable profit *may* reduce, but only if the payment is salary or a bonus (and it meets the criteria set out in Section 12.4 below).

It is important to remember, therefore, that receiving additional salary, a bonus or a dividend, may itself push the director into a higher Income Tax band. (Although, in the case of a director moving 'up' into the income bracket between £40,040 and £40,835, their marginal tax rate will actually reduce - see Section 2.6.)

Similarly, the payment of salary or a bonus and its associated employer's secondary National Insurance may cause the company to drop from one marginal Corporation Tax rate bracket to another. The same is not true of a dividend, which has no impact on the company's Corporation Tax.

However, 'dropping' from one marginal Corporation Tax bracket to another does not necessarily mean a drop in the marginal rate of Corporation Tax – it could mean an increase (see Section 2.1).

Whenever the extra salary, bonus or dividend to be paid has the potential to span more than one marginal tax rate bracket for either the director or the company, it is necessary to consider the results shown in Chapter 3 in two stages:

a) The part of the salary, bonus or dividend *before* any change in marginal tax rate occurs, and

b) The part *after* any change in marginal tax rates.

However, if a <u>dividend</u> is paid as the best solution to part (a), it is not possible to then pay <u>salary</u> or a <u>bonus</u> as the best solution to part (b). The reverse, however, <u>is</u> possible.

This is because dividends are always treated as the top part of an individual's taxable income. Hence, if a dividend were paid first and then a bonus (within the same tax year), the bonus would be treated as if *it* had been paid first for Income Tax and National Insurance purposes.

In other words, when planning the best way to make a payment to a director/shareholder, you <u>can</u> start with salary or a bonus and then change to dividends but you <u>cannot</u> start with dividends and then change to salary or a bonus for any later part of the payment. Examples of these principles in practice are given in Sections 4.11 and 4.12.

In some cases, the payment to the director/shareholder will be large enough to span two or more changes in marginal tax rates and the part of the payment which follows each change should then be considered separately.

However, the fact remains that once a dividend is being paid as the best solution to one part of the desired payment, it is not possible to revert to a salary or bonus for the later parts which follow.

For this reason, it is often necessary to also look at the overall picture for the whole of the desired payment, as well as the individual elements, before being able to finally conclude what the optimum solution is.

Simple and Complex Situations

Having said all that, there are many situations where planning the optimum structure for a payment to the director/shareholder turns out to be reasonably simple, even when the payment spans one or more changes in marginal tax rates.

This is because many changes in marginal tax rates do not result in a change to the recommended payment method. The change in marginal tax rates will alter the net tax cost of the payment but if the recommendation per our model (see Table D) is unchanged, the structure of the optimum payment remains simple.

In Section 4.3, we will look at the situations which can safely be regarded as falling into this 'simple' category.

Sadly, however, there are also still many situations where matters become rather more complex and require a good deal more 'number-crunching' in order to get to the optimum result.

We will cover the mechanics of this 'number-crunching' in Sections 4.4 to 4.8 and then look at some practical examples of how to plan your optimum mix of dividend and salary or bonus in a complex scenario in Sections 4.11 and 4.12.

4.2 PLANNING FOR PROFIT

Because of the 'Step by Step' approach referred to above, we need to bear in mind that when carrying out our planning, the company's taxable profit may be altered as we proceed.

Throughout this chapter, therefore, when I talk about a company's 'profit', I am talking about its taxable profit *before* payment of any extra salary, bonus or dividend which we are in the process of calculating.

If, however, the director already has a regular salary then our 'profit' for planning purposes will already have taken this into account.

When we discuss the accounting periods out of which payments are to be taken there are two possibilities:

a)   We are talking about the company's current accounting period.
b)   We are talking about the company's previous accounting period.

In reality, we obviously will not yet actually know the company's taxable profit for its current accounting period. However, for the purposes of the planning techniques discussed in this chapter, we are assuming that the profit *is* known. In practice, the planning will need to be based on the best estimate of the company's likely taxable profit for the period.

The position will be more certain when payments are being taken out of the company's previous accounting period. To do this in practice, a number of additional criteria must be met. We will look at these additional criteria in Section 6.1.

4.3   KEEPING LIFE SIMPLE

In the next few sections we will look at how to deal with complex situations where the payment to a director/shareholder actually has the potential to change the payment method recommended by our model.

Before we do that, however, it is possible to identify a number of cases where we simply do not need to consider these complexities because we know that the model's recommendation will not change.

Readers whose companies have taxable profits of no more than £300,000 for a twelve month accounting period (and no active associated companies) may also wish to skip to Section 4.10 which neatly summarises the position for director/shareholders extracting funds from such a company.

The 'Down and Left' Technique

As explained in Section 4.1, a payment to a director/shareholder will increase the director's income and may also reduce the company's profit.

Looking at Table D, our overview table in Appendix A, this means that the payment will cause us to move **down** the table and, in the case of salary or bonus payments, may also cause us to move to the **left**.

We must, however, consider not only what **does** happen but also what **might** happen if an alternative payment method were followed.

This narrows down the number of cases where a simple solution is always possible since we must always consider both a move down the table and a move to the left, even when the current recommendation is actually to pay a dividend (see Section 4.7 for an example of this in action).

Nevertheless, when every part of the table lying directly below, to the left, or below and to the left, of our current position gives the same recommendation as that already given, then we know that a simple solution to the 'Salary versus Dividends' question will always be possible, no matter how large the payment to be made to the director.

Example

Let us suppose that the company has a profit of between £300,000 and £1,500,000 and the director has existing income of between £6,035 and £40,040. This puts us in the part of the table shaded dark grey below.

To decide if we have a simple solution without the need to resort to further calculations, we must consider the results shown in every part of the table shaded light grey.

Director's Income	Company Profit		
	Up to £300,000	£300,000 to £1.5M	Over £1.5M
Up to £5,435	Bonus	Bonus	Bonus
£5,435 to £6,035	Dividend for APs ending by 30/4/2009	Bonus	Bonus
£6,035 to £40,040	Dividend	Dividend	Dividend
£40,040 to £40,835	Dividend	Bonus for APs ending by 28/2/2009	Dividend
Over £40,835	Dividend	Bonus for APs ending by 31/12/2008	Dividend

This tells us the simple solution is to always pay dividends if the company's accounting period ends after 28th February 2009.

Reviewing the table, we can now see that under the scenarios described below the optimum solution to the 'Salary versus Dividends' question is always simply to pay a dividend:

i) Director's income is £5,435 or more, company profit is no greater than £300,000 and the company's accounting period ends on or before 30th April 2009.

ii) Director's income is £6,035 or more and the company's accounting period ends after 28th February 2009.

iii) Director's income is £40,835 or more and the company's accounting period ends after 31st December 2008.

The company accounting periods referred to above mean the accounting period ('AP') in which salary or a bonus would be eligible for Corporation Tax relief if they were paid. As explained in Section 2.1, we are only considering accounting periods ending at the end of a calendar month.

These 'safe' scenarios where we know that we can simply pay a dividend can also be represented diagrammatically as follows:

Director's Income	Company Profit		
	Up to £300,000	£300,000 to £1.5M	Over £1.5M
Up to £5,435	Bonus	Bonus	Bonus
£5,435 to £6,035	■	Bonus	Bonus
£6,035 to £40,040	Dividend	Dividend	Dividend
£40,040 to £40,835	Dividend	Bonus for APs ending by 28/2/2009	Bonus for APs ending by 31/3/2008
Over £40,835	Dividend	Bonus for APs ending by 31/12/2008	Dividend

▓	- Dividends preferred for all periods
■	- Dividends preferred for APs ending on or before 30/4/2009
▓	- Dividends preferred for APs ending 31/1/2009 or later
▓	- Dividends preferred for APs ending 31/3/2009 or later

Where your situation falls into one of the scenarios described above, you can effectively ignore all of the complex calculations set out in Sections 4.4 to 4.9.

With one small proviso:

Where the amount to be paid to the director might be large enough to give rise to a loss for the company if paid in the form of salary or bonus, the potential impact on the company's Corporation Tax position in other years will need to be considered. We will discuss the issue of loss-making companies in more detail in Section 9.6.

4.4 USING THE MODEL FOR MORE COMPLEX DECISIONS

Tables A, B and C in Appendix A take the approach of calculating a net tax cost for each bonus or dividend payment. This enables us to establish the optimum payment method at any given level of director's income and company profit (i.e. the 'snapshot' approach).

For more complex tax planning decisions, however, we will often need to refer to two further important sets of statistics:

i)   How much does the director's taxable income increase by?

ii)   How much does the company's taxable profit reduce by?

These statistics are required to enable us to work out how much extra dividend, salary or bonus can be paid before either the director's or the company's marginal tax rate will change.

This, in turn, is important in establishing whether, and when, we have reached a point where the payment method should be changed.

However, we now know that this will only be relevant when we do not fall into one of the scenarios set out in Section 4.3 above.

4.5 INCREASING DIRECTOR'S INCOME

In Chapter 3, we looked at the net tax cost involved in putting a net sum of £100 into a director's hands through the payment of a bonus or dividend.

Based on the same assumptions as we followed in that chapter, the increase in the director's gross taxable income resulting from those net payments will be as follows:

Director's Income	Increase caused by £100 net Bonus	Increase caused by £100 net Dividend
Up to £5,435	£100.00	£111.11
£5,435 to £6,035	£112.36	£111.11
£6,035 to £40,040	£144.93	£111.11
£40,040 to £40,835	£126.58	£111.11
Over £40,835	£169.49	£148.15

The level of the company's profit has no impact on these results.

Naturally, these results only remain valid as long as the director's income stays within the relevant bracket after adding the extra amount of bonus or dividend.

These figures are important because they tell us the rate at which each of the director's marginal tax rate bands is used up.

For example, the income bracket from £6,035 to £40,040 covers a range of gross taxable income totalling £34,005 (i.e. the difference between £6,035 and £40,040). However, this income bracket is used up by *net* salary or bonus payments of:

£34,005 x £100/£144.93 = £23,463

The same income bracket will also be used up by *net* dividend payments of:

£34,005 x £100/£111.11 = £30,605

The above table plays an essential role in enabling us to work out the optimum structure of payments to directors in more complex situations and it is therefore reproduced again as Table E in Appendix A.

Deriving Director's Gross Income Figures

The figures in the 'bonus' column of the above table are derived by 'grossing up' the £100 net sum received by the director to take account of the Income Tax and National Insurance payable (see Section 2.6 for the relevant rates).

For example, where the director has existing taxable income between £6,035 and £40,040, their combined marginal tax rate is 31%. Hence, this means that to get £100 net into the director's hands requires a gross *before-tax* bonus of: £100 x 100/69 (we get 69 by deducting 31 from 100).

This works out at £144.93, which is supported by the fact that £144.93 less 31% comes back to £100 exactly.

The first four figures in the 'dividend' column include the tax credit of one ninth, or £11.11, as explained in Section 2.8. This produces a 'gross' dividend of £111.11. The key point for our purposes however, as we saw in Section 2.8, is the fact that each £100 of dividend paid to the director uses up £111.11 of each of the first four Income Tax brackets described in the table above.

The final figure in the dividend column is derived by 'grossing up' the £100 net sum received by the director to take account of the 25% effective tax rate on the dividend (see Section 2.7) and then also adding the tax credit of one ninth.

Net to Gross Calculations for Director's Income

The table above can be used to convert net sums received by the director into the gross amount by which their taxable income will be increased.

Example

Let us suppose that we want to get a net sum of £2,000 into the director's hands after tax and that the director has existing income of £35,000.

Using the above table, we can work out how much extra taxable gross income is required to get this sum into the director's hands, as follows:

If paid by way of bonus: £2,000 x £144.93/£100 = £2,899.

If paid by way of dividend: £2,000 x £111.11/£100 = £2,222.

In both cases, the increase in the director's gross taxable income is less than the £5,040 (£40,040 - £35,000) which would take the director into a different marginal tax bracket.

Hence, in this case, we know that the payment will not affect the director's marginal tax rate.

When we come to review the results in Table D we will therefore only need to consider other results to the left of our current position (we know that the size of the payment is insufficient to move us down the table).

In this case this means that we can stick to one simple dividend payment, as recommended by the model, without resorting to further calculations.

In other cases, however, the position will also depend on whether any change in the company's marginal tax rate might occur. That requires another set of calculations which we will look at in the next section.

Gross to Net Calculations for Director's Income

A better way to use the above table in many cases is to convert gross sums into the net amount which will be received by the director.

We can use this conversion to see how much net payment we can get into the director's hands before altering his or her marginal tax rate.

Example

Harry has an existing salary of £40,040 from his company, Shrewsbury Hotspurs Limited. He now wishes to take out a further payment but does not wish to push his income above the £40,835 higher rate tax threshold.

Harry can therefore take a payment which increases his gross taxable income by £795.

If he takes the payment as a bonus, he will receive the following sum:

£795 x £100/£126.58 = £628.

Alternatively, if Harry takes his payment by way of dividend, he will receive the following sum:

£795 x £100/£111.11 = £716.

Note that this does not necessarily mean that a dividend is better here. Table D in Appendix A has already told us the answer to that question.

What the above figures do tell us are the maximum amounts which Harry can receive net of tax before his marginal tax rate changes. To use these results in practice, we need to put them into the context of the model's recommendations in Table D. We will therefore return to take a detailed look at using 'gross to net' calculations in practice in Section 4.7.

Before that, however, we need to look at the other side of the equation: reductions in the company's taxable profit.

4.6   REDUCING   THE   COMPANY'S   TAXABLE PROFIT

Having looked at how the director's gross taxable income is increased by salary, bonus and dividend payments, we now need to look at the other side of the coin: how much is the company's taxable profit reduced by?

In the case of dividend payments, the answer is simple: **Nothing!**

In the case of additional salary or bonus payments, the reduction in the company's taxable profit is equal to the gross payment to the director (as per the table in the previous section) *plus* the resultant employer's National Insurance.

Subject to the further points covered in Section 12.4, the following table sets out the amount by which the company's taxable profit reduces when paying a bonus sufficient to leave a net sum of £100 in the director's hands.

Director's Income	Reduction in profit caused by £100 net Bonus
Up to £5,435	£100.00
£5,435 to £6,035	£126.74
£6,035 to £40,040	£163.48
£40,040 to £40,835	£142.78
Over £40,835	£191.19

These figures are derived simply by adding the 12.8% employer's National Insurance to the equivalent figures in the table in the previous section. (Apart from the first figure: where the director's income lies below £5,435, no employer's National Insurance is payable.)

These figures are again reproduced as Table F in Appendix A for ease of reference.

The figures in the above table tell us how much a bonus paid to a director actually costs the company before Corporation Tax relief. As we shall see in the next few sections, this will often be useful in helping us to plan the optimum payment to the director.

The above table is also important because it enables us to calculate how much additional net salary or bonus may be paid to a director before the company's marginal Corporation Tax rate is altered.

Example

Boudica has an existing salary of £50,000 from her company, Watling Street Limited, and now wishes to also take a large bonus. The company's taxable profit before paying Boudica's bonus, but after paying her normal salary, is £400,000.

Using the above table, we can work out how much net bonus will be received by Boudica before the company's taxable profit is reduced by £100,000 to £300,000 and the company therefore experiences a change in its marginal Corporation Tax rate.

The maximum net bonus which can be paid before the company's marginal Corporation Tax rate changes is £100,000 x £100/£191.19 = £52,304

4.7   PLANNING A PAYMENT

The tables in Appendix A now provide all of the information we need to enable us to plan the optimum method for making a payment to a director under almost any circumstances.

We have already seen in Section 4.3 that there are a number of cases where the process of planning the payment can be kept very simple.

In other cases, however, we are faced with the task of establishing the optimum payment method in a situation where the model may actually change its recommended payment method as the payment progresses.

Furthermore, we may also need to consider what might have happened if we had taken the alternative route. The reason we must do this is best explained by way of an example.

Example

James takes an annual salary of £50,000 out of his company, Sedgemoor Limited. The company has a taxable profit of £1,501,000 for the accounting period ended 31ˢᵗ March 2008 and James now wishes to extract a further net sum of £50,000. (We are assuming that a bonus paid now could still attract Corporation Tax relief in the year ended 31ˢᵗ March 2008 – see Section 6.1.)

If we look at Table D, we see that a dividend is currently the best method for James to extract funds from the company.

If James takes the whole net sum of £50,000 as a dividend, Table C tells us that this will have a net tax cost of:

£50,000 x £33.33/£100 = £16,667

However, we can also see that James only needs to take a small bonus before the company's taxable profit falls below £1,500,000 and Table D then recommends a different payment method.

Whilst this does initially mean going against the table's first recommendation, we need to know whether it might actually be better overall if James simply took a bonus instead of a dividend.

To work out the net tax cost of paying James a net bonus of £50,000, we first need to work out how much the bonus will cost Sedgemoor Limited before Corporation Tax relief.

Using Table F and the 'net to gross' calculation method explained in Section 4.5, we can work out the total cost of James's bonus to the company as follows:

£50,000 x £191.19 / £100 = £95,595

This tells us that the total Income Tax and National Insurance suffered by both James and Sedgemoor Limited amounts to £45,595 (£95,595 - £50,000).

Next, we need to work out how much Corporation Tax relief Sedgemoor Limited will receive for the bonus. From the table in Section 2.3, we can see that the first £1,000 (£1,501,000 - £1,500,000) of the cost suffered by the company will benefit from Corporation Tax relief at 30% and the remainder, £94,595 (£95,595 - £1,000), at 32.5%.

The total Corporation Tax relief for the bonus will therefore be as follows:

£1,000 @ 30% =	£300
£94,595 @ 32.5% =	£30,743
Total:	£31,043

Deducting the Corporation Tax relief from the Income Tax and National Insurance costs calculated above gives us the total net cost of the bonus, as follows:

£45,595 - £31,043 = £14,552

This is £2,115 LESS than the cost of a dividend.

So, we can now see that the optimum method to get a net sum of £50,000 into James's hands under these circumstances is actually to pay a bonus despite the fact that the model's initial recommendation is to pay a dividend.

This example demonstrates the fact that the optimum solution will sometimes only be found by exploring what happens if we do **not** follow the model's recommendations. This happens for two reasons.

Firstly, as explained in Section 4.1, a bonus cannot follow a dividend but a dividend can follow a bonus. This means that once the model tells us to pay a dividend, we have a problem if it then tells us to pay a bonus for any later part of the payment.

In order to grasp this idea, it may be useful to think of salary or bonus payments as being like bricks and dividends as being like layers of whipped cream. You can put cream on top of bricks, but you cannot balance bricks on top of cream!

Secondly, where a dividend is paid, the company's marginal rate of Corporation Tax cannot change. As we saw in the example above, however, there are cases where the payment of a bonus would change the company's marginal Corporation Tax rate so that the bonus then becomes preferable. Without exploring the possible outcome of paying a bonus in the first place we would never know what the optimum solution for the whole payment would be.

Because of these factors, once the model has told us to pay a dividend for any part of the payment to the director, from then onwards we will need to explore what might happen if we use the alternative payment method to the one recommended by the model.

Have We Lost Faith in the Model?

None of this means that the model is wrong. Remember, the model is only a tool which provides a 'snapshot' of the position at any given level of director's income and company profit. In practice, we must deal with what happens when we start to alter the position by actually making a payment to the director.

This does not mean ignoring the model altogether. In fact, as we have already seen in Section 4.3, there are many situations where it is safe to rely on the model.

In other situations, not included in Section 4.3, it is not that the model is misleading us, but rather that its initial recommendation is sometimes outweighed by the savings generated through following a revised recommendation which results when we actually start making the payment to the director. This, in effect, is what occurred in the case of James and Sedgemoor Limited above.

Hence, what we need to establish in any case which is not covered in Section 4.3 is whether the net payment required by the director may be large enough to cause the model to change its recommendation.

This also includes cases, like our example above, where following the alternative route to the initial recommendation causes a change in the model's recommendation.

In the next section we will look at how to determine whether the payment is large enough to potentially cause a change in the model's recommendation. After that, in Sections 4.10 to 4.12, we will look at what to do when the required payment does (or might) cause such a change.

4.8   CAN WE STILL KEEP LIFE SIMPLE?

If the net sum required by the director is not large enough to cause any change in the model's recommended payment method, we can still 'keep life simple' and simply make the whole payment in the form which the model recommends for the existing level of director's income and company profit.

As explained in the previous section, however, as part of this exercise we may need to consider whether the model's recommendation might change if we were to make the payment under the alternative method to the one which the model actually recommends.

Hence, to know whether we can 'keep life simple', we may need to establish up to three key numbers:

i)   How much net dividend could be paid to the director before his or her income is increased to the point where the model's recommendation changes.

ii)   How much net salary or bonus could be paid to the director before his or her income is increased to the point where the model's recommendation changes.

iii)   How much net salary or bonus could be paid to the director before the company's taxable profit is reduced to the point where the model's recommendation changes or would change if the director had a higher level of income.

I call these three numbers the *'trigger points'*.

The amount derived under point (i) is the 'dividend trigger point'; the amount derived under point (ii) is the 'bonus trigger point' and the amount derived under point (iii) is the 'company trigger point'.

We will not always need all three trigger points. In some cases, no amount of increase in the director's income will change the model's recommendation, meaning that the first two trigger points do not exist.

Furthermore, where the model recommends paying a bonus at the existing level of director's income and company profit, we will not need the 'dividend trigger point' at this stage (although it could come into play later).

The 'company trigger point' will always apply, since even when there is no apparent possibility of a change in the recommended payment method, there still remains the possibility that a large enough bonus payment could eliminate the company's profit altogether.

Such a payment could radically alter the situation and is the reason for the proviso given at the end of Section 4.3 regarding the potential for creating a loss in the company. The position for loss-making companies is examined in Section 9.6.

How to Use the Trigger Points

If the net sum actually required by the director is less than each of the trigger points then we know that we can simply follow the model's current recommendation for the whole payment required.

Let's look at an example to see how all of this might work in practice.

Example

Wallace takes a salary of £20,000 from his company, Stirling Bridge Limited. The company has a taxable profit of £310,000 for the year ended 30th June 2008 and Wallace now wishes to make a further payment to himself out of the profits for this period.

Looking at Table D, we see that the model initially recommends paying a dividend at this level of director's income and company profit.

We can also see that the model's recommendation changes to a bonus if Wallace's income increases by £20,040, from £20,000 to £40,040.

We can therefore calculate the first two trigger points using the 'gross to net' calculation method explained in Section 4.5 and the figures provided by Table E in Appendix A.

The 'dividend trigger point' is therefore:

£20,040 x £100/£111.11 = £18,036

In other words, a dividend of £18,036 would increase Wallace's taxable income to £40,040, the point at which the model's recommendation would change.

The 'bonus trigger point' is as follows:

£20,040 x £100/£144.93 = £13,827

This means that a net bonus of £13,827 would increase Wallace's taxable income to £40,040.

From the current position in Table D, we can see that a reduction in the company's profit will not change the recommended payment method.

As explained above, however, in a case like this, the 'company trigger point' occurs when a bonus would have reduced the company's profit to zero. Using Table F, we can therefore calculate the 'company trigger point' as follows:

£310,000 x £100/£163.48 = £189,626

The lowest of our three trigger points in this case is therefore £13,827 (the 'bonus trigger point').

We may therefore safely say that Wallace can take a net payment of up to £13,827 in the form of a dividend, as recommended by the model, secure in the knowledge that this is his optimum payment method.

If, however, Wallace wants any more than £13,827, then I am afraid that we still have more work to do!

As explained in the above example, a key step is to establish which is the lowest of up to three possible trigger points.

Where the net sum required by the director is less than the lowest trigger point, we can simply make one payment following the model's recommendation for the current level of director's income and company profit.

Where, however, the director requires any greater amount, further analysis will be required before we can determine the optimum mix of dividend and bonus or salary for the payment.

The best way to explain how this is done is to look at each possible situation in turn. In Sections 4.10 to 4.12 we will therefore take a detailed look at all of the possible outcomes for every level of director's income and company profit.

As we proceed through this analysis, it is worth remembering the principle explained in Section 4.3: that we can only ever move either down or to the left within the table of model recommendations: Table D (subject to the Wealth Warning given below).

Before we commence our detailed analysis, however, I will give you one warning and one useful shortcut.

Wealth Warning

Remember that any payment which is large enough to create a loss in the company if it were paid by way of a bonus will always require some further consideration. See Section 9.6 for further details.

All of the results and analysis given in Sections 4.10 to 4.12 and in Chapter 5 are subject to this over-riding principle.

4.9   A USEFUL SHORTCUT

Before we go on to a detailed analysis of how to deal with more complex situations where a payment is large enough to cause a change in the model's recommended payment method, I can provide you with a useful shortcut which will often reduce the amount of detailed work required.

As explained in the previous section, the 'company trigger point' will always exist.

Often, however, the 'company trigger point' will be considerably larger than the other trigger points. Indeed, just such a situation did occur in the example in the previous section.

In many other cases, the 'company trigger point' will be the only figure which we are interested in.

Very often, therefore, we simply want to know one of two things:

a)   Which is the lowest of the possible trigger points?
b)   Does our payment exceed the 'company trigger point'?

As a shortcut to answering these questions there is a very simple way to quickly derive a figure which is always less than the 'company trigger point'.

The Shortcut

Our shortcut comes in two easy steps:

i)   Work out the amount by which the company's taxable profit needs to be reduced before the model's recommendation changes. (Or, where no such change occurs, simply take the amount of the company's taxable profit, since, as explained previously, the creation of a company loss has a significant impact on the whole 'Salary versus Dividends' question.)

ii)   Halve it.

Example

Edward already has existing taxable income of over £100,000 and now wishes to extract a large sum of money from his company, Falkirk Limited.

Falkirk Limited has a taxable profit of £450,000 for the year ending 31st December 2008.

From Table D, we can see that the model's recommended payment method will change when Falkirk Limited's taxable profit has been reduced by £150,000, from £450,000 to £300,000.

Our shortcut figure for the 'company trigger point' is therefore half of £150,000, i.e. £75,000.

As Edward is already in the highest income bracket, the other two trigger points do not exist in this case.

Hence, we can very quickly see that if the sum required by Edward is no greater than £75,000, we can safely follow the model's recommendation to pay a bonus without doing any further detailed work.

Using the Shortcut

The shortcut is simply a quick way to derive a 'failsafe' figure.

In a case like the example above, the shortcut can be used to give us a very quick answer to our question.

It will also work in other cases where the other trigger points do exist and we need to know which of them is the lowest amount. If our shortcut figure is greater than at least one of the other trigger points then this will be enough to tell us that there is no need to calculate an accurate figure for the 'company trigger point' at this stage.

The shortcut figure is merely a way to avoid doing further unnecessary work. It is not an accurate figure and should not be used to actually calculate the amount of part of an optimum payment structure.

The answer it provides is also just a question of eliminating payments which are small enough not to warrant any further detailed work.

Hence, in our example, if Edward wanted a net payment of £75,000 or less, the shortcut is sufficient to provide the answer.

If, however, Edward requires a greater sum, the shortcut has merely told us that we need to do an accurate calculation.

Failsafe Figures

The same basic technique can be used whenever we need to establish a 'failsafe' minimum figure for the amount of net bonus which will reduce the company's profit to any given level.

Some good examples of the use of this 'failsafe figure' are given in Sections 4.11 and 4.12.

4.10 SMALL COMPANIES: PROFITS NOT EXCEEDING £300,000

The situation for companies with existing taxable profits not exceeding £300,000 is generally fairly simple and will not usually require any detailed analysis.

Where the director's income is currently less than £5,435, a bonus should first be paid until his or her income reaches that level. There is no need for any 'gross to net' calculations here since the increase in the director's taxable income is simply equal to the net amount received.

For accounting periods ending after 30th April 2009, the bonus should be increased slightly, to bring the director's taxable income up to the level of the personal allowance (£6,035).

Any additional amount which may be required should then be paid as a dividend.

Example

Arthur takes a salary of £300 per month out of his company, Camelot (499AD) Limited. Arthur's existing salary is therefore £3,600 (12 x £300). Camelot (499AD) Limited makes an annual profit of around £50,000 and draws up its accounts to 31st December each year.

In March 2009, Arthur decides that he would like to take out a further net sum of £10,000.

As the payment will be accounted for in the company's accounting period ending 31st December 2009, the first £2,435 (£6,035 - £3,600) should be taken as a bonus. The first £1,835 (£5,435 - £3,600) of the bonus is tax free and the remaining £600 (£6,035 - £5,435) yields a net sum of:

£600 x £100/£112.36 = £534

In total, therefore, Arthur receives a net sum of £2,369 (£1,835 + £534) out of his gross bonus of £2,435.

The remaining £7,631 (£10,000 - £2,369) which Arthur requires should be taken as a dividend.

Where the director's taxable income for 2008/9 is already:

i)   £5,435 or more (for company accounting periods ending on or before 30th April 2009), or

ii)   £6,035 or more (for company accounting periods ending after 30th April 2009);

our model simply recommends that a dividend is paid.

This simple strategy is generally the best route to follow. In practice, however, it is essential to observe all of the necessary formalities and other criteria set out in Chapter 12.

Furthermore, any payments which might be large enough to generate a loss in the company, if paid by way of a bonus, warrant some further consideration. The implications of such a payment are explained further in Section 9.6.

Subject to these points, however, the position for companies with profits not exceeding £300,000 is pretty simple.

4.11 MEDIUM-SIZED COMPANIES: PROFITS BETWEEN £300,000 AND £1,500,000

The position for medium-sized companies with profits between £300,000 and £1,500,000 is the most complex and is also in a state of flux. Much depends on which accounting period the payment is to be taken out of.

For accounting periods ending after 28th February 2009 however, the position at all levels of director's income above £6,035 is quite simple. In these cases, the model will generally recommend a simple dividend payment, as explained in Section 4.3.

To examine the position for medium-sized companies not falling into the simple position dealt with in Section 4.3, we will need to break it down into the different levels of director's income before the payment under consideration is made.

If you have already worked out the relevant trigger points (see Section 4.8), you will already have some of the figures which you need to carry out the detailed analysis. In this section, I will refer back to the three trigger points explained in Section 4.8 where relevant, but I will also work from basic principles for the benefit of readers who may have decided to skip Section 4.8 on the basis that the payment was bound to be large enough to fall into a complex scenario.

We will start with the highest income level and work downwards.

Director's Income over £40,835

For accounting periods ending on or before 31st December 2008, the model tells us to pay a bonus.

Since the director is already in the top income bracket, we only have one 'trigger point' to be concerned about: the 'company trigger point' (see Section 4.8). This is reached when sufficient bonus has been paid to reduce the company's taxable profit to £300,000.

After this point is reached, the model's recommendation changes to paying a dividend.

As explained in Section 4.1, we do not have a problem with paying a bonus first and then a dividend later (it is the reverse which creates problems).

Hence, the approach required here is therefore fairly simple. First we work out how much bonus to pay in order to reduce the company's taxable profit to £300,000 (i.e. the 'company trigger point') and then we pay any additional amount required by way of dividend.

Example

John already has a salary of £100,000 from his company Jutland Limited. He now wishes to extract a further net sum of £80,000 from the company. The payment will be taken out of the company's accounts for the year ending 31st October 2008 which currently show a taxable profit of £350,000.

The first step is to work out the 'company trigger point': the amount of net bonus which will reduce the company's taxable profit by £50,000 to £300,000. Using Table F, this is calculated as:

£50,000 x £100/£191.19 = £26,152

This leaves John requiring a further £53,848 (£80,000 - £26,152). As John is a higher rate taxpayer, we know that he will suffer an effective tax rate of 25% on any dividends he receives, so the total dividend required is £53,848 x 100/75 = £71,797.

The optimum payment to John is therefore a net bonus of £26,152 and a dividend of £71,797.

For accounting periods ending after 31st December 2008, the model simply recommends the payment of a dividend in these circumstances.

Director's Income between £40,040 and £40,835
Accounting periods ending on or before 31st December 2008

For accounting periods ending on or before 31st December 2008, the model tells us to pay a bonus at this level of director's income.

We can see from Table D that the model's recommendation will only change when the company's taxable profit is reduced to £300,000.

This effectively creates the same situation as in the previous scenario except that we may have an additional stage in our calculations to deal with the change in the director's marginal tax rate when his or her income reaches £40,835.

Example Revisited

Let's take the same facts as in the example above except that John only takes a salary of £40,500 out of the company (and not £100,000 as before).

Our first step remains to work out the 'company trigger point': how much net bonus will be needed to reduce the company's profit from £350,000 to £300,000. This time, however, we need to do this in three stages.

First we calculate the amount of the net bonus required to increase John's taxable income by £335 from £40,500 to £40,835 using the appropriate figure from Table E.

£335 x £100/£126.58 = £265

Next, using Table F, we work out how much this will cost the company:

£265 x £142.78/£100 = £378

(We could have just added 12.8% to £335 to get this last figure, but I did it this way because we will need our first figure later on.)

Now, using Table F again, we work out how much more net bonus we can pay before the company's profit is reduced by a further £49,622 (£50,000 - £378) to £300,000.

£49,622 x £100/£191.19 = £25,954

This brings the total net bonus paid to John up to £26,219 (£265 + £25,954). He now needs a further net sum of £53,781 (£80,000 - £26,219) and, as his bonus has pushed him into the higher rate tax bracket, this means paying a dividend of:

£53,781 x 100/75 = £71,708

This time, therefore, the optimum solution is to pay John a net bonus of £26,219 and a dividend of £71,708.

Director's Income between £40,040 and £40,835
Accounting periods ending on 31st January or 28th February 2009

The model continues to tell us to pay a bonus at this level of director's income.

However, once the director's income reaches £40,835, the model tells us to pay a dividend instead. The model also tells us to switch to a dividend if and when the company's taxable profit is reduced to £300,000.

In most cases, the answer will simply be to pay sufficient bonus to bring the director's total taxable income up to £40,835 and then pay any further sum required by way of dividend.

In a small handful of cases, the bonus should be restricted to the amount which reduces the company's taxable profit to £300,000.

Director's Income between £40,040 and £40,835
Accounting periods ending on or after 31st March 2009

The model now simply recommends the payment of a dividend.

Director's Income between £6,035 and £40,040

At this level of director's income, the model recommends paying a dividend.

However, for accounting periods ending on or before 28th February 2009, we can see from Table D that the model changes its recommended payment method to a bonus when the director's taxable income reaches £40,040.

However, the model only recommends paying a bonus until the company's taxable profit is reduced to £300,000 or, in the case of accounting periods ending after 31st December 2008, until the director's income reaches £40,835.

We can therefore see that a simple dividend payment must be preferable if paying a bonus would reduce the company's taxable profit to £300,000 before it increased the director's taxable income to £40,040.

In other cases, we must compare the cost of the following two possible approaches:

i)   Pay the whole of the required amount as a dividend, or
ii)   First pay a bonus sufficient to reduce the company's taxable profit to £300,000 (or to increase the director's income to £40,835 in the case of accounting periods ending on 31st January or 28th February 2009) and then pay the rest as a dividend.

Where the required amount is not actually sufficient to reduce the company's taxable profit to £300,000 (or to increase the director's income to £40,835 in the case of accounting periods ending on 31st January or 28th February 2009), then a straight comparison between the cost of a bonus and the cost of a dividend is all that is required.

94

Example

Horatio's company, Trafalgar Limited, anticipates a taxable profit of £550,000 for the year ending 30th September 2008.

In August 2008, Horatio decides that he needs to take a net sum of £20,000 out of the company. He is already paying himself a gross annual salary of £30,000.

From Table D we can see that the model currently recommends paying a dividend to Horatio but that this recommendation changes when Horatio's taxable income reaches £40,040. Using Table E, we can therefore calculate the 'bonus trigger point': the net bonus required to increase Horatio's taxable income by £10,040 from £30,000 to £40,040, as follows:

£10,040 x £100/£144.93 = £6,927

We can also quickly calculate a 'failsafe figure' (see Section 4.9) for the minimum net bonus required to reduce Trafalgar Limited's taxable profit by £250,000 from £550,000 to £300,000, as follows:

£250,000 x ½ = £125,000

As the 'failsafe figure' exceeds the 'bonus trigger point' we know that Horatio's income will be increased to £40,040 before the company's profit is reduced to £300,000 and we therefore cannot yet simply conclude that it is preferable to pay a dividend.

Our 'failsafe figure' also exceeds the total net sum actually required by Horatio and this tells us that the sum to be extracted from the company cannot possibly be sufficient to reduce its taxable profit to £300,000.

Hence, we therefore know that all that is required in this case is a comparison between the total net cost of a bonus and the cost of a dividend.

Bonus

From our calculation above, we know that a net bonus of £6,927 will increase Horatio's taxable income by £10,040 to £40,040.

Next, using Table E, we calculate how much further net bonus will use up Horatio's next income band from £40,040 to £40,835:

£40,835 - £40,040 = £795 x £100/£126.58 = £628

So far, this gives Horatio a total net bonus of £7,555 (£6,927 + £628). This leaves a further net bonus of £12,445 (£20,000 - £7,555) to be paid. Using Table E we see that this equates to a total gross bonus of:

£12,445 x £169.49/£100 = £21,093

The total gross bonus paid to Horatio is therefore £10,040 + £795 + £21,093 = £31,928. We can therefore now work out the total net cost of this bonus as follows:

	£
Total gross bonus paid:	31,928
Add:	
Employer's National Insurance @ 12.8%:	4,087

Total cost to company before Corporation Tax relief:	36,015
Less:	
Corporation Tax relief @ 31.125% (Section 2.3):	(11,210)

Net cost to company after Corporation Tax relief:	24,805
	======

Deducting the £20,000 received by Horatio, this leaves us with a total net cost of paying him by way of bonus of £4,805.

Dividend

From Table E we can calculate how much dividend Horatio could receive tax free:

£40,835 - £30,000 = £10,835 x £100/£111.11 = £9,752

This leaves Horatio requiring a further net sum of £10,248 (£20,000 - £9,752). To get this net sum requires a further dividend of £13,664 (£10,248 x 100/75).

This dividend will give Horatio an Income Tax bill of:

£13,664 x 25% = £3,416

Hence, in this case, we can see that the dividend route is preferable and will save Horatio £1,389 (£4,805 - £3,416).

Director's Income less than £6,035

The first step here is to pay sufficient bonus to increase the director's income to £6,035.

If, after making this payment, the company's taxable profit is still in excess of £300,000, then the remaining payment required should be dealt with exactly as explained above for 'director's income between £6,035 and £40,040'.

Otherwise, the remaining sum required should be paid by way of dividend.

A Minor Exception

There is a minor exception to the above recommendation for companies with taxable profits not exceeding £306,111 prior to the payment to the director and accounting periods ending on or before 30th April 2009.

In these cases, a bonus should be paid to the director equal to the lower of:

i)   The amount required to increase the director's income to £6,035, and

ii)   The greater of the amount required to increase the director's income to £5,435 and the amount required to reduce the company's taxable profits to £300,000.

Any remaining sum required should then be paid by way of dividend.

4.12 LARGE COMPANIES: PROFITS EXCEEDING £1,500,000

The position for large companies with profits in excess of £1,500,000 also depends on which accounting period the payment is to be taken out of.

As explained in Section 4.3, for accounting periods ending after 28th February 2009, the position at all levels of director's income above £6,035 is quite simple and, in these cases, a simple dividend payment can generally be made.

For accounting periods ending 31st January or 28th February 2009 where the director's income is already £40,835 or more, a simple dividend payment is again the optimum solution.

Even in other cases, the position for large companies is generally much simpler than for medium-sized companies and, for all levels of director's income above £6,035, a simple dividend payment usually remains the best solution - with one major exception.

The major exception, of course, is the fact that there is sometimes the possibility that the payment itself will reduce the company's taxable profit below £1,500,000 and thus make it a medium-sized company. As we saw in Section 4.11, this makes life rather more complicated!

Hence, in most cases not falling within the one of the simple scenarios in Section 4.3, a useful first step is to establish whether the required payment is large enough to potentially reduce the company's taxable profit below £1,500,000.

In fact, in most cases where the director's existing taxable income exceeds £6,035, if we can prove that the payment would not reduce the company's taxable profit below £1,500,000 if paid by way of a bonus, then it should simply be paid by way of dividend.

And, of course, the quick way to do this in many cases is to use our 'failsafe figure' from Section 4.9.

Example

Alamein Limited has a taxable profit of £1,750,000 for the year ending 31st August 2008. Bernard, the company's director/shareholder has existing taxable income in excess of £6,035 and now wishes to extract a large sum of money from the company as tax efficiently as possible.

Using the shortcut in Section 4.9, we can calculate a 'failsafe figure' as follows:

£1,750,000 - £1,500,000 = £250,000 x ½ = £125,000

We can therefore immediately tell Bernard that if he requires a net sum of no more than £125,000 after tax, he can safely withdraw the necessary funds by way of dividend.

"Could do with a little more than that, old boy," says Bernard, so we need to do a more accurate calculation.

We therefore now need to consider what amount of net bonus would reduce the company's taxable profit to £1,500,000. Using Table F, we can calculate this as follows:

£250,000 x £100/£191.19 = £130,760

Hence, we know from this slightly more accurate calculation that any required net sum of up to £130,760 can safely be paid by way of dividend.

If Bernard wants any more than that, however, we will need to think again!

Director's Income exceeding £6,035
Payments potentially reducing profit below £1,500,000

Where the payment is large enough to reduce the company's profit below £1,500,000 if paid by way of a bonus then, for accounting periods ending on or before 28th February 2009, there is a possibility that a bonus may be preferable overall.

For periods ending on 31st January or 28th February 2009, however, this possibility is pretty slight and the maximum tax saving at stake is a mere £2.14, so it makes sense to simply pay dividends in these cases.

In practical terms, therefore, this issue is generally only relevant for accounting periods ending on or before 31st December 2008.

For these accounting periods, a bonus will become the model's recommended payment method when the company's taxable profit has been reduced to £1,500,000 and the director's income has been increased to at least £40,040.

A dividend can therefore still safely be paid when the required payment would not increase the director's income above £40,040 *if* it had been paid by way of a bonus.

In all other cases, unless the payment is large enough to reduce the company's taxable profit below £300,000, it will be a case of a simple alternative – pay the whole sum as a bonus or pay the whole sum as a dividend.

We will therefore need to do the exercise of comparing the total net cost of a bonus with the total net cost of a dividend in order to work out which method is preferable.

Example Continued

Bernard, from our example above, decides that he would like to take a net sum of £350,000 out of Alamein Limited.

We know that this sum is large enough to reduce the company's profits below £1,500,000 if paid by way of a bonus and we also know that it is large enough to increase Bernard's income over £40,040 regardless of its current level.

In fact, for the sake of illustration, let's assume that Bernard's existing income is £50,000.

We therefore know that we have a straight choice between paying a bonus and paying a dividend and we now need to compare the cost of each method.

Bonus

Bernard is already a higher rate taxpayer so, using Table F, we can calculate the total cost of his bonus to the company (before Corporation Tax relief) as follows:

£350,000 x £191.19/£100 = £669,165

The company's Corporation Tax relief on this sum will come at two different rates: one rate for the first £250,000, which reduces its taxable profit to £1,500,000, and a different rate on the remaining sum of £419,165.

The relevant marginal Corporation Tax rates for an accounting period ending on 31st August 2008 given in Section 2.3 can be used to calculate the company's Corporation Tax relief as follows:

£250,000 @ 29.164% =   £72,910
£419,165 @ 31.35% =   £131,408

Total Corporation Tax relief: £204,318

Deducting the Corporation Tax relief from the total cost of £669,165 leaves the company with a net cost of £464,847. If we then deduct the net sum of £350,000 received by Bernard, this gives us an overall net tax cost for the bonus of £114,847.

Dividend

As Bernard is already a higher rate taxpayer, we know that to get a net sum of £350,000 into his hands after tax by way of dividend requires a total dividend payment of:

£350,000 x 100/75 = £466,667

The tax suffered by Bernard on this dividend at an effective rate of 25% is thus:

£466,667 x 25% = £116,667

So, in conclusion, we can see that it is preferable to pay Bernard a bonus. This generates an overall saving of £1,820 (£116,667 - £114,847).

(Whilst this is technically the correct solution, the saving is small enough to potentially be outweighed by some of the cashflow considerations discussed in Chapter 2.)

Director's Income less than £6,035

In the unlikely event that the director/shareholder of a company with profits in excess of £1,500,000 has income of less than £6,035 the model always recommends paying a bonus.

Hence, the first step here should always be to pay sufficient bonus to increase the director's income to £6,035.

If, after making this payment, the company's taxable profit is still in excess of £1,500,000, then the remaining payment required should be dealt with as explained above.

Otherwise, the remaining sum required should be dealt with according to the procedure for 'director's income between £6,035 and £40,040' given in Section 4.11.

4.13 SUMMARY

Set out below is a 12-step procedure for planning the optimum payment to a director/shareholder under any circumstances.

This procedure summarises everything we have covered so far and also provides a few pointers to refer you to other chapters of the guide which may be relevant in certain circumstances.

In particular, you will see at Step 6 that there is effectively an 'opt out' clause where the director does not yet have any taxable income for the period in question. This refers you to the next chapter, where we are going to look at 'bottom-up planning': how to plan payments to director/shareholders when you have the opportunity to start with a 'clean sheet'.

How to Plan the Optimum Payment to a Director/Shareholder

Step 1

Start by establishing four basic facts:
- i) What company accounting period will the payment be made out of?
- ii) How much is the director's taxable income *before* making the payment?
- iii) How much is the company's taxable profit for the relevant accounting period *before* making that payment?
- iv) How much is the net payment required?

Step 2

Consider whether there is any risk that the payment could give rise to a loss in the company if made by way of a bonus or extra salary. If so, you will need to refer to Section 9.6.

Step 3

Remind yourself that the key figures of £300,000 and £1,500,000 for the company's taxable profit need to be reduced if you do not have a twelve-month accounting period or your company has any active associated companies. Refer to Chapter 9 before proceeding if either of these apply.

Step 4

If you will be over state retirement age before 6th April 2009 or you have a spouse or civil partner born before 6th April 1935, refer to Chapter 10 before proceeding any further.

Step 5

If you are claiming Tax Credits refer to Chapter 11 before proceeding any further.

Step 6

If the director/shareholder does not have any taxable income for the current tax year, refer to Chapter 5 for a guide to the best payment strategy and then proceed straight to Step 12.

Step 7

Refer to Section 4.3 to see whether your situation falls within one of the simple scenarios. If so, you know that the model recommends paying the whole required sum as a dividend and you can go straight to Step 12.

Step 8

Refer to Table D to see the recommended payment method for your current level of director's income and company profit.

Step 9

Work out your relevant trigger points as explained in Section 4.8. Use the shortcut explained in Section 4.9 to work out the 'company trigger point' if you wish. If the net payment required which you established at Step 1 is less than all relevant trigger points, you know that the model's recommendation will not change from the recommended payment method found at Step 8. You can therefore now go straight to Step 12.

Step 10

If you used the shortcut from Section 4.9 to establish your 'company trigger point' and it turned out to be the lowest trigger point, you should now calculate the 'company trigger point' accurately. If this results in the net payment required now being less than all the relevant trigger points, you know that the model's recommendation will not change from the recommended payment method found at Step 8. You can therefore now go straight to Step 12.

Step 11

If the net payment required exceeds one or more of the relevant trigger points, you will need to carry out a detailed analysis in order to establish the optimum payment method. Refer to Section 4.10, 4.11 or 4.12, as appropriate, for guidance.

Step 12

You have now established your theoretical optimum payment method. You should now refer to Chapter 12 for further factors which need to be considered in practice.

Chapter 5

Bottom-Up Planning

5.1 A CLEAN SHEET

In the previous chapter, we were faced with the task of dealing with the myriad different situations which may arise over the course of a tax year, where the director may already have some income.

It is now worth looking at the basic planning strategies which apply where we are able to start with a 'clean sheet' – i.e. the director does not yet have any taxable income for the year.

Note that, when we start with a 'clean sheet', the company's 'profit' for our planning purposes is its profit before payment of any director's salary or bonus.

Readers may notice that the conclusions produced by 'bottom-up' planning differ from some of the optimum solutions produced in our examples in the previous chapter. This demonstrates the difference between a 'clean sheet', where we can truly achieve the optimum result, and an existing situation which is already less than ideal.

The 'ideal' solutions produced in this chapter must be viewed in the context of the practical aspects of payments to director/shareholders which we will cover in Chapter 12.

We are also assuming in this chapter that there will be no payments made which would be large enough to create a loss in the company.

For ease of reference, our detailed findings in Sections 5.2 to 5.7 are summarised in Section 5.8.

5.2 ALL COMPANIES: ACCOUNTING PERIODS ENDING AFTER 30TH APRIL 2009

For all companies with accounting periods ending after 30th April 2009 there is one simple solution.

The first £6,035 should be paid by way of salary or bonus. After deducting primary National Insurance at 11% from the amount in excess of the earnings threshold (£5,435), this will yield a net sum of £5,969.

Any additional sum required should then be paid by way of dividend.

5.3 SMALL COMPANIES: PROFITS NOT EXCEEDING £305,435 ACCOUNTING PERIODS ENDING ON OR BEFORE 30TH APRIL 2009

A quick review of Table D reveals a simple answer: pay salary or bonus of £5,435 and the rest as dividends. Easy!

Why £305,435 and not £300,000? Simple: because once that first £5,435 of salary or bonus has been paid, the company's profit will be no greater than £300,000.

5.4 MEDIUM-SIZED COMPANIES: PROFITS BETWEEN £305,435 AND £306,112 ACCOUNTING PERIODS ENDING ON OR BEFORE 30TH APRIL 2009

For this small group of companies, the optimum solution is to pay the exact amount of salary or bonus which will reduce the company's profit to £300,000 (taking account of the employer's secondary National Insurance at 12.8% due on the amount in excess of the £5,435 earnings threshold).

As usual, any further amount required should then be paid by way of dividend.

(The cost to the company of a £6,035 salary or bonus payment is £6,112. This is made up of the payment itself plus secondary National Insurance of £77 [£600 x 12.8%].)

5.5 MEDIUM AND LARGE COMPANIES: PROFITS EXCEEDING £306,112 ACCOUNTING PERIODS ENDING BETWEEN DECEMBER 2008 AND APRIL 2009

The same simple solution given in Section 5.2 above is again the optimum solution for these companies; namely, pay salary or bonus of £6,035 (yielding a net sum of £5,969) and pay any further sum required by way of dividend.

Is The Model Wrong?

At first glance, Table D would appear to suggest that bonus or salary might sometimes be preferable for accounting periods ending between December 2008 and February 2009.

However, when we are carrying out 'bottom up' planning, we see that the savings which are sometimes generated by bonuses after the director's income reaches £40,040 are not sufficient to make up for the extra cost of a bonus in the £6,035 to £40,040 income bracket in these accounting periods.

For these periods, therefore, salary or bonus should be restricted to just £6,035 as stated above.

5.6 MEDIUM-SIZED COMPANIES: PROFITS BETWEEN £306,112 AND £1,506,112 ACCOUNTING PERIODS ENDING BEFORE DECEMBER 2008

From Table D, we can see that the initial recommendation in this scenario is to start with a salary or bonus of £6,035. As we know from Section 5.2, this will yield a net sum of £5,969.

According to Table D, dividends are then preferable until the director's taxable income reaches £40,040, after which salary or bonus becomes preferable once more.

A salary of £6,035, plus 'gross' dividends (see Section 2.8) of £34,005, will give us the required £40,040.

The total <u>net</u> amount received at this point will be as follows:

£5,969 + £34,005 x £100/£111.11 = £36,574

So far, therefore, we can safely conclude that if no more than a net £36,574 is required, the best strategy remains simply to pay a salary of £6,035 and the rest as dividends.

But What If More Income Is Required?

So, what do we do when profits exceed £306,112 and the director wishes to extract more than £36,574 net?

The director's taxable income has now reached £40,040 and Table D is telling us that salary or bonus is now preferable, but we know that we cannot pay this on top of the dividends which have already been paid.

Hence, this leaves us with a choice between continuing to pay additional sums as a dividend or changing the whole payment to salary or bonus.

Clearly, if we only require slightly more than £36,574, the dividend route must remain preferable. Eventually, however, there must come a point where it is preferable to pay the whole amount as salary.

The critical question, therefore, is how much does the director need to be extracting from the company before it becomes preferable to do it **all** as bonus or salary?

Calculating this figure becomes pretty horrendous, so I won't bore you with the details. The answer to this question also depends on the company's accounting period. I have therefore summarised the position in the table below.

The figures given in the middle column below represent the minimum amount of net income to be withdrawn by the director which is required before it becomes preferable to pay the whole amount by way of salary or bonus (or at least until the company's taxable profit is reduced to £300,000). In the right-hand column, I have also summarised the minimum taxable profit which the company must have before paying the director's salary or bonus.

If the company's taxable profit before the relevant payment is not at least this minimum level, the payment will reduce its taxable profits below £300,000. Hence, for companies without at least this profit level, a dividend will remain the best method to make any payment after the initial salary of £6,035.

Year Ending:	Minimum Net Income	Minimum Profit
31-Jul-2007	£93,000	£465,699
31-Aug-2007	£93,772	£467,174
30-Sep-2007	£94,532	£468,627
31-Oct-2007	£95,331	£470,155
30-Nov-2007	£96,118	£471,660
31-Dec-2007	£96,947	£473,243
31-Jan-2008	£97,790	£474,856
29-Feb-2008	£98,568	£476,344
31-Mar-2008	£99,440	£478,011
30-Apr-2008	£109,858	£497,929
31-May-2008	£123,393	£523,806
30-Jun-2008	£140,349	£556,223
31-Jul-2008	£163,939	£601,323
31-Aug-2008	£197,607	£665,692
30-Sep-2008	£247,453	£760,992
31-Oct-2008	£336,315	£930,883
30-Nov-2008	£519,241	£1,280,613

The method for paying a bonus from an accounting period which has already ended is explained in Section 6.1.

Where the total net payment required lies below the figure given in the middle column above, it remains more beneficial to restrict the salary or bonus to £6,035 and pay the remainder as dividends. As explained above, the same applies when the company's taxable profit before the payment is less than the figure given in the right-hand column.

Where, however, the company's profit exceeds the amount shown in the right-hand column **and** the total net payment required exceeds the amount shown in the middle column above, the payment should be made by way of salary or bonus until it reduces the company's taxable profit to £300,000. Only after the company's profit has been reduced to this level should any excess be paid by way of dividend.

5.7 LARGE COMPANIES: PROFITS EXCEEDING £1,506,112 ACCOUNTING PERIODS ENDING BEFORE DECEMBER 2008

At first glance, the position indicated by Table D appears pretty simple: the first £6,035 should be paid out as salary or bonus and dividends are then always preferable thereafter.

But what about a salary or bonus so large that it reduces the company's taxable profit below £1,500,000 and thus takes it into the 'medium-sized companies' scenario which we explored in Section 5.6. Could a salary become preferable in such a situation?

We know already that a salary in excess of £6,035 cannot be worthwhile unless the total net amount required by the director exceeds the relevant amount given in the table in Section 5.6.

Furthermore, as we are starting with a profit of over £1,500,000, the first part of the salary will attract a lower rate of Corporation Tax relief until we reach the point where the company's taxable profit is reduced to £1,500,000.

This means that it must take an even bigger total net payment to the director before a salary of more than £6,035 becomes worthwhile.

Nevertheless, there are situations where a large company could pay sufficient salary to reduce its profits far enough down below £1,500,000 that the large salary route actually does work out better than the small £6,035 salary plus dividends.

Example

Marston Moor Limited has a taxable profit of £1,600,000 for the year ended 30th June 2008. Rupert, the company's sole director/shareholder now wishes to withdraw a net sum of £500,000 from the company. Rupert has no other taxable income for 2008/9. (We will assume that a bonus paid now can be validly claimed as an expense of the year ended 30th June 2008 – see Section 6.1 for further details.)

We already know that we should start by paying Rupert a bonus of £6,035 and that this will cost the company £6,112 (see Section 5.4) and yield a net sum of £5,969 for Rupert (see Section 5.2). The company therefore now has a taxable profit of £1,593,888 (£1.6M - £6,112) and we need to get a further net sum of £494,031 (£500,000 - £5,969) to Rupert. As we know that we will definitely start with a bonus of £6,035, we will use this position as our starting point for the rest of our calculations.

Dividend

Rupert can receive some dividends tax free until his taxable income reaches £40,835. From Table E, we can see that his tax free dividend is thus:

£40,835 - £6,035 = £34,800 x £100/£111.11 = £31,320

Rupert will then need a further £462,711 (£494,031 - £31,320). To get this sum to Rupert after tax requires a further dividend of:

£462,711 x 100/75 = £616,948

The tax cost of this method of payment is therefore:

£616,948 x 25% = £154,237

Bonus

Using Table E, we can see that Rupert will be able to receive the following further net sums before his taxable income is increased to £40,835, the higher rate tax threshold:

£40,040 - £6,035 = £34,005 x £100/£144.93 = £23,463
£40,835 - £40,040 = £795 x £100/£126.58 = £628
Total: £24,091

This still leaves Rupert needing a further net sum of:

£494,031 - £24,091 = £469,940

Using Table E, we can see that this equates to a gross bonus of:

£469,940 x £169.49/£100 = £796,501

Excluding the original £6,035, this means that the total additional gross bonus required to get a net sum of £494,031 to Rupert is therefore:

£34,005 + £795 + £796,501 = £831,301

Adding employer's National Insurance gives us the cost to the company before Corporation Tax relief in paying this bonus:

£831,301 x 112.8% = £937,708

We can now use the marginal Corporation Tax rates from Section 2.3 to work out Marston Moor Limited's Corporation Tax relief.

Firstly, we must deal with the part of the total cost to the company which reduces its taxable profit to £1,500,000:

£1,593,888 - £1,500,000 = £93,888 @ 29.503% = £27,700

Next, we deal with the remaining part of the cost to the company. This attracts a higher rate of Corporation Tax relief as the company's profit is now below £1,500,000:

£937,708 - £93,888 = £843,820 @ 31.816% = £268,470

The total amount of Corporation Tax relief obtained by the company is therefore £296,170 (£27,700 + £268,470). This leaves a net cost for the company after Corporation Tax relief of:

£937,708 - £296,170 = £641,538

Deducting the net £494,031 received by Rupert, we get a final net total tax cost of £147,507 for the additional bonus paid over and above the first £6,035.

And the Answer Is....

Paying the whole of the required sum to Rupert by way of bonus is the better alternative in this case and saves a total net sum of £6,730 (£154,237 - £147,507).

From this example, we can see that there **are** cases where the required payment is large enough for a salary or bonus to become preferable for the whole payment.

At this point you are probably looking for a nice table to tell you exactly when the net sum required by the director is large enough for it to be better to pay it all as salary or bonus.

However, if I showed you the algebraic equations which I used to produce the table in Section 5.6, you would realise that this situation, which is even more complex, has way too many variable factors to enable me to produce a definitive guide.

What I can do, however, is to give you one of my useful shortcuts. It goes like this:

Step 1: Take the company's taxable profit and deduct £1,506,112.

Step 2: Take the figure from Step 1 and halve it.

Step 3: Add the figure from Step 2 to the figure from the middle column of the table in Section 5.6 for the relevant accounting period.

Step 4: If the net amount required by the director is less than the sum derived at Step 3 then it is safe to conclude that it would not be beneficial to pay the whole amount by way of salary. You can therefore safely pay a salary or bonus of £6,035 and the rest as a dividend without doing any further work.

Step 5: If the net amount required by the director is more than the sum derived at Step 3 then I'm afraid you will have to work it out properly using the method followed in the example above.

In Rupert's case, this shortcut approach would have told us that we needed a net payment of at least £187,293 (£140,349 + £93,888/2). As Rupert needed £500,000, it was worth exploring whether a bonus was preferable and, in the end, we found out that it was.

Remember that the shortcut described above is again merely a way to produce a 'failsafe' figure to save on unnecessary work in some cases and is not a substitute for the accurate calculations.

Don't go Too Far

For very large payments, where a salary or bonus is preferable, it will not be beneficial to continue paying salary beyond the point where the company's taxable profit has been reduced to £300,000. If this point is reached, a dividend should be used to pay any further sums still required.

5.8 SUMMARY OF 'BOTTOM-UP' PLANNING

We can now summarise our conclusions for planning the optimum method of making payments to director/shareholders on a 'clean sheet' basis:

Accounting Periods Ending After 30th April 2009:

> Pay salary or bonus of £6,035 and then pay any further sums required as a dividend.

Accounting Periods Ending Between December 2008 and April 2009:

i) **Companies with profits not exceeding £305,435:**
Pay salary or bonus of £5,435 and then pay any further sums required as a dividend.

ii) **Companies with profits between £305,435 and £306,112:**
Pay sufficient salary or bonus to reduce the company's profits to £300,000 and then pay any further sums required as a dividend.

iii) **Companies with profits over £306,112:**
Pay salary or bonus of £6,035 and then pay any further sums required as a dividend.

Accounting Periods Ending Between July 2007 and November 2008:

i) Companies with profits not exceeding £305,435:
Pay salary or bonus of £5,435 and then pay any further sums required as a dividend.

ii) Companies with profits between £305,435 and £306,112:
Pay sufficient salary or bonus to reduce the company's profits to £300,000 and then pay any further sums required as a dividend.

iii) Companies with profits between £306,112 and £465,699:
Pay salary or bonus of £6,035 and then pay any further sums required as a dividend.

iv) Companies with profits between £465,699 and £1,506,112:
Pay salary or bonus of £6,035 and then pay any further sums required as a dividend.

Except
When the director wishes to extract large sums in excess of the amounts shown in the table in Section 5.6 and the company has sufficient profit as per that table.

In these cases, the whole payment should be made by way of salary or bonus.

Until
You have reduced the company's taxable profits to £300,000, after which dividends should be paid.

v) Companies with profits over £1,506,112:
Pay salary or bonus of £6,035 and then pay any further sums required as a dividend.

Except
When the director wishes to extract very large sums, it may be more beneficial to take the whole payment as salary or bonus. (The shortcut described in Section 5.7 may help you to decide whether your payment is large enough.)

Until

You have reduced the company's taxable profits to £300,000, after which dividends should be paid.

5.9 THE BIGGER PICTURE

Everything that we have examined in this chapter has, of course, been based purely on tax considerations. Many other factors will need to be considered in practice and we will look at these in Chapter 12.

We have also, so far, only looked at the position for one single shareholder/director. We will look at a company with two or more owners in Chapter 8.

Furthermore, the principles examined in this chapter are based on the assumption that you want, or need, to extract funds from the company. In Chapter 7 we will look at the payment of a bonus or dividend as a tax planning measure in itself.

Before that, however, we need to look at the issue of timing.

Chapter 6

Timing Your Payments

6.1 ACCELERATING CORPORATION TAX RELIEF

In many cases, the company will obtain Corporation Tax relief for a bonus or salary payment in the accounting period during which it is actually paid.

However, Corporation Tax relief may sometimes be obtained for a bonus by making provision for it in the company's accounts. Nevertheless, to obtain Corporation Tax relief in the accounting period before payment is actually made, a number of criteria must be met.

Firstly, there must be some form of obligation on the company to make the payment and this obligation must already exist at the end of the relevant accounting period.

Where there is a long-standing practice of paying bonuses, this may sometimes be sufficient to ensure that this criterion is met.

In other cases, it will be necessary to have some form of memorandum, completed before the accounting period ends, that a bonus will be paid, even though the amount is yet to be ascertained.

To create a sufficiently strong obligation on the company to pay the bonus, there should be some indication of the way in which the bonus is to be computed. This could be by reference to some other earlier agreement.

A suitable example of such a memorandum is included in Appendix B. You will see that this refers to a formula to be used to determine the amount of the bonus. The precise nature of the formula will depend on the particular circumstances of each individual case but, ideally, the formula should be certain enough to create an obligation for the company to pay a bonus but flexible enough to enable you to plan the optimum amount of the bonus.

Secondly, the bonus must actually be deemed to be paid to the director within nine months of the company's accounting date.

A bonus is deemed to be paid when an obligation to pay it is recorded in the company's records. This time, we are talking about a more 'concrete' obligation, including the exact amount to be paid and actual entries in the company's accounting records. This will also trigger the liabilities for both Income Tax under PAYE and National Insurance.

Thirdly, the bonus must be a justifiable business expense for the company. We will return to this point in Section 12.4.

If these criteria can be met, the bonus, and any relevant employer's National Insurance, may be allowable for Corporation Tax purposes in the earlier accounting period.

Hence, one can readily see that Corporation Tax relief might be obtained in respect of a bonus deemed payable out of the company's profits for the year ended 31st December 2007, for example, even though the bonus is not deemed to be paid to the director until after 5th April 2008 and thus falls into the 2008/9 tax year for Income Tax purposes.

Any company with an accounting date not falling between 6th April and 5th July (inclusive) might be able to achieve a similar result.

Furthermore, the nine-month period required to fulfil the second criterion above means that it is actually possible to arrange for Corporation Tax relief to be obtained **before** PAYE and National Insurance is due on a bonus!

Example

Charlotte is the director and shareholder of Naseby Limited. The company's accounts for the year ended 31st December 2007 include a provision for a bonus of £50,000 to be paid to Charlotte.

The provision for Charlotte's bonus meets all of the criteria set out above, so the company obtains relief for the bonus in its Corporation Tax computation for the year ended 31st December 2007, thus reducing the amount of tax payable by the company on 1st October 2008.

*The amount of Charlotte's bonus was, however, only finalised and recorded in the company's books on 15th September 2008. Hence, the PAYE and National Insurance due on the bonus is not payable until 19th October 2008 – 18 days **after** Corporation Tax relief has been obtained!*

To achieve this positive cashflow requires two main steps:

i)   The obligation to pay the bonus must be established by the company's accounting date.

ii)   The amount of the bonus must be finalised and recorded in the company's accounting records some time between the 6th day and the last day of the ninth calendar month after the end of the accounting period (assuming that the period ended on the last day of a calendar month).

More details on the practical aspects of paying bonuses out of the profits of an earlier accounting period are given in Section 12.4.

6.2   TIMING DIVIDEND PAYMENTS

Since April 2006, the timing of a dividend has been irrelevant for Corporation Tax purposes, although it remains important for company law and accounting purposes (see Section 12.5).

For Income Tax purposes, however, most dividends are taxable in the tax year in which they are paid.

Again, however, 'paid' might mean recorded as having been paid – perhaps by being posted to a loan account to the credit of the director/shareholder.

A dividend 'paid' in, say, 2008/9 might be paid out of the company's profits for an earlier accounting period ending before 6th April 2008. (Again, this requires a number of criteria to be met.) This does not affect its treatment for Income Tax purposes and such a dividend continues to be treated as part of the director's 2008/9 income.

More details on the practical aspects of paying dividends out of the profits of an earlier accounting period are given in Section 12.5.

6.3 SPREADING THE COST

In Chapters 4 and 5, we saw several instances where salary or a bonus was preferable until the company's taxable profits had been reduced down to the small companies' rate threshold at £300,000. After this, it is generally preferable to pay dividends.

However, it is worth remembering that, whilst a bonus paid within nine months of a company's accounting period **may** sometimes be treated as a cost of that accounting period, it does not generally **have** to be.

Hence, where a company is anticipating profits over £300,000 for its next accounting period, it may sometimes be better to treat all or part of a bonus as being a cost of that later period.

Example

Bannockburn Limited's draft accounts for the year ended 31st October 2007 are showing a taxable profit of £320,000 after having already paid a salary of £50,000 to Robert, the company's sole director/shareholder.

Robert now wishes to extract a net sum of £100,000 from the company and has met the necessary criteria to be able to pay himself a bonus out of the profits for the year ended 31st October 2007.

However, Table D tells us that it is only beneficial for Robert to pay himself with a bonus until Bannockburn Limited's profits are reduced by £20,000 to £300,000.

From Table F, we can see that this will only yield the following net sum for Robert:

£20,000 x £100/£191.19 = £10,461

To get the remaining £89,539 which he requires, our model now tells Robert to take a dividend (see Table D). As Robert is a higher rate taxpayer, this would entail taking a dividend of:

£89,539 x 100/75 = £119,385

This dividend would give Robert an additional Income Tax bill of:

£119,385 x 25% = £29,846

However, Robert is confident that Bannockburn Limited will make a taxable profit of between £500,000 and £600,000 in the current year ending on 31st October 2008.

He therefore restricts his bonus for the year ended 31st October 2007 to a net sum of £10,461 (as calculated above) but takes a further net bonus of £89,539 out of the profits for the year ending 31st October 2008.

Robert's 2008 bonus will have the following net tax cost:

	£
Cost of bonus to Bannockburn Limited	
£89,539 x £191.19/£100 =	*171,189*
Less:	
Corporation Tax Relief @ 30.892% (see Section 2.3)	*(52,884)*
Net amount received by Robert	*(89,539)*

Net Cost of Bonus:	*28,766*
	=======

By taking a bonus out of the profits for the later accounting period, instead of a dividend, Robert has therefore saved £1,080 (£29,846 - £28,766).

Note that there are some important cashflow issues to be considered here, as explained in Section 2.13. In many cases, the adverse cashflow impact of paying a bonus out of a later accounting period, instead of a dividend, may outweigh the apparent advantage produced by the Corporation Tax relief.

In other cases, however, for a variety of possible reasons, it may be that a bonus will be paid in preference to a dividend regardless of our model's recommendations. This will often occur, for example, where the company has multiple shareholders (see Chapter 8).

In these cases, the rate of Corporation Tax relief obtained for the bonus will frequently outweigh any adverse cashflow impact of paying it out of a later accounting period.

Example

In September 2008, Bruce decides to pay himself a gross bonus of £50,000 out of the profits of his company, Teba Limited.

Adding employer's National Insurance at 12.8% to the bonus will produce a total cost of £56,400.

Bruce anticipates that Teba Limited will make a profit of around £250,000 for the year ending 30th September 2008.

Hence, if Bruce pays his bonus out of the profits for the year ending 30th September 2008, Teba Limited will receive Corporation Tax relief at just 20.5% (see Section 2.3), i.e. £11,562.

In the next year to 30th September 2009, however, Bruce is expecting Teba Limited to make profits of over £500,000. He therefore delays taking his bonus until October 2008 and makes no provision for it in the company's 2008 accounts (this is perfectly acceptable as the company had no obligation to pay the bonus at 30th September 2008).

From Section 2.3 we see that Teba Limited will therefore receive Corporation Tax relief at 29.625% for the bonus in the year ending 30th September 2009. This amounts to £16,709 (£56,400 x 29.625%).

By delaying the Corporation Tax relief for his bonus, Bruce has increased the amount of relief by £5,147, or __45%__!

Such an increase is certainly well worth the adverse cashflow impact of waiting an extra year for the relief.

Generally, of course, we like to get tax relief sooner rather than later. However, Corporation Tax relief at nearly 30% next year is worth so much more than relief at 20% or 21% this year that this is often a case where two birds in the bush **are** worth more than one in the hand!

After all, we are talking about an effective rate of return of 45%, backed by the Government. Just as long as your company does make the requisite level of profits, that is!

6.4 DELAYING PAYMENTS

The tables reproduced in previous chapters all deal with income received by the director, which is taxed as part of their 2008/9 income. The question arises as to whether it may sometimes be worth delaying payments to the director where possible, so that they can be taxed as part of their 2009/10 income instead.

After all, we know from Section 6.1 that this does not necessarily have to mean a delay in claiming Corporation Tax relief if the appropriate criteria have been met. However, as we shall see in Chapter 7, such a delay will **not** be advisable where the payment can be made in 2008/9 at a zero or negative tax cost.

In fact, in Chapter 7, I will actually be explaining why 'payments' should always be made to director/shareholders under these circumstances, even when there is no desire to extract the funds from the company.

As we can see from Tables A, B and C, funds can always be extracted from the company at either zero or negative cost whenever the director/shareholder has taxable income of less than the higher rate tax threshold (i.e. £40,835 for 2008/9).

Hence, in other words, **the director/shareholder should always take sufficient payment from the company each tax year to bring their income up to the higher rate tax threshold.** (Subject to some possible issues for older directors and those claiming Tax Credits which we will look at in Chapters 10 and 11 respectively)

Generally speaking, therefore, the only instance where it will make sense to delay payments will be when the director/shareholder already has taxable income of at least £40,835 for 2008/9.

Nevertheless, where the director/shareholder *does* have existing taxable income of at least £40,835 for 2008/9, it generally *will* make sense to delay further payments until at least 6th April 2009.

124

Before we move on to the consequences of delaying payments to director/shareholders until 2009/10, however, I just want to add two important points:

i)   Where payment is delayed until after the end of the accounting period for which Corporation Tax relief is to be claimed, remember that the three criteria set out in Section 6.1 must be met.

ii)   Remember that merely recording the obligation to make the payment in the company's accounting records may create a deemed 'payment' for Income Tax purposes.

6.5   A GLIMPSE INTO THE FUTURE

Where a payment to a director is to be delayed until 2009/10, it is worth thinking about what it will cost when it is made.

Not all of the changes coming into force on 6th April 2009 are known yet. Furthermore, given the Government's dramatic 'U-Turn' on 13th May 2008 and the sensational debacle over the abolition of the 10% starting rate, it now seems highly likely that even those changes which have been announced to date will be revised significantly. The Government has little choice in this matter, as the unprecedented change to the Income Tax personal allowance announced on 13th May 2008 will cost them an estimated £2.7 billion which they cannot afford to repeat next year.

Nevertheless, as we cannot predict what the Government will do to the tax system in 2009/10 (nor how many times they will subsequently change their mind), we will base our forecasts on the existing proposals, as this is the best information that we currently have.

Based on what we know to date, our current best estimate of the marginal rates of combined Income Tax and National Insurance payable by directors on salary and bonus payments received in 2009/10 is as follows:

Income up to £5,635:   0%
Income from £5,635 to £6,255:   11%   (Tax-Nil + NI-11%)
Income from £6,255 to £43,155:   31%   (Tax-20% + NI-11%)
Income over £43,155:   41%   (Tax-40% + NI-1%)

Note that there is no 21% band for 2009/10 as there is in 2008/9 (see Section 2.6). This is because it is currently proposed that the thresholds at which 40% Income Tax starts and 11% National Insurance ends will be aligned from 6th April 2009, thus eliminating that quirky little band where Income Tax is paid at basic rate but National Insurance paid at only 1%.

Whether our other new quirky little tax band, where National Insurance is payable below the level of the Income Tax personal allowance, will actually survive for more than a year remains to be seen. For the moment, we are assuming that it will.

The **effective** rate of Income Tax on dividend income received during 2009/10 can also be estimated as follows:

Income up to £43,155:   0%
Income over £43,155:   25%

(The taxation of dividends is explained in detail in Section 2.8.)

Subject to the usual criteria given in Section 6.1, a salary or bonus payment made to a director during 2009/10 may attract Corporation Tax relief in a company accounting period ending anywhere between July 2008 and March 2011.

Hence, putting the estimated marginal personal tax rates set out above together with the known forthcoming changes in Corporation Tax rates (see Section 2.2), we can produce our estimated 2009/10 versions of Tables A, B and C. These are set out in the next section.

6.6   FORECAST MODEL RESULTS 2009/2010

Subject to the notes set out below and also the major proviso that the figures below are based on estimates, the net tax suffered on an additional *net* £100 of bonus or dividend paid during 2009/10 at different levels of company profit and director's income is expected to be as follows:

Annual company profits up to £300,000

Director's Income	Total Tax on £100 (net) of:		Dividend
	Bonus		
	From	To	
Up to £5,635	£20.33	£22.00	£0.00
£5,635 to £6,255	£0.97	-£1.14	£0.00
£6,255 to £43,155	£30.24	£27.51	£0.00
Over £43,155	£52.31	£49.13	£33.33

Annual company profits £300,000 to £1,500,000

Director's Income	Total Tax on £100 (net) of:		Dividend
	Bonus		
	From	To	
Up to £5,635	-£31.58	-£29.50	£0.00
£5,635 to £6,255	£13.29	£10.65	£0.00
£6,255 to £43,155	£11.85	£15.25	£0.00
Over £43,155	£30.80	£34.79	£33.33

Annual company profits over £1,500,000

Director's Income	Total Tax on £100 (net) of:		Dividend
	Bonus		
	From	To	
Up to £5,635	-£29.33	-£28.00	£0.00
£5,635 to £6,255	£10.44	-£8.75	£0.00
£6,255 to £43,155	£15.52	£17.70	£0.00
Over £43,155	£35.11	£37.65	£33.33

Notes to the Tables

1. 'Total Tax' means the total Income Tax and National Insurance suffered by both the company and the director, less the Corporation Tax relief obtained by the company.
2. In each case, the £100 referred to above is the net sum left in the director/shareholder's hands after payment of all applicable taxes.

3. 'Director's Income' represents the salary and bonuses which will already be received by the director during 2009/10 without paying the additional salary, bonus or dividend under consideration. It is assumed that the director has no other sources of income and will not yet have taken any other dividends out of the company after 5th April 2009.
4. It is also assumed that the director has no applicable tax reliefs or credits beyond the personal allowance and will still be of normal working age by 5th April 2010.
5. The company is assumed to be paying the bonus out of a twelve-month accounting period and to have no associated companies.
6. The total net tax cost of a bonus will vary according to the company accounting period for which Corporation Tax relief is being obtained. The costs given in the 'From' column represent those applying for an accounting period ending on 31st July 2008. The costs given in the 'To' column represent those applying for an accounting period ending on or after 31st March 2010. The costs applying for an accounting period ending between 1st August 2008 and 30th March 2010 will lie somewhere between those given in the 'From' column and those given in the 'To' column.
7. Notes 7, 8 and 9 to the tables in Section 3.2 and the notes in Section 3.3 on how to interpret those tables all continue to apply again here.

As in 2008/9 (see Section 3.4), we can see from the above tables that the recommended strategy for some bands of director's income and company profit changes according to the company accounting period out of which the payments are to be made.

Further detailed analysis of the relevant results enables us to summarise the changes to our model's recommendations which occur as follows:

Company profits not exceeding £300,000
Director's income: Dividends preferable for accounting periods
                       ending up to:
£5,635 to £6,255   30th April 2009

Company profits £300,000 to £1,500,000

Director's income:	Bonus preferable for accounting periods ending up to:
Over £43,155	31st December 2008

Note that we have again restricted our analysis to accounting periods ending at calendar month ends. The notes to the tables above also continue to apply.

6.7 OVERVIEW OF MODEL RECOMMENDATIONS FOR PAYMENTS MADE IN 2009/2010

On the basis of the assumptions set out in Sections 6.5 and 6.6, our model recommends that payments to directors made, or deemed to be made, in 2009/10 should be structured as follows:

Director's Income	Company Profit		
	Up to £300,000	**£300,000 to £1.5M**	**Over £1.5M**
Up to £5,635	Bonus	Bonus	Bonus
£5,635 to £6,255	Dividend for APs ending by 30/4/2009	Bonus	Bonus
£6,255 to £43,155	Dividend	Dividend	Dividend
Over £43,155	Dividend	Bonus for APs ending by 31/12/2008	Dividend

'AP' = Accounting Period

As before, the model recommends that payments out of accounting periods ending after the dates shown above should be structured in the opposite way.

Wealth Warning

Dividend payments made on or after 6th April 2009 may be subject to the proposed new 'income shifting' legislation. See Section 16.2 for further details.

Chapter 7

Using Loan Accounts

7.1 EXPLOITING TAX ADVANTAGES

As we can see from Tables A, B and C in Appendix A, there are a number of scenarios where paying salary or a bonus will actually result in an overall net tax saving (the negative numbers in the tables).

In addition, there are many further scenarios where dividends may be paid without any tax cost.

A company director/shareholder should generally exploit these situations as fully as possible as they will usually lead to either current or long-term tax savings.

The current savings are quite clearly beneficial. These arise simply from the fact that bonus or salary payments are attracting more Corporation Tax relief than they are costing in Income Tax and National Insurance.

Where funds may be 'extracted' from the company tax-free but do not generate an actual current saving, the benefit is less clear-cut. Nevertheless, these opportunities should also generally be maximised whenever possible. I will show you why in the next few sections.

7.2 LEND TO SAVE

Why extract funds from the company when you don't really need them?

A sensible question; to answer it I need to introduce you to the concept of the director's loan account.

Unwelcome tax charges will generally arise if a company lends money to one of its directors, including Income Tax and National Insurance charges on notional interest.

There is nothing, however, to prevent a director from lending money to the company.

A director can, of course, obtain funds elsewhere and then lend them to the company.

Or, the director can be 'paid' a bonus or a dividend and then lend it back to the company. When I say 'paid' here, we only need to make it an effective payment for Corporation Tax and Income Tax purposes, it is not always necessary for any actual cash to change hands. This is very useful if the company does not actually have the funds to make these tax efficient payments or if the director would rather keep money invested in the company (subject to the wealth warning given below).

To make the payment effective for tax purposes, it is important to meet the criteria set out in Sections 6.1 and 12.4 in the case of a bonus or, in the case of a dividend, to make sure that it is validly declared, as explained in Section 12.5.

Wealth Warning

There is a school of thought that a dividend which is not actually paid out in cash is only valid if the company would have had sufficient funds to pay it.

There is no legal basis for this view but I understand that HM Revenue and Customs sometimes takes this stance when it suits them.

For the avoidance of doubt, it may therefore sometimes be necessary to make sure that a cash payment does take place, perhaps by borrowing the necessary funds for a few days until the director's loan back to the company has cleared the banking system.

7.3 MEDIUM-TERM BENEFITS

Having money outstanding on a loan account enables a director to withdraw funds from the company as and when required, subject, of course, to the company's own cashflow requirements.

A withdrawal of funds due to the director has no tax cost. It is just like withdrawing money from a bank.

Example

Olivia has just started up a new business run through her company, Preston Roundheads Limited. She is currently living off the proceeds of a previous capital disposal and has no other taxable income for 2008/9.

In the year ending 31ˢᵗ December 2008, Preston Roundheads Limited makes a taxable profit of £50,000.

Olivia does not wish to withdraw any funds from Preston Roundheads Limited at this critical stage in its development but realises that paying herself a bonus or salary of £5,435 will actually save the company £1,128 in Corporation Tax (at 20.751% - see Section 2.3).

Furthermore, Olivia realises that she can also take a dividend of £31,860 with no tax cost (see Section 2.9).

Hence, without actually extracting any cash funds from the company, Olivia takes a bonus and dividend totalling £37,295 by declaring them payable but leaving them outstanding on director's loan account.

Olivia does the same thing for the next two tax years and, by early 2011, Preston Roundheads Limited owes her £111,885.

In March 2011, when the company is now quite stable, Olivia is able to withdraw this sum of £111,885 with absolutely no tax cost, having also saved the company £3,506 in the process.

For the sake of illustration, I have assumed in this example that the National Insurance earnings threshold and Income Tax personal allowance and basic rate tax band will remain at their 2008/9 levels. (See Section 6.5 for a better prediction of the likely position for 2009/10.) To keep things simple, I have also restricted Olivia's salary to the level of the National Insurance earnings threshold, although we know that for accounting periods ending after April 2009 it would be beneficial to increase it to the level of the Income Tax personal allowance (if they are still different at that time).

I have, however, taken account of the fact that the company's tax saving on Olivia's bonus increases to £1,182 and £1,196 in the second and third years respectively due to the changes in Corporation Tax rates (see Section 2.2).

This example provides a perfect illustration of the benefits of 'extracting' the maximum tax-free sum from the company each tax year.

As discussed in Section 7.1, I would therefore generally advocate that director/shareholders always take at least these maximum tax-free sums out of their company each tax year in most cases. As explained in Section 7.2 above, the funds can always be 'lent back' to the company where desired.

Possible exceptions, however, include:

- Directors with other sources of income (see Section 2.9)
- Companies with insufficient profits (see Chapter 12)
- Companies with insufficient funds (see Section 7.2)
- Some directors aged over 65 (see Chapter 10)
- Directors claiming Tax Credits (see Chapter 11)
- Directors with a short life expectancy (see Section 7.5)
- After 5th April 2009: cases where the 'income-shifting' rules might apply (see Section 16.2)

7.4 LONG-TERM BENEFITS

But what if you never wish to extract the funds from the company?

Even then, you should probably still ensure that bonuses and dividends are deemed to be paid and then left on loan account whenever there is a tax saving or a zero tax cost.

Although the long-term rate for capital gains on the sale of a small trading company is usually effectively only 10% (see further in Chapter 15), even this can't beat having a director's loan account which has been accumulated tax free and can be repaid tax free too.

Example

Gonville runs a small trading company, Rorke's Drift Limited. The company makes sufficient profit each year to pay Gonville a bonus of £5,435 and a dividend of £31,860. Gonville lives very modestly, however, and lends £30,000 of this back to the company every year.

After ten years, Gonville negotiates to sell Rorke's Drift Limited for £1,000,000. On a straight sale of shares for this price, Gonville would face a Capital Gains Tax bill of up to £100,000 (or £180,000 if entrepreneur's relief is not available – see Section 15.3 for details).

However, because of his loan account, Gonville sells the company for just £700,000 and then arranges to have the outstanding balance of £300,000 on the loan account repaid.

This saves Gonville £30,000 in Capital Gains Tax (or £54,000 if entrepreneur's relief is not available).

It will also save the purchaser £1,500 in Stamp Duty, so everyone (except HM Revenue & Customs) is happy.

7.5   VERY LONG TERM

One major drawback to using a director's loan account is the fact that some or all of the value of the loan account may be subject to Inheritance Tax at 40% if you should die whilst the loan is still outstanding.

Conversely, where you have a private trading company, the value of your shares in the company will usually be exempt from Inheritance Tax due to the operation of business property relief.

The problem is that the loan account is a separate asset to your shares and is fully exposed to Inheritance Tax. The loan account also reduces the value of your shares in the company. In other words, using the loan account shifts value from an Inheritance Tax exempt asset (the shares) to an asset which is fully taxable for Inheritance Tax purposes (the loan account).

Hence, whilst the loan account may provide significant savings for other tax purposes, it could prove quite disadvantageous for Inheritance Tax purposes in the case of a private trading company.

One way to avoid this problem would be to issue further shares in the company in exchange for the amount outstanding on the loan account. This effectively converts your loan account into additional share capital. If the new shares are issued as a 'rights issue' they should be eligible for business property relief, and thus exempt from Inheritance Tax, immediately. Otherwise, they will need to be held for two years to gain exemption.

The conversion of a loan account to share capital will generally also still preserve your Capital Gains Tax savings in the event of a sale of your company (see Section 7.4), as your new shares will be treated as part of the 'cost' of your company.

The only problem with converting a loan account into share capital, however, is that it then becomes difficult to withdraw the funds at a later date. The original advantage described in Section 7.3 might thus be lost.

In practice, therefore, it is usually only wise to convert loans into share capital to the extent that the outstanding sums are surplus to the director/shareholder's own personal requirements.

Nevertheless, where the owner of a private trading company has a short life expectancy, I would generally recommend that they leave funds in the company wherever possible and convert any outstanding loan account into share capital using a 'rights issue' in order to maximise the benefit of business property relief on their death.

In the case of an investment company, however, the shares in the company would be ineligible for business property relief in any case, so using a loan account makes no difference to the owner's Inheritance Tax position. Given its other tax advantages, therefore, the loan account should generally be maximised, as described in the previous sections.

For more information on the availability of business property relief for Inheritance Tax purposes, see the Taxcafe.co.uk guide *'How to Avoid Inheritance Tax'*.

7.6   INTEREST ON LOAN ACCOUNTS

There is no requirement for a director to charge interest on a loan account with their own company but they can charge interest if they want to, as long as it does not exceed a reasonable commercial rate.

Subject to the commercial rate requirement, interest paid to a director on their loan account will usually be an allowable business expense for the company. The interest will therefore provide Corporation Tax relief at the company's marginal rate (subject to meeting the practical considerations covered in Section 12.10).

Which takes us back to the question of whether it is worthwhile charging the interest?

A director in receipt of interest is subject to the following Income Tax rates for 2008/9:

Up to £6,035:	0%
£6,035 to £8,355:	10%
£8,355 to £40,835:	20%
Over £40,835:	40%

As usual, these are marginal rates based on a director whose total income falls into the above brackets. (As explained in Section 2.18, the 10% starting rate continues to apply to interest where the director's other income, excluding dividends, does not exceed £8,355.)

National Insurance is not payable on interest income.

The company must, however, deduct Income Tax at source at 20% on the payment of interest and must pay this over to HM Revenue & Customs quarterly.

If this results in an overpayment, the director can reclaim the excess through their Self-Assessment Tax Return.

Sadly, this means that an interest charge cannot be made without any cashflow consequences, even if the sum charged is to be paid back into the company and added to the loan account.

Subject to these cashflow considerations, the ultimate total net tax cost of putting a net sum of £100 into a director's hands as interest in 2008/9 is as follows:

Total Net Tax Cost of Putting a Net Sum of £100 Into a Director's Hands as Interest

Annual company profits up to £300,000

Director's Income	Interest		Bonus	
	From	To	From	To
Up to £5,435	-£19.33	-£22.00	-£19.33	-£22.00
£5,435 to £6,035	-£19.33	-£22.00	£2.24	-£1.14
£6,035 to £8,355	-£10.09	-£13.33	£31.87	£27.51
£8,355 to £40,040	£1.15	-£2.50	£31.87	£27.51
£40,040 to £40,835	£1.15	-£2.50	£15.18	£11.37
Over £40,835	£34.86	£30.00	£54.22	£49.13

Annual company profits £300,000 to £1,500,000

Director's Income	Interest		Bonus	
	From	To	From	To
Up to £5,435	-£32.67	-£29.50	-£32.67	-£29.50
£5,435 to £6,035	-£32.67	-£29.50	-£14.66	-£10.65
£6,035 to £8,355	-£25.25	-£21.67	£10.08	£15.25
£8,355 to £40,040	-£15.91	-£11.88	£10.08	£15.25
£40,040 to £40,835	-£15.91	-£11.88	-£3.86	£0.66
Over £40,835	£12.12	£17.50	£28.73	£34.79

Annual company profits over £1,500,000

Director's Income	Interest		Bonus	
	From	To	From	To
Up to £5,435	-£30.00	-£28.00	-£30.00	-£28.00
£5,435 to £6,035	-£30.00	-£28.00	-£11.28	-£8.75
£6,035 to £8,355	-£22.22	-£20.00	£14.43	£17.70
£8,355 to £40,040	-£12.50	-£10.00	£14.43	£17.70
£40,040 to £40,835	-£12.50	-£10.00	-£0.05	£2.81
Over £40,835	£16.67	£20.00	£33.83	£37.65

The costs for bonuses are included again here for comparative purposes. As in Section 3.2, the 'From' and 'To' columns represent the costs for the earliest and latest accounting periods out of which the payments, or charges, could be taken when paid, or deemed to be paid, to the director in 2008/9.

In the case of interest charges, however, the earliest accounting period in which the charge could be made is the year ended 30th April 2007, as opposed to 31st July 2007 for a bonus (see Sections 7.10 and 6.1 respectively). The latest period remains the year ending 31st March 2010 in both cases.

Conclusions

The above tables give rise to some fairly clear conclusions with important consequences for planning payments to directors when the opportunity exists to pay interest instead of salary, bonus or dividends.

Firstly, we see that interest payments, where available, are always preferable to salary or bonus payments, except where the National Insurance earnings threshold (£5,435) has not yet been used, when they are equal. (For the reasons explained in Section 12.8, salary or bonus should, in fact, usually be paid in preference to interest when the director's earnings threshold has not yet been used.)

Secondly, we can see that, in nearly every case, interest payments actually save tax overall whenever the director's income does not exceed £40,835.

The only exception to this arises when the company's profits are £300,000 or less, the director's existing income is between £8,355 and £40,835 and the accounting period in which the interest would be charged (see Section 7.10) ends on or before 31st March 2008.

Lastly, comparing these tables with Tables A, B and C, we can see that interest payments are almost always preferable to dividends. (Again, the only exceptions arise when the company's profits are £300,000 or less, the director's existing income is over £8,355 and the accounting period in which the interest would be charged ends on or before 31st March 2008.)

At this stage, the position therefore appears to be fairly simple. The above tables tell us that whenever the option to pay interest is available:

i) Interest should always be paid in preference to salary, bonus or dividends once the director's National Insurance earnings threshold (£5,435) has been used, Except

ii) In the case of interest charges which would be made in an accounting period ended on or before 31st March 2008, where the director's existing income exceeds £8,355 and the company's taxable profit is less than £300,000.

In the latter case, the first table above tells us that a dividend would be preferable.

Loan Repayments

Naturally, the very existence of the loan which creates the potential to pay interest provides another means for the director to extract funds from the company – a loan repayment!

As we saw in Section 7.3, the loan can effectively be repaid tax free. (Except in some special cases where the loan has arisen as a result of an earlier capital disposal by the director.)

Hence, once the director's taxable income has reached £40,835, the best way for them to extract any further sums required will be by way of a loan repayment.

7.7 AN INTERESTING STRATEGY

Combining the results in the previous section with our conclusions from earlier chapters, we can produce a fairly simple summary of the optimum strategy for making payments to directors where the opportunity to pay interest is available.

i) First, pay salary or bonus of £5,435.

ii) Next, pay as much interest as can be justified commercially (subject to the limitations set out below).

iii) A dividend should then be paid until the director's total taxable income reaches £40,835.

iv) Any further sum required should be paid by way of loan repayment.

In most cases, the amount paid under step (ii) should not exceed £35,400 gross before tax.

In the case of a company with an accounting period ended on or before 31st March 2008 and taxable profits of no more than £308,355 before making any payments to the director, the amount paid under step (ii) should not exceed £2,320 gross before tax.

In the case of a company with an accounting period ended on or before 31st March 2008 and taxable profits of between £308,355 and £340,835, before making any payments to the director, the amount paid under step (ii) should not exceed the amount which, when combined with the payment under step (i), reduces the company's taxable profit to £300,000.

For example, where the company has a taxable profit of £330,000 for an accounting period ended on or before 31st March 2008, before making any payments to the director, a bonus of £5,435 should be paid first followed by a maximum interest charge of £24,565 gross before tax (£330,000 - £5,435 - £26,565 = £300,000).

Where interest of £35,400 gross before tax is paid, this will ultimately yield a net sum of £28,672 after Income Tax at Nil on the first £600, 10% on the next £2,320 and 20% on the rest (although tax at 20% will need to be deducted from the whole payment in the first instance, as explained in Section 7.6, leaving the director to reclaim the excess payment of £352 at a later stage).

Any interest paid in excess of the amounts outlined above would give rise to an overall tax cost which can be avoided quite simply by moving on to step (iii) or (iv) instead.

Whilst steps (iii) and (iv) are both tax free, putting step (iii) first preserves more of the loan account for future use.

Where the director wishes to extract more than the total amount yielded by steps (i) to (iv) above, the best strategy will usually be to follow steps (i) and (ii) above, then repay the loan account and then follow the appropriate strategy as set out in Chapter 4 in respect of the further amount required.

In a few cases, however, there is an additional complication which may need to be taken into account and we will return to this in Section 7.9.

As usual, all of this is subject to the practical issues discussed in Chapter 12 and also to the fact that the position will be altered if the payment is potentially large enough to create a loss (see Section 9.6).

7.8 COMPOUND INTEREST

The strategy outlined in the previous section does not alter the advice given in Section 7.3 above. In other words, subject to the possible exceptions described in Section 7.3, it will be worth ensuring that any payments which may be made at a zero or negative tax cost are indeed deemed to be made, even when the funds are not actually required.

What the previous section does mean, however, is that the most beneficial way to follow this strategy may be to charge interest on the balance already brought forward on the director's loan account.

In other words, since interest paid to a director with total income of less than £40,835 will usually **save** tax overall, it will generally make sense for the director to always charge interest equal to the lower of:

    i)   The maximum amount which can be justified commercially, or

    ii)   The amount required to bring their total taxable income up to £40,835.

Where the interest will be charged in an accounting period ended on or before 31st March 2008 and the company's taxable profit before any payments to the director is no more than £340,835, the interest should be restricted to the amount derived under step (ii) in Section 7.7 above.

Where the resultant interest payment is more than the director actually wishes to extract from the company, the excess can be loaned back to the company to further enhance the director's loan account.

This may create a slight cashflow disadvantage, since 20% of the interest charges will need to be paid over to HM Revenue & Customs, as explained in Section 7.6 above. However, in Section 7.10 we will see how this cashflow disadvantage can be avoided with careful planning.

Where the director's existing income is less than £8,355, some or all of the tax deducted at source will eventually be recovered via the Self-Assessment system, at which point the director could again lend it back to the company if desired.

Where the interest charged by the director is not sufficient to bring their total taxable income up to £40,835, it will continue to be beneficial to 'pay' sufficient dividend to bring their income up to that level and lend the resultant sum back to the company as outlined in Section 7.3.

7.9 LOAN ACCOUNT LIMITATIONS

The strategy set out in Section 7.7 is based on the assumption that the director can and will get the company to repay their loan account.

In some cases, however, there may be restrictions which prevent the company from immediately repaying some or all of the director's loan account.

Furthermore, there is a school of thought that it may be better to preserve the loan account, rather than repay it, as it may yield greater savings in the future. We won't go into that topic in detail here but it does give rise to further situations where we do not have the loan repayment option and must rely on salary, bonus, dividends and interest only.

Lastly, as already discussed in Section 7.7, there is the situation where the total amount required by the director is large enough to exhaust the loan account when following the strategy set out in that section.

In each of these cases, the best strategy for making a payment to the director will generally be as follows:

    i)   Pay enough salary or bonus to bring their income up to 5,435.
    ii)   Pay as much interest as can be justified commercially.
    iii) Repay as much of the loan account as is permitted or desired.
    iv) Pay any further sum required by following the appropriate strategy set out in Chapter 4.

Exceptions

Where the company accounting period in which any interest payment would be charged ends on or before 31st March 2008, the interest payment should be restricted to the greater of:

    i)   The amount required to bring the director's taxable income up to £8,355, or
    ii)   The amount required to reduce the company's taxable profit to £300,000.

Where the company's taxable profits are no more than £300,000 before the payment then the payment should simply be restricted to the amount under (i).

Another exception to the above strategy also arises for later accounting periods where the company's taxable profit after making the payment would be less than £300,000 and the net sum required by the director is sufficient to take their total taxable income over the critical £40,835 threshold (in other words, when the director's taxable income is less than £40,835 before the payment and will, or may (depending on how it is paid), be more than £40,835 after the payment).

This exception arises because a net sum of £100 received by a basic rate taxpayer by way of interest uses up £125 of their basic rate band whereas a dividend of £100 uses up only £111.11 of their basic rate band.

Hence, whilst interest payments may often produce an overall tax saving, each £100 of net interest received effectively uses up more of the director's basic rate tax band than £100 of net dividend. It therefore takes less net income to push the director into the higher rate tax band and this can lead to a greater tax cost overall when the company's marginal Corporation Tax rate is 22% or less (i.e. where the company's profits are under £300,000).

Where this position exists, it may sometimes be more beneficial to make the whole payment as a dividend instead of paying any interest.

Example

Frances pays herself a salary of £8,500 from her trading company, Golden Hind Limited. She has no other sources of income and has previously loaned a total of £500,000 to the company. Frances has made a commitment to Armada Bank (Golden Hind Limited's bank) that she will not take any loan repayments out of the company for the next five years. She is, however, permitted to charge interest on her loan account.

Golden Hind Limited is expected to make a taxable profit of around £280,000 for the year ending 31st March 2009 after paying Frances's salary but before making any other payments to her.

Frances would now like to extract a further net sum of £29,000 from Golden Hind Limited.

Clearly, Frances has loaned a sufficient sum to the company to justify charging enough interest to give her the net additional income that she needs, so she sets about working out the required sum.

Her remaining basic rate tax band amounts to £32,335 (£40,835 - £8,500). Hence, after basic rate tax at 20%, the first £32,335 of interest paid to her will yield net income of £25,868.

This leaves Frances needing a further net sum of £3,132 (£29,000 - £25,868). This further sum, however, will be after deducting tax at 40%, so it equates to a further gross interest payment of £3,132 x 100/60 = £5,220.

In total, therefore, Frances will need to pay herself gross interest of £37,555 (£32,335 + £5,220) in order to give her the required net sum of £29,000.

This equates to an interest charge of 7.5% on Frances's unsecured loan to the company, so it would seem to represent a reasonable commercial rate and should be allowable for Corporation Tax purposes (subject to the provisos set out in Section 12.10).

Using the appropriate rate given in Section 2.3, we can therefore see that the interest charge will produce the following Corporation Tax saving for Golden Hind Limited:

£37,555 x 21% = £7,887

The overall net tax cost of the interest payment is thus £37,555 - £29,000 - £7,887 = £668.

However, let's look at what would have happened if Frances had withdrawn the net £29,000 as a dividend.

Adding the tax credit of one ninth (see Section 2.8), the dividend would have increased Frances's taxable income by £32,222 (£29,000 x 10/9 or £29,000 x £111.11/£100 using Table E).

This would give Frances total taxable income of £40,722 (£8,500 + £32,222). She would therefore still be a basic rate taxpayer and the dividend would be tax free!

In this example, we can see that paying a dividend is the better option and saves Frances a net sum of £668 despite the results given by the tables in Section 7.6.

Once more this arises because the tables produced in Section 7.6 are based on a 'snapshot' approach and are not always appropriate when the director's marginal tax rate is altered by the payment, or might be altered depending on the payment method used.

This does not, however, mean that an interest payment will always be inappropriate in these circumstances.

As the total net sum required by the director increases and takes their total taxable income further above £40,835, there will eventually come a point where making the payment by way of an interest charge becomes more beneficial again (if this level of interest can be justified commercially).

Hence, in cases where this exception may apply, detailed analysis along the lines used in our example above will be required in order to determine the optimum result.

As a shortcut though, remember that this potential exception can safely be ignored if:

a) The company's taxable profits after making any payment required by the director will still be in excess of £300,000,
b) The director's taxable income for the year is already at least £40,835,
c) The net sum required by the director does not exceed 80% of their remaining basic rate Income Tax band (i.e. the amount by which their existing taxable income is less than £40,835), or
d) The accounting period in which the interest would be charged ends on or before 31st March 2008 (in which case, follow the advice given for our other exception above).

7.10 ACCRUING INTEREST

To claim Corporation Tax relief for interest paid to a director, the company must meet two important criteria:

i) The interest must be a valid business expense. This means ensuring that the rate of interest charged does not exceed a reasonable commercial rate and also meeting the further points which we will look at in Section 12.10.

ii) The interest must be 'paid' within twelve months of the company's accounting date.

The second criterion opens up some opportunities to gain an extra cashflow advantage or, to be more precise, to ameliorate the cashflow <u>disadvantage</u> discussed in Sections 7.6 and 7.8.

Firstly, it is worth pointing out that, as long as the first criterion above is met, 'paid' will include crediting the director's loan account with the interest charged. The drawback, of course, is that this triggers the need to deduct and account for tax at 20% and, if the director is a higher rate taxpayer, also triggers a further personal Income Tax liability for them.

Interest can, however, be 'accrued' in the company's accounts before it is paid to the director. Where interest is 'accrued' it is charged in the accounts but it is not credited to the director's loan account yet; the credit goes to a more general area in the company's accounts known as 'accruals'.

As explained above, accrued interest which meets the other necessary criteria will be eligible for Corporation Tax relief as long as it is paid, or deemed to be paid, to the director within a year.

The upshot of all this is that the company can claim tax relief for the interest in one year whilst the income is only taxable on the director in the next year.

Hence, for example, interest could be accrued in the company's accounts for the year ended 30th April 2008 but not paid to the director until 6th April 2009. The company would then obtain Corporation Tax relief in its 2008 accounts, thus reducing the Corporation Tax payable on 1st February 2009; but the director would not be taxable on this income until 2009/10.

Chapter 8

Multiple Owners

8.1 BACKGROUND

So far, we have looked only at the position for a single director/shareholder.

Many companies are, however, owned by two or more people. This adds another dimension to our planning.

In principle, bonus or salary should be paid according to the level of effort which each person puts into the company's business. This makes these payments infinitely variable and the payment to each person can be quite independent of the payment to any other director/shareholder.

Admittedly, commercial pressures will alter this position in some companies but, that aside, we can pay each director a different salary.

Dividends, on the other hand, must usually be paid to all shareholders in proportion to the shares held. There are ways around this, but this book is long enough already!

Wealth Warning

Many companies with multiple owners, most particularly family companies and companies owned by couples, may be affected by the proposed 'income shifting' legislation due to be introduced with effect from 6th April 2009. We will look at this subject in detail in Section 16.2 at the end of the guide.

8.2 CORPORATE COUPLES

For smaller companies, the most common scenario is probably the situation where a couple own all the shares in the company equally between them.

If both of them also work in the business then it will often be possible to treat them both equally as far as planning for salary or dividends is concerned.

Life gets more complicated if one person has more existing income from other sources than the other. Generally, for couples, 'equalisation' is the best tax planning strategy.

Example

Henry and Joan each own 50 of the 100 issued shares in Agincourt Limited.

Joan takes a modest salary of £6,035 out of the company.

Agincourt Limited has a profit of £400,000 for the year ended 31st December 2008 and Henry and Joan wish to take a net total sum of £50,000 out of the company.

Henry has no other income for 2008/9, so the first step must be to pay him a salary or bonus of £6,035, as this produces an overall tax saving (see Table B). This yields a net sum of £5,969 (see Section 5.2).

The remaining £44,031 which the couple wish to extract from the company can then be paid out as a dividend.

Each partner will receive a dividend of £22,015.50, leaving them both still comfortably below the higher rate Income Tax threshold.

This is far preferable to paying the whole £50,000 to either person which would inevitably have had a greater tax cost. (We know from Section 5.6 that it is preferable to avoid salaries over £6,035 in this situation and paying the required amount as a dividend to one person would have pushed them into higher rate Income Tax.)

We are, of course, assuming here that Henry and Joan are equally happy whichever of them receives funds from the company. In practice, this assumption is true for many, but not all, couples.

Actually, if Henry and Joan had read Chapter 7, they would have known they should 'pay' a dividend of £31,320 each. The extra £9,304.50 each which is 'surplus to requirements' should be posted to loan accounts for each of them. Pay nothing now, save tax later!

Wealth Warning

Couples owning companies have been the subject of a concerted attack by HM Revenue and Customs in recent years, culminating in the infamous 'Arctic Systems' case and the proposed new 'income shifting' legislation.

Despite the taxpayers' final victory in the 'Arctic Systems' case, couples owning a company together may not necessarily be able to follow their optimum tax planning strategy in practice. We will return to this subject in Section 16.2.

8.3   UNEQUAL COUPLES

Sometimes we may find that one person is already taking salary from a company before we commence our planning. Not ideal, but let's take a look.

Example

Charles and Nell both own shares in Worcester Limited. The company is expected to make a taxable profit of around £450,000 for the year ending 30th September 2008.

Nell has already taken a salary of £40,040 from the company but, so far, Charles has no other taxable income for the year.

The couple now wish to extract a further net sum of £20,000 from the company as tax efficiently as possible.

*In this case, our first step is **NOT** to pay Charles the same salary as Nell has already taken. That would have a substantial tax cost and also means extracting far more funds than the couple currently need.*

The first step does remain to pay Charles a salary of £6,035 however. As usual, this will yield a net sum of £5,969 (see Section 5.2).

For our next step, we should turn to Table D but, this time, we have three choices:

i)   *Pay more salary to Nell,*

ii)   *Pay more salary to Charles, or*

iii)   *Pay a dividend*

From Table B we can see that option (i) will produce an overall tax saving of up to £3.86 per £100 paid to Nell (we know that there is a saving because Table D tells us that it is better to pay Nell a salary than a dividend under this scenario when the company's accounting period ends on or before 28th February 2009).

Table B also tells us that option (ii) will cost between £10.08 and £15.25 per £100 and option (iii) initially has no tax cost.

We have a clear winner – we should pay sufficient further salary to Nell to increase her total taxable income by £795 to £40,835. Using Table E, we can calculate that this produces further net income of:

£795 x £100/£126.58 = £628

So far, therefore, we have managed to get net income of £6,597 (£5,969 + £628) to the couple. However, we still have £13,403 (£20,000 - £6,597) to go.

Again, we face the same three choices as before. This time, we can see from Table B that option (i) gives a cost of between £28.73 and £34.79 and option (ii) still produces a cost of between £10.08 and £15.25.

For option (iii), we have two different costs - £0.00 for Charles, and £33.33 for Nell. Here, we take the average - £16.67.

The winner this time is therefore option (ii), so we should pay more salary to Charles in order to provide the couple with the additional net £13,403 they require.

This situation is far from ideal. The couple already had an existing payment structure in place which was 'inefficient' from a tax perspective.

We were only able to use our planning technique to 'make the best of a bad lot'.

Nevertheless, this example does demonstrate the basic technique of the three-way comparison which we should use to optimise the payment of bonuses or dividends to a couple who co-own, and both work for, a company.

Note that the 'averaging' used on the tax rate applying to a dividend was based on 50/50 ownership of the company's shares.

If, for example, Nell had owned just 25% of the shares, and Charles the other 75%, we would have calculated the cost for option (iii) in the last stage above as £0.00 x 75% + £33.33 x 25% = £8.33.

This would then have been our best option and a dividend payment would have produced the best result.

8.4   BOTTOM-UP PLANNING FOR COUPLES

Subject to the problems highlighted in Section 16.2, the best tax strategies for couples owning a company equally together and each having no other income in the tax year, may be summarised as follows:

Accounting periods ending after 30th April 2009:

Pay salaries of £6,035 each and then pay any further sums required as a dividend.

Accounting periods ending between October 2008 and April 2009:

i)   Companies with profits not exceeding £310,870:
Pay salaries of £5,435 each and then pay any further sums required as a dividend.

ii)   Companies with profits between £310,870 and £312,224:
First, pay salaries of £5,435 each. Next, pay sufficient further salary or bonus to one or both directors to reduce the company's profits to £300,000 without paying either

director more than £6,035 (gross) in total. Pay any further sums required as a dividend.

In a few cases, it will be necessary to ensure that the couple's salaries are equal in order to achieve the best result.

iii) Companies with profits over £312,224:
Pay salaries of £6,035 each and then pay any further sums required as a dividend.

Accounting periods ending between July 2007 and September 2008:

i) Companies with profits not exceeding £631,398:
Follow the same strategy as set out above for accounting periods ending between October 2008 and April 2009.

ii) Companies with profits between £631,398 and £1,512,224:
Pay salaries of £6,035 each and then pay any further sums required as a dividend.

Except
When the couple wish to extract very large sums in excess of the amount shown in the middle column of the table below and the company has sufficient profit as per the right-hand column of the table.

Year Ending:	Minimum Net Income	Minimum Profit
31-Jul-2007	186,001	631,398
31-Aug-2007	187,544	634,348
30-Sep-2007	189,064	637,253
31-Oct-2007	190,662	640,309
30-Nov-2007	192,237	643,320
31-Dec-2007	193,893	646,487
31-Jan-2008	195,581	649,713
29-Feb-2008	197,137	652,688
31-Mar-2008	198,881	656,022
30-Apr-2008	219,717	695,858
31-May-2008	246,786	747,611

30-Jun-2008	280,698	812,446
31-Jul-2008	327,877	902,646
31-Aug-2008	395,213	1,031,383
30-Sep-2008	494,907	1,221,984

When
The optimum method will be to pay each director a salary of at least £40,835 and pay the remainder as further salary or bonus, split between the directors in whatever manner is desired.

Until
You have reduced the company's taxable profits to £300,000, after which dividends should be paid.

iii) **Companies with profits over £1,512,224:**
Pay salaries of £6,035 each and then pay any further sums required as a dividend.

Except
When the couple wish to extract very large sums in excess of the amounts described under (ii) above plus at least half of the amount by which the company's profit exceeds £1,512,224.

When
It may be more beneficial to take the whole payment as salaries. If so, each director should be paid at least £40,835. The excess may be split between the directors in whatever manner is desired.

Until
You have reduced the company's taxable profits to £300,000, after which dividends should be paid.

As before, these strategies are ideal from a theoretical point of view but will need to be considered in the light of a great many other factors.

An additional factor which may sometimes be present in the case of a 'corporate couple' is the fact that one member of the couple may not actually wish to pay over an equal sum to their spouse or partner.

The issues discussed in Chapter 7 regarding dividends or salary paid but left outstanding on loan account continue to apply equally when the company is owned by a couple – but with double the potential impact!

8.5 OTHER CO-OWNERS

As far as tax planning is concerned, the position for any other co-owning director/shareholders is exactly the same as outlined above for a couple.

Here, however, commercial requirements are much more likely to take precedence.

Nevertheless, where equality of treatment is desired, the guidelines given in the previous section remain valid.

Furthermore, where co-owners have a purely commercial relationship, there is far less likelihood of any attack under the new 'income-shifting' legislation (see Section 16.2).

8.6 FAMILY COMPANIES

Companies are also often owned by three or more director/shareholders. In such cases, the dictates of commercial necessity are likely to be stronger still.

Nevertheless, where a bonus or dividend is proposed, following the advice given in Table D will continue to provide the theoretical optimum result for taxation purposes.

In the case of a family company, perhaps owned by siblings, we will often still get sufficient equality of treatment to enable the table to be followed in practice.

Example

The Wessex brothers: Alfred, Ethelred, Ethelbert and Ethelbald each own a 25% share in Eddington Limited and are all directors of the company.

The company is forecast to make a profit of £400,000 in the year ending 30th September 2008 after having already paid the directors salaries of £40,000 each.

The directors now wish to extract a further net sum of £20,000 each from the company. To begin with, Table D shows us that dividends appear to be preferable. However, after paying a mere £40 (gross) to each director, the table's advice switches to bonus, so we know that we have to carry out a comparison.

Following a bonus strategy, each director would receive a net sum of £13,240 through bonus payments which will cost the company a total of £100,000 and bring its profits down to the small companies rate threshold of £300,000. This is made up as follows:

Gross   **Net**
£40,000 to £40,040 = £40   x £100/£144.93 =   £28
£40,040 to £40,835 = £795   x £100/£126.58 =   £628
£40,835 to £62,163 = £21,328 x £100/£169.49 =   £12,584

Total net sum received: £13,240

The gross payments totalling £22,163 will attract employer's National Insurance at 12.8%, bringing the total cost for each director up to £25,000, or a total of £100,000 for all four.

Having thus reduced the company's taxable profits to £300,000, the directors should then extract the remaining funds required by way of dividend. To get the additional net £6,760 (£20,000 - £13,240) which each director requires will necessitate a dividend of £9,013 each (£6,760 x 100/75).

Each director's dividend will thus produce an Income Tax cost of:

£9,013 x 25% = £2,253

This gives the following total tax cost for the exercise:

	£
Total cost of bonuses to Eddington Limited	100,000
Less:	
Corporation Tax relief @ 31.125% (see Section 2.3)	(31,125)
Net cost of bonuses after Corporation Tax relief	68,875

Less:

Net bonuses received by directors (4 x £13,240)	*(52,960)*

Total net tax cost of bonuses	*15,915*
Add:	
Income Tax on dividends (4 x £2,253)	*9,012*

Total net tax cost of payments:	*24,927*
	======

Now we have to compare this with the cost of a simple dividend.

Each director would have been able to receive a tax free dividend of £751.50. This is arrived at as £40,835 - £40,000 (existing salary) = £835 x £100/£111.11.

To get the additional £19,248.50 required for each director would necessitate further dividends of £25,664 each (£19,248.50 x 100/75).

This would give each director a higher rate Income Tax bill of:

£25,664 x 25% = £6,416

The total cost would thus be £25,664 (£6,416 x 4) meaning that the bonus route is preferable (subject to cashflow considerations).

8.7 MINORITY SHAREHOLDERS

Where a company has one or more minority shareholders, a majority director/shareholder attempting to follow Table D may run into a problem.

If this senior director wishes to pay himself extra, the table will continue to provide the best tax solution. If that solution is to pay a bonus, there is no problem – the senior director just pays himself extra salary or a bonus.

If, however, a dividend appears to be the best solution, there will be a dilemma. To pay this dividend will mean also paying funds out to the minority shareholders.

If the minority holdings are small, however, it could still remain the best solution.

Example

William owns 90% of Hastings Limited. The other 10% is owned by Harold, a former director who has now retired.

After deducting William's basic salary of £20,000, the company has a taxable profit of £100,000 for the year ended 31ˢᵗ March 2009. William now wishes to take a further net sum of £9,000 out of the company.

Table F tells us that the total cost to Hastings Limited if William takes a net bonus of £9,000 will be:

£9,000 x £163.48/£100 = £14,713

After Corporation Tax relief at 21% (see Section 2.3) this would leave a net cost to Hastings Limited of £11,623. Deducting the £9,000 received by William leaves a net total tax cost of £2,623.

Instead of this, however, William could declare a total dividend of £10,000, of which he would receive £9,000. This would have no tax cost and the £1,000 paid to Harold would be a lot better than a tax cost of £2,623.

Harold will be happy too – not only has he received £1,000, but the value of his investment has not been reduced to fund a bonus payment to William which would have cost the company a total of £14,713.

Things will not always work out this well of course and larger minority shareholdings are more likely to prevent dividends from being the best solution.

If Harold had held 40% of the shares in Hastings Limited, for example, the total dividends paid would need to be increased to £15,000 and his share would have amounted to £6,000. William would then have been better off to pay himself extra salary or a bonus.

In reality, a situation like this tends to be governed by the nature of the relationship between William and Harold and that, of course, is always something to keep an eye on!

Things are different, of course, if we actually want to make payments to the minority shareholders.

Example

Winston is the managing director of Dunkirk Ltd and owns 75% of its shares. His co-directors, Clementine and Spencer, own 15% and 10% each respectively.

The company's profits for the year ended 30th June 2008 are estimated at £1,000,000 after paying salaries of £100,000 to Winston, £40,040 to Clementine and £26,000 to Spencer. The company has taken the necessary steps to ensure that any amounts paid by way of directors' bonuses can also be deducted from its profits for the year ended 30th June 2008 for Corporation Tax purposes (see Section 6.1).

Winston decides that they all deserve a bit of a reward and wishes to pay out a total sum of £100,000 to the director/shareholders. He is content to pay this sum in the same 75/15/10 ratio as their shareholdings.

Paying a total dividend of £100,000 would mean that Winston, as a higher rate taxpayer, would suffer Income Tax at an effective rate of 25% on his dividend (see Section 2.7). This would give him an Income Tax bill of £18,750 on his £75,000 share, leaving him with a net sum of just £56,250.

Clementine would escape tax on the first part of her dividend before her taxable income reached £40,835. From Table E, we can see that the further £795 required to bring her taxable income up to this level equates to a dividend of:

£795 x £100/£111.11 = £715.50

Clementine would then suffer Income Tax at an effective rate of 25% on the remaining £14,284.50 (£15,000 - £715.50). This would give her an Income Tax bill of £3,571 (£14,284.50 x 25%), leaving her with a net sum of £11,429 (£15,000 - £3,571).

Spencer would be able to keep his entire £10,000 dividend as his taxable income would still remain below £40,835.

In total, the directors receive a net £77,679 (£56,250 + £11,429 + £10,000).

Winston isn't really happy with this prospect, so he looks at using the same sum of £100,000 to fund bonus payments. He knows that he can 'gross up' this sum to account for the Corporation Tax relief which the company will obtain at 31.816% (see Section 2.3). This produces a sum of £146,662 (£100,000 x 100/68.184).

Accounting for employer's National Insurance at 12.8% means that the total gross bonus payments to be paid would then be £130,020 (£146,662 x 100/112.8). This is then split as:

Winston:	£97,515
Clementine:	£19,503
Spencer:	£13,002

This time, Winston keeps £57,534 after Income Tax at 40% and National Insurance at 1%.

Clementine is taxed as follows:

£795 (£40,835 - £40,040) @ 21% =	£167
£18,708 (£19,503 -£795) @ 41% =	£7,670
Total Tax:	£7,837

Clementine therefore retains net income of £11,666 (£19,503 - £7,837) under this approach.

Spencer will suffer Income Tax at 20% and National Insurance at 11% on his entire £13,002 bonus, leaving him with a net sum of £8,971.

In total, the three directors will receive net sums of £78,171 (£57,534 + £11,666 + £8,971) by following the bonus strategy, which is £492 more than under the dividend strategy.

Winston's happy, Clementine is happy, and Spencer?

Admittedly, Spencer does lose out here. Winston may say it's just tough, or could adjust the payments to ensure that Spencer doesn't lose out. Since the overall tax burden is lower, this could be done and still leave Winston and Clementine with more net income than under the dividend route (see Section 8.10 below).

8.8   COMPANY BUDGETS

The last example in the previous section showed a different approach to the 'Salary/Bonus or Dividend' question.

This time, we started with a budget of how much the company could afford, rather than a net sum required by the director/shareholder.

For companies with several shareholders this will often be the more appropriate approach, as it is less a case of what shareholders want and more a case of what the company can afford. In these situations, the director/shareholders will generally also have a basic salary before we start our tax planning.

Where Does Our Model Fit In?

Nevertheless, using Table D would still have shown Winston the best route to follow, as we shall see in the next section.

8.9   THE COMPOSITE RATE APPROACH

Before payment of the additional sum in the last example in Section 8.7, the marginal net tax rates for the three shareholders were £30.36, -£2.64 and £11.47 respectively per £100 of net bonus received.

These numbers are derived by taking the net cost to the company of paying these bonuses as per Table F then deducting Corporation Tax relief at 31.816% (see Section 2.3) and the £100 actually received by the director. This works as follows:

Winston: £191.19 – 31.816% =   £130.36 - £100 =   £30.36
Clementine: £142.78 – 31.816% =   £97.36 - £100 =   -£2.64
Spencer: £163.48 – 31.816% =   £111.47 - £100 =   £11.47

We can thus work out an appropriate 'composite rate' as follows:

£30.36 x 75% =   £22.77
-£2.64 x 15% =   -£0.40
£11.47 x 10% =   £1.15

Total: £23.52

The composite rate for the payment of a dividend would be 75% x £33.33 = £25.00.

Hence, we can see that the table clearly indicates that bonus payments would be preferable overall. The answer to Winston's situation lay in our table all along!

Furthermore, we also know that, after payment of part of the bonus, Clementine moved up into the 'Over £40,835' income bracket. This alters the composite rate for a bonus payment as follows:

£30.36 x 75% =   £22.77
£30.36 x 15% =   £4.55
£11.47 x 10% =   £1.15

Total: £28.47

However, the composite rate for the payment of a dividend now becomes 90% x £33.33 = £30.00, so we can see that the bonus strategy remains preferable.

Using the composite rate approach will always point you in the right direction to make your payment at the lowest overall tax cost.

This is, however, based on the assumption that we are comparing 'like with like'; namely that you are happy to pay bonuses in the same proportions as a dividend would have been paid in.

Nevertheless, the approach can be further refined to compensate anyone who individually loses out under the strategy which provides the optimum overall result. Effectively, this is done by 'sharing' the overall tax savings.

8.10 EVERY LOSER WINS

Using the composite rate approach, Winston knows that the directors, as a whole, will be better off taking bonuses out of the company.

We have also worked out that total gross bonuses of £130,020 can be paid to leave the company with an overall net cost of £100,000.

Winston has now decided, however, that he would like each director to receive at least the same net sum as they would have received under the dividend route.

To get a net £10,000 into Spencer's hands (the sum he received under the dividend route) we will need to pay him a bonus of £14,435.

The first £14,040 of this bonus suffers Income Tax and National Insurance totalling 31%, leaving Spencer with £9,688. The remaining £395 suffers just 21%, thus providing Spencer with the required additional net sum of £312.

In Section 8.7, we saw that Clementine would have received a net sum of £11,429 under the dividend route.

We also saw that the first £795 of her bonus suffers total tax of £167, leaving her with a net sum of £628. To put her in the same position as if a dividend had been paid, therefore, she needs a further net bonus of £10,801 (£11,429 - £628). From Table E, we can see that this equates to a gross bonus of:

£10,801 x £169.49/£100 = £18,307

The total bonus to be paid to Clementine is therefore £795 + £18,307 = £19,102.

This will leave Winston to take the remaining bonus of £96,483 (£130,020 - £14,435 - £19,102). After Income Tax and National Insurance, he will be left with £56,925, still £675 better off than when he simply paid everyone a dividend.

Summary

We have now managed to put Clementine and Spencer back where they started and yet still leave Winston better off than under the dividend route.

In fact, the move to improve Spencer's position by £1,129 has cost the other directors just £846. Not only have we shared the tax savings, we've actually improved them!

What this revised example shows is that the composite rate approach can easily be adapted to ensure that everyone benefits.

Chapter 9

Companies with Different Tax Rates

9.1 ASSOCIATED COMPANIES

As explained in Section 2.1, whenever the company paying a salary, bonus or dividend has any active associated companies, the tax bands for Corporation Tax purposes must be divided equally between the paying company itself and all of its active associated companies.

This means amending the Corporation Tax thresholds included in the tables in Appendix A and throughout the guide as follows:

Associated Companies:	Normal Thresholds £300,000	£1,500,000
1	£150,000	£750,000
2	£100,000	£500,000
3	£75,000	£375,000
4	£60,000	£300,000
5	£50,000	£250,000

Hence, for example, if we look at a company with annual profits of £65,000 and four active associated companies, we see that its profits lie in the band '£60,000 to £300,000' per the above table.

This band equates to the '£300,000 to £1,500,000' band for a company with no associated companies.

Hence, to find the total net tax cost of a net £100 bonus or dividend paid by this company, we look at the results for a company profit of '£300,000 to £1,500,000' given in Table B.

It is only the Corporation Tax thresholds which are affected by the existence of any associated companies, everything else remains the same.

9.2   WHAT IS AN ASSOCIATED COMPANY?

Any company controlled by the same person or persons is an associated company for Corporation Tax purposes. Additionally, where one company controls another, they are associated. Group companies must generally therefore be counted as associated companies.

Example

Ike, Montgomery and George each own one third of Gold Limited.

Ike, Montgomery and Edwin each own one third of Sword Limited.

Gold Limited and Sword Limited are associated companies because Ike and Montgomery together own more than 50% of each company.

Furthermore, a company controlled by the same persons and their spouses, civil partners and minor children must also be included as an associated company.

Example

Claudia owns 90% of a small trading company, Conquest AD43 Limited; her husband Antedios owns the remaining 10%.

Antedios also owns another trading company, Iceni Limited.

Each company must count the other as an associated company for Corporation Tax purposes and all the Corporation Tax thresholds for both companies are therefore halved.

In general, companies controlled by other relatives need not be counted as associated companies unless there is a significant commercial relationship between the companies.

All active associated companies worldwide must be counted.

To be 'active', a company must be carrying on a business. Simply holding funds on deposit or owning vacant property will not, however, render it 'active'.

9.3 SHORT ACCOUNTING PERIODS

Again, as explained in Section 2.1, a company with an accounting period of less than twelve months will need to reduce its Corporation Tax thresholds. The reduced thresholds are approximately as follows:

Months in Period:	Normal Thresholds £300,000	Normal Thresholds £1,500,000
1	£25,000	£125,000
2	£50,000	£250,000
3	£75,000	£375,000
4	£100,000	£500,000
5	£125,000	£625,000
6	£150,000	£750,000
7	£175,000	£875,000
8	£200,000	£1,000,000
9	£225,000	£1,125,000
10	£250,000	£1,250,000
11	£275,000	£1,375,000

The above figures are only approximate since, in practice, the reduced thresholds must actually be calculated on the basis of the number of days in the accounting period.

Again, for our purposes, it is only the Corporation Tax thresholds which are affected.

9.4 LONG ACCOUNTING PERIODS

Where a company has an accounting period of more than twelve months, this is treated as two periods for Corporation Tax purposes.

The first period for Corporation Tax purposes is the twelve month period beginning on the first day of the long accounting period; the second period for Corporation Tax purposes comprises the remainder of the long accounting period.

However, as far as any Corporation Tax relief for salaries or bonuses is concerned, the effect is the same as if we had one single long accounting period.

For example, if we have a profit of £450,000 for a fifteen month accounting period this is treated as a twelve month period with a £360,000 profit (12/15 x £450,000) and a three month period with a £90,000 profit (3/15 x £450,000). (These figures are again approximate since in practice the allocation must be based on the number of days in each period rather than months.)

If, however, we then make a provision for a bonus of £30,000 (including National Insurance) in the accounts for this fifteen month period (meeting the criteria set out in Section 6.1), it is not all treated as a cost of the final three month period. Instead, the profit of the whole fifteen month period is reduced to £420,000 before being apportioned between the two periods which we have for Corporation Tax purposes. This, of course, would mean earlier Corporation Tax relief for approximately 12/15ths of the bonus.

As far as our tables in Appendix A are concerned, therefore, in planning for bonus or dividend payments with a long accounting period, the revised Corporation Tax thresholds for this purpose are effectively approximately as follows:

Months in Period:	Normal Thresholds	
	£300,000	£1,500,000
13	£325,000	£1,625,000
14	£350,000	£1,750,000
15	£375,000	£1,875,000
16	£400,000	£2,000,000
17	£425,000	£2,125,000
18	£450,000	£2,250,000

9.5 THE CORPORATION TAX THRESHOLD FORMULA

We've now covered most situations which affect the Corporation Tax thresholds we need to know for 'Salary or Dividend' planning.

We are still left with those companies with more than five associated companies, as well as those with any associates and an accounting period with a duration of anything other than twelve months.

So, I'll give you a formula.

'A' is the number of active associated companies which your company has.

'M' is the number of months in your company's accounting period.

'N' is the normal Corporation Tax threshold for a company with no associated companies and a twelve month accounting period (i.e. the £300,000 threshold or the £1,500,000 threshold).

Your threshold is: $M/12 \times N/(1 + A)$

9.6 LOSS-MAKING COMPANIES

Where a company is making a loss for Corporation Tax purposes, there cannot usually be any relief in the current accounting period for the payment of salaries or bonuses.

In most cases, for any payments in excess of £5,435, this will render payments of salaries or bonuses more expensive than the payment of a dividend. (Although a dividend cannot be paid if the company has no distributable profits – see Section 12.5.)

Unless the company's losses are carried back to be set against the profits of the previous accounting period, they are generally carried forward to be set off against future profits of the same business.

From a tax planning perspective, therefore, further payments of salary or bonus in excess of £5,435 may sometimes still be worthwhile where:

- The company's losses can be carried back for relief in the previous accounting period, or
- It is anticipated that the company will have taxable profits in the near future.

In these cases, the effective rate of Corporation Tax relief on any salary or bonus payment will be the company's marginal Corporation Tax rate for the year in which its losses are expected to be utilised.

Example

On 6th June 2008, Ryan's company, Omaha Limited, launched its product in a new market. The company has a difficult first trading period in the new market and, as a result, anticipates making overall losses of £100,000 for Corporation Tax purposes for the year ending 31st December 2008.

In the previous year to 31st December 2007, however, the company made a taxable profit of £500,000.

The company's loss of £100,000 for the year ending 31st December 2008 can therefore be carried back and set off against the previous year's taxable profits. This will reduce Omaha Limited's taxable profits for the year ended 31st December 2007 to an estimated £400,000.

Ryan is already taking a salary of £50,000 from Omaha Limited and, in December 2008, the company pays him a further net bonus of £50,000. Using Table F, we can see that the total cost of this bonus to the company will be:

£50,000 x £191.19/£100 = £95,595

This bonus will thus increase the amount of loss for the year ending 31st December 2008 to £195,595. As we know, that loss can be carried back and set off against the company's profits for the previous year. By increasing the loss carried back, Ryan will therefore effectively further reduce the previous year's taxable profit.

Hence, by paying the bonus during the year ending 31st December 2008, Omaha Limited will effectively obtain Corporation Tax relief in the year ended 31st December 2007 when its marginal Corporation Tax rate was 32.562% (see Section 2.3).

A situation like this has the added advantage that the bonus will effectively produce almost instant Corporation Tax relief by increasing the repayment due for the previous year.

Group Companies

Where the loss-making company is a member of a group of companies, it may be able to surrender its losses to a profitable company in the group (e.g. a subsidiary company). In these cases, the marginal Corporation Tax rate of the company benefiting from the surrendered losses will be the effective rate at which relief is obtained for any salary or bonus payments.

Creating Losses

Where the payment of salary or bonus reduces the company's taxable profit to nil, any further salary or bonus paid will create a loss for Corporation Tax purposes (subject to the points in Section 12.4).

Hence, when considering whether such further salary or bonus payments should be made, the considerations set out above should be applied.

9.7   CLOSE INVESTMENT HOLDING COMPANIES

Broadly speaking, a private company is a 'Close Company' if it is under the control of five or fewer persons. 'Control' is based on voting power vested in share capital held by those persons. Shares held by 'connected' persons such as spouses, civil partners and other close relatives are included when considering the application of this rule.

As complex as the above definition may seem, what it means is that the vast majority of private companies are Close Companies for tax purposes.

This, in itself, is not a problem. We only start to run into difficulty if the close company is also a Close Investment Holding Company.

A close company will be a Close Investment Holding Company unless it exists wholly or mainly for one or more 'qualifying purposes'. Thankfully, these 'qualifying purposes' include carrying on a trade or 'making investments in land let, or intended to be let, other than to connected persons'.

Hence, all trading companies and most property investment companies should not, therefore, be Close Investment Holding Companies.

This is very important because Close Investment Holding Companies must pay Corporation Tax at the main rate on all of their profits. In other words, a Close Investment Holding Company always pays Corporation Tax at the rate which normally only applies to companies with profits in excess of £1,500,000.

For the purposes of this guide, therefore, anyone extracting funds from such a company should follow the recommendations given for a company with profits of 'over £1,500,000' in Table D, regardless of what the actual level of profit in their company may be.

Chapter 10

Older Directors

10.1 PRIVILEGES OF AGE

The marginal tax rates set out in Sections 2.6 and 2.7 need to be modified in the case of some older directors who may be entitled to:

- A higher personal allowance,
- Exemption from National Insurance,
- The married couples allowance, or
- Some combination of the above.

The people affected by one or more of the matters described in this chapter may be summarised as:

- Men who will be aged 65 or more at the end of the tax year,
- Women aged 60 or more, and
- Any person who is married to, or is a registered civil partner of, a person born before 6th April 1935.

(When referring to 'married people' or 'spouses' throughout this chapter, I will also be referring to registered civil partners.)

Directors over state retirement age (see Section 10.4) will, of course, also generally be entitled to a state pension. Many of the 'older directors' discussed in this chapter will also be receiving private pension income.

Fortunately, unlike some other forms of income, pension income does not give rise to too many additional complications, but it will nevertheless still need to be taken into account. In Section 10.15, we will therefore look at the impact of pension income on the issues discussed in this chapter.

10.2 AGE-RELATED ALLOWANCES

Anyone aged 65 or over at the end of the tax year is entitled to a higher personal allowance in place of the usual £6,035 available to younger people. The current (2008/9) amounts of these higher 'age-related' personal allowances are as follows:

Taxpayers aged 65 to 74:   £9,030
Taxpayers aged 75 and over: £9,180

Each of the age limits described above is applied according to the taxpayer's age at the end of the tax year. Hence, for example, a person born on 3rd April 1944 will be entitled to a personal allowance of £9,030 for the 2008/9 tax year (subject to the potential withdrawal of relief described in the next section).

For married couples, where one or both of them were born before 6th April 1935, there is also still a 'Married Couples Allowance' available. The married couples allowance is given in the form of a 10% tax credit on the following amounts of income:

- Where the older member of the couple was born before 6th April 1935, but is aged under 75: £6,535
- Where the older member of the couple is aged 75 or more: £6,625.

Only one married couples allowance is available to the couple. It remains available, subject to the potential withdrawal explained below, for the whole of the tax year of divorce, separation or the death of a spouse. A suitably reduced proportion, however, may be claimed in the year of marriage.

Tax Tip – 'Grab a Granny'

Note that the married couples allowance is available whenever the older member of the couple was born before 6th April 1935.

Hence, whatever age **you** are, you can qualify for married couples allowance by marrying someone who is old enough.

With a maximum tax saving available of just £662.50 per annum, however, it is rather questionable whether it is worth marrying for this reason alone!

For those who married before 5th December 2005, the allowance is usually claimed by the husband, although these couples may elect for the spouse with the higher income to claim the allowance instead.

In the case of eligible couples marrying on or after 5th December 2005, the allowance must be claimed by the spouse or civil partner with the higher income.

The minimum amount of the married couples allowance (£2,540) may be transferred to the other spouse or may be shared between the couple equally.

10.3 WITHDRAWAL OF ALLOWANCES

The benefit of the age-related allowances detailed in the previous section is progressively withdrawn when the taxpayer's income exceeds £21,800 per annum.

Withdrawal is at the rate of £1 for every £2 of income over this threshold. This creates a higher effective marginal tax rate for such taxpayers with income between £21,800 and an amount somewhere between £27,790 and £36,260, depending on age and marital status.

Those eligible for married couples allowance will, however, always still be entitled to a minimum allowance of at least £2,540 and everyone will continue to receive at least the normal personal allowance of £6,035.

Where there is both a higher personal allowance and a married couples allowance available, the personal allowance is withdrawn first. This usually increases the marginal tax rate in the relevant band of income by 10%, although this can increase to 15% in certain circumstances (see Example 3 in Section 10.10).

Where income lies in a band in which the married couples allowance is being withdrawn, there is a 5% increase in the effective marginal rate of tax.

Tax Tip

As explained in the last section, for many couples married before 5th December 2005, the married couples allowance is still withdrawn solely by reference to the husband's income.

Hence, where such a married couple eligible for the allowance are both involved in a company, it will often be better to ensure that the wife gets a greater income than her husband, thus avoiding any loss of the available married couples allowance.

10.4 NATIONAL INSURANCE FOR OLDER DIRECTORS

Directors (and other employees) over state retirement age are not liable for employee's primary National Insurance. Unlike the higher Income Tax allowances, however, it is not sufficient to be the requisite age by the end of the tax year and the exemption only commences on the date that state retirement age is reached.

Sadly, employer's secondary National Insurance at 12.8% continues to apply to any salary or bonus in excess of £5,435 paid to any director (or other employee), regardless of the recipient's age.

At present, state retirement age is 60 for women and 65 for men. From 6th April 2010, the female state retirement age will begin to increase until reaching 65 on 6th April 2020.

A payment of salary or bonus which would **normally** be paid to a director after they reach state retirement age will be exempt from employee's primary National Insurance.

This means that a simple delay in the payment of salary will not be sufficient to avoid employee's National Insurance.

Example

Arthur was born on 1st August 1943. He normally takes a salary out of his company, Talavera Limited, on the last Friday of each month.

However, he delays his July 2008 salary payment to 2nd August in an attempt to avoid employee's National Insurance.

Sadly, this does not work; the normal payment date for Arthur's salary would be before his birthday, so employee's National Insurance is due.

His normal salary payments from August 2008 onwards, however, will be exempt from employee's National Insurance.

Potentially, however, if Arthur had adopted the 2nd of the month as his regular salary payment date some years earlier, he should then have managed to avoid employee's National Insurance on his 2nd August 2008 payment. (The 6th would be even better, as we saw in Section 2.14.)

The 'normal due date' rule will be more critical when we are talking about the payment of a large bonus to a director near to state retirement age.

Tax Tip

The most obvious and critical point is to make sure that bonus payments are delayed until after the director reaches state retirement age.

Where large sums are at stake, I would not advocate reliance on the 'normal due date' rule!

Even then, there still remains the danger that the 'normal due date rule' could be used against you:

Example

Harriet was born on 15th February 1949. For several years, she has paid herself a bonus in January each year, based on the profits which her company, Salamanca Limited, has made for the previous year.

In 2009, she delays her bonus until 20th February in an attempt to avoid employee's National Insurance.

Employee's National Insurance may, however, still be due since there is an argument that her bonus would normally be due in January.

To avoid the risk of an argument that a bonus would normally be paid before the director reaches state retirement age, it will be sensible to either avoid any regular pattern for bonus payments or, better still, to establish a regular pattern of paying bonuses on a suitable date falling after the director is expected to reach state retirement age in a few years' time.

Example

Every year, Anne pays herself a bonus out of the profits made by her company, Vimiero Limited. Anne will reach state retirement age on 5th June 2011 (see below) and she wants to ensure that the bonus which she receives in 2011 will be exempt from employee's National Insurance.

She therefore pays herself a bonus on 10th June in 2008, 2009 and 2010, so that, by the time she pays herself a bonus on 10th June 2011, this has become the normal due date and she can be sure that it will be exempt from employee's National Insurance.

In fact, to be really clever, in 2008 Anne also changes the normal payment date for her salary to the 10th of each month, so that, three years later, her June 2011 salary is also exempt from employee's National Insurance.

To make it extra safe for someone like Anne, it will also be sensible to ensure that the company's records, director's board minutes, etc, all show that the bonus is due on the appropriate date.

Wealth Warning

Women born after 5th April 1950 will not reach state retirement age until some time after their 60th birthday.

Broadly, these women will reach state retirement age two months after 5th April 2010 for every month, or part month, after 5th April 1950 that they were born.

For example, a woman born on 24th August 1951 was born between 16 and 17 months after 5th April 1950. She will therefore reach state retirement age 34 months (2 x 17) after 5th April 2010, i.e. on 5th February 2013.

It is important to remember that employee's primary National Insurance will continue to be payable on any salary or bonus due to be paid to such a woman before she reaches her revised state retirement age under these rules.

Women born after 5th April 1955 will have the same state retirement age as men. Further increases in the state retirement age for both genders are proposed after 2025.

10.5 MARGINAL TAX RATES ON SALARIES AND BONUSES FOR OLDER DIRECTORS

As a result of the additional allowances described in Section 10.2 and the National Insurance rules described in Section 10.4, there are a great many different potential marginal tax rate scenarios applying to older directors receiving salary or bonuses.

We will examine these marginal rates in detail over the next few sections.

The reason for establishing all of these marginal tax rates, of course, is to understand how the different rules applying to older directors affect the whole 'Salary or Dividend' question.

Once we have established the relevant marginal tax rates, therefore, we will then summarise how this impacts on the optimum payment strategy for older directors in Sections 10.13 and 10.14.

Please note the following important points when referring to the marginal tax rate tables given in Sections 10.6 to 10.9:

a) The term 'unmarried' includes divorced or separated taxpayers, as well as widows and widowers, who have not remarried. However, it excludes taxpayers who have entered into a registered civil partnership. As explained in Section 10.2, it also excludes those who have separated or been widowed or widowered during the same tax year.

b) Headings are given for ease of reference only. Be sure to read the more detailed descriptions given afterwards to check your eligibility.

c) The 75 age limit refers to age at the end of the tax year.

d) Directors who are under state retirement age at the time of a salary or bonus payment (see Sections 10.8 and 10.9), and who have other income in the same tax year, will continue to be affected by the factors discussed in Section 2.18 and may suffer higher marginal tax rates as a result.

e) Where the director has some interest or other savings income, their marginal tax rates may sometimes differ from those set out in Sections 10.6 to 10.9, as explained in Section 10.10.

f) Directors with dividend income may also suffer a slightly higher marginal tax rate on some salary or bonus payments, as detailed in Section 10.11.

Subject to points (e) and (f) above, the marginal rate bands given for directors over state retirement age in Sections 10.6 and 10.7 apply to the director's <u>total</u> income for the tax year. Naturally, this will often include pension income (see Section 10.15 for further details).

All of the marginal rates quoted in Sections 10.6 to 10.11 apply to payments made, or deemed to be made, to directors in the 2008/9 tax year.

10.6 DIRECTORS AGED 65 OR OVER

i) Unmarried People Aged 65 to 74 and Married People Aged 65 to 73

For a taxpayer aged between 65 and 74 who is:
  a) unmarried,
  b) married but both spouses were born after 5th April 1935, or
  c) married but not personally claiming any part of the married couples allowance,

the effective marginal tax rate on a bonus would be as follows:

Income up to £9,030 (personal allowance):	0%
Income from £9,030 to £21,800:	20%
Income from £21,800 to £27,790:	30%
Income from £27,790 to £40,835:	20%
Income over £40,835:	40%

ii)   Unmarried People Aged 75 Or More

For a taxpayer aged 75 or over who is either:
   a) unmarried, or
   b) married but not claiming any part of the married couples allowance,
the marginal rates on a bonus are as follows:

Income up to £9,180 (personal allowance):	0%
Income from £9,180 to £21,800:	20%
Income from £21,800 to £28,090:	30%
Income from £28,090 to £40,835:	20%
Income over £40,835:	40%

iii)   Married People aged 73 or 74

For a married person aged between 65 and 74, where:
   a) either they or their spouse were born before 6th April 1935,
   b) their spouse is under 75 years of age, and
   c) they personally are claiming the married couples allowance,
the effective marginal tax rate on a bonus would be as follows:

Income up to £9,030:	0%
Income from £9,030 to £15,565:	10%
Income from £15,565 to £21,800:	20%
Income from £21,800 to £27,790:	30%
Income from £27,790 to £35,780:	25%
Income from £35,780 to £40,835:	20%
Income over £40,835:	40%

iv) Married People aged 65 to 74 With a Spouse Aged 75 Or More

For a married person aged between 65 and 74, where:
  a) their spouse is aged 75 or more, and
  b) they personally are claiming the married couples allowance,
the effective marginal tax rate on a bonus would be as follows:

Income up to £9,030:	0%
Income from £9,030 to £15,655:	10%
Income from £15,655 to £21,800:	20%
Income from £21,800 to £27,790:	30%
Income from £27,790 to £35,960:	25%
Income from £35,960 to £40,835:	20%
Income over £40,835:	40%

v) Married People Aged 75 & Over

For a married person aged 75 or over, who personally claims the married couples allowance, the effective marginal tax rates on a bonus are as follows:

Income up to £9,180:	0%
Income from £9,180 to £15,805:	10%
Income from £15,805 to £21,800:	20%
Income from £21,800 to £28,090:	30%
Income from £28,090 to £36,260:	25%
Income from £36,260 to £40,835:	20%
Income over £40,835:	40%

10.7 FEMALE DIRECTORS AGED 60 TO 64

The state retirement age for women is currently 60, rather than 65. (But see Section 10.4 for forthcoming changes). Hence, women in the 60 to 64 age bracket represent another special class of 'older directors'.

These female directors are over the state retirement age and hence are exempt from employee's primary Class 1 National Insurance. They are not yet, however, entitled to a higher personal allowance.

Note, however, that a 64-year-old woman who will be 65 before the end of the tax year *is* entitled to a higher personal allowance. Any female director falling into this category can follow the rules given in the previous section and should ignore the rest of this section.

Just to make it really complicated, there will also be many women aged 60 to 64 with a husband or civil partner born before 6th April 1935. They may therefore be claiming half or all of the minimum married couples allowance entitlement of £2,540 or, since 5th December 2005, even perhaps all of the couple's available married couples allowance.

This gives us some further potential marginal rate scenarios to consider.

vi) Women Aged 60 to 64 and Not Claiming Any Married Couples Allowance

For a woman aged 60 to 64 who is:
  a) unmarried,
  b) married to someone born after 5th April 1935, or
  c) married to an older person but not personally claiming any married couples allowance,
the marginal tax rates applying to a bonus are as follows:

Income up to £6,035 (personal allowance):	0%
Income from £6,035 to £40,835:	20%
Income over £40,835:	40%

vii) Women Aged 60 to 64 With Husbands Aged 73 or 74

For a woman aged 60 to 64 with a husband or civil partner who:
  a) is aged under 75, but
  b) was born before 6th April 1935,
  c) and who is herself personally claiming the whole of the couple's available married couples allowance,

the marginal tax rates applying to a bonus are as follows:

Income up to £6,035:	0%
Income from £6,035 to £12,570:	10%
Income from £12,570 to £21,800:	20%
Income from £21,800 to £29,790:	25%
Income from £29,790 to £40,835:	20%
Income over £40,835:	40%

viii) Women Aged 60 to 64 With A Husband Aged 75 or Over

For a woman aged 60 to 64, whose husband or civil partner is aged 75 or more and who herself is personally claiming the whole of the couple's available married couples allowance, the marginal tax rates applying to a bonus are as follows:

Income up to £6,035:	0%
Income from £6,035 to £12,660:	10%
Income from £12,660 to £21,800:	20%
Income from £21,800 to £29,970:	25%
Income from £29,970 to £40,835:	20%
Income over £40,835:	40%

10.8 WHEN I'M 64

About half of all male directors aged 64 will also present a special case.

If a 64-year-old man's next birthday falls before the end of the tax year, he will be due a higher personal allowance. Until he reaches that birthday, however, any salary or bonus paid to him will usually still be subject to employee's primary National Insurance, as explained in Section 10.4. For the part of the tax year preceding their 65th birthday, the marginal rates applying to salary or bonus paid to these directors will be as set out below:

ix) Unmarried Men Aged 64
Men Aged 64 With A Wife Aged Under 73

For a man aged 64, who will be 65 before the end of the tax year, and who is:
  a) unmarried,
  b) married to someone born after 5th April 1935, or
  c) married to an older person but not personally claiming any married couples allowance,

The marginal tax rates applying to a bonus are as follows:

Income up to £5,435:	0%
Income from £5,435 to £9,030:	11%
Income from £9,030 to £21,800:	31%
Income from £21,800 to £27,790:	41%
Income from £27,790 to £40,040:	31%
Income from £40,040 to £40,835:	21%
Income over £40,835:	41%

x) Men Aged 64 With A Wife Aged 73 or 74

For a man aged 64, who will be 65 before the end of the tax year, and who is married to someone born before 6th April 1935, but aged under 75, and who is personally claiming the whole of the married couples allowance available to the couple, the marginal tax rates applying to a bonus are as follows:

Income up to £5,435:	0%
Income from £5,435 to £9,030:	11%
Income from £9,030 to £15,565:	21%
Income from £15,565 to £21,800:	31%
Income from £21,800 to £27,790:	41%
Income from £27,790 to £35,780:	36%
Income from £35,780 to £40,040:	31%
Income from £40,040 to £40,835:	21%
Income over £40,835:	41%

xi)   Men Aged 64 With A Wife Aged 75 or Over

For a man aged 64, who will be 65 before the end of the tax year, and who is married to someone aged over 75 and who is personally claiming the whole of the married couples allowance available to the couple, the marginal tax rates applying to a bonus are as follows:

Income up to £5,435:	0%
Income from £5,435 to £9,030:	11%
Income from £9,030 to £15,655:	21%
Income from £15,655 to £21,800:	31%
Income from £21,800 to £27,790:	41%
Income from £27,790 to £35,960:	36%
Income from £35,960 to £40,040:	31%
Income from £40,040 to £40,835:	21%
Income over £40,835:	41%

Tax Tip

Subject to the points discussed in Section 10.4, men aged 64 can easily avoid the higher tax rates given above by delaying any salary or bonus payments in excess of £5,435 until after their 65th birthday.

10.9 YOUNGER DIRECTORS WITH OLDER SPOUSES

Yet another 'special' class of directors arises where the director is under state retirement age but has a spouse born before 6th April 1935.

These taxpayers are still liable for primary Class 1 National Insurance and are not eligible for the higher age-related personal allowances.

However, due to the age of their spouse or partner, they <u>are</u> sometimes eligible for the married couples allowance.

This gives rise to our final two marginal rate scenarios for salaries or bonuses.

xii)   People Under 65, With Spouses Aged 73 or 74

For a person below state retirement age but personally claiming the whole married couples allowance available, whose spouse is aged under 75, but born before 6th April 1935, the marginal tax rates for a bonus are:

Income up to £5,435:	0%
Income from £5,435 to £6,035:	11%
Income from £6,035 to £12,570:	21%
Income from £12,570 to £21,800:	31%
Income from £21,800 to £29,790:	36%
Income from £29,790 to £40,040:	31%
Income from £40,040 to £40,835:	21%
Income over £40,835:	41%

xiii)   People Under 65 With Spouses Aged 75 Or More

For a person below state retirement age but personally claiming the whole married couples allowance available, whose spouse is aged 75 or more, the marginal tax rates applying to a bonus are as follows:

Income up to £5,435:	0%
Income from £5,435 to £6,035:	11%
Income from £6,035 to £12,660:	21%
Income from £12,660 to £21,800:	31%
Income from £21,800 to £29,970:	36%
Income from £29,970 to £40,040:	31%
Income from £40,040 to £40,835:	21%
Income over £40,835:	41%

10.10 OLDER DIRECTORS WITH SAVINGS INCOME

Where a director has some interest or other savings income, they may be subject to slightly different effective marginal tax rates on a bonus or salary payment.

Where the director is below state retirement age at the time that the salary or bonus is paid (or due to be paid – see Section 10.4), they will be affected by the factors discussed in Section 2.18.

For those over state retirement age at the time of the salary or bonus payment, different effective marginal tax rates may arise unless they are:

i)   A woman aged 60 to 64 at the end of the tax year who has at least £8,355 of other income, excluding dividends, in the tax year,

ii) A person aged 65 to 74 at the end of the tax year who has at least £11,350 of other income, excluding dividends, in the tax year, or

iii) A person aged 75 or more at the end of the tax year who has at least £11,500 of other income, excluding dividends, in the tax year.

Where the director's other income, excluding dividends, exceeds these levels, the marginal rates set out in Sections 10.6 or 10.7, as appropriate, will continue to apply.

The different rates applying where other income is below these levels arise due to the fact that only interest or other savings income attracts the 10% starting rate of Income Tax on the first £2,320 of taxable income after deducting the director's personal allowance, combined with the effect of the tax band 'pecking order' which we discussed in Section 2.18.

As a result of the tax band 'pecking order', we may see several different effective marginal tax rates arising on the payment of bonuses or salary in these circumstances. As for younger directors, there are an infinite variety of possibly outcomes, but the principles can be demonstrated by way of a few examples.

In our first three examples we will look at three scenarios:

i)   A male director aged 64 at the time of the payment but who will be aged 65 at the end of the tax year ('64').

ii) A director over state retirement age at the time of the payment who will be aged between 65 and 74 at the end of the tax year ('65 to 74').

iii) A director aged 75 or over at the end of the tax year ('Over 75').

In each case, we are ignoring any married couples allowance. Where this allowance is available, further appropriate adjustments will need to be made.

Example 1: Overall effective marginal tax rates on payment of a bonus or salary to a director with £1,000 of savings income:

Bonus/Salary	64	65 to 74	Bonus/Salary	Over 75
Up to £5,435	0%	0%	Up to £8,180	0%
£5,435 to £8,030	11%	0%		
£8,030 to £9,030	21%	10%	£8,180 to £9,180	10%
£9,030 to £10,350	31%	20%	£9,180 to £10,500	20%
£10,350 to £11,350	41%	30%	£10,500 to £11,500	30%
£11,350 to £20,800	31%	20%	£11,500 to £20,800	20%
£20,800 to £26,790	41%	30%	£20,800 to £27,090	30%
£26,790 to £39,835	31%	20%	£27,090 to £39,835	20%
£39,835 to £40,040	51%	40%	Over £39,835	40%
Over £40,040	41%	40%		

The figures used above are derived as follows:

£5,435	Earnings threshold for National Insurance
£8,030/£8,180	Age-related personal allowance less savings income
£9,030/£9,180	Age-related personal allowance
£10,350/£10,500	Point at which savings income begins to be taxed at 20%
£11,350/£11,500	Point at which salary or bonus has exhausted the 10% starting rate band (i.e. personal allowance plus £2,320)
£20,800	Point at which age-related personal allowance starts to be withdrawn (i.e. £21,800, as per Section 10.3, less savings income)
£26,790/£27,090	Point at which age-related personal allowance has been fully withdrawn (i.e. £27,790/£28,090, as per Section 10.6, less savings income)
£39,835	£40,835 less savings income
£40,040	Upper earnings limit for National Insurance

Example 2: Overall effective marginal tax rates on payment of a bonus or salary to a director with £10,000 of savings income:

Bonus/Salary	64	65 to 74	Bonus/Salary	Over 75
Up to £1,350	10%	10%	Up to £1,500	10%
£1,350 to £5,435	20%	20%	£1,500 to £9,180	20%
£5,435 to £9,030	31%	20%		
£9,030 to £11,350	41%	30%	£9,180 to £11,500	30%
£11,350 to £11,800	31%	20%	£11,500 to £11,800	20%
£11,800 to £17,790	41%	30%	£11,800 to £18,090	30%
£17,790 to £30,835	31%	20%	£18,090 to £30,835	20%
£30,835 to £40,040	51%	40%	Over £30,835	40%
Over £40,040	41%	40%		

The figures used above are derived as follows:

£1,350/£1,500	Point at which savings income begins to be taxed at 20% (i.e. £11,350/£11,500 less savings income)
£5,435	Earnings threshold for National Insurance
£9,030/£9,180	Age-related personal allowance
£11,350/£11,500	Point at which salary or bonus has exhausted the 10% starting rate band (i.e. personal allowance plus £2,320)
£11,800	Point at which age-related personal allowance starts to be withdrawn (i.e. £21,800, as per Section 10.3, less savings income)
£17,790/£18,090	Point at which age-related personal allowance has been fully withdrawn (i.e. £27,790/£28,090, as per Section 10.6, less savings income)
£30,835	£40,835 less savings income
£40,040	Upper earnings limit for National Insurance

Example 3: Overall effective marginal tax rates on payment of a bonus or salary to a director with £15,000 of savings income:

Bonus/Salary	64	65 to 74	Bonus/Salary	Over 75
Up to £5,435	20%	20%	Up to £6,800	20%
£5,435 to £6,800	31%	20%		
£6,800 to £8,287	41%	30%	£6,800 to £8,387	30%
£8,287 to £9,833	56%	45%	£8,387 to £9,933	45%
£9,833 to £12,790	41%	30%	£9,933 to £13,090	30%
£12,790 to £25,835	31%	20%	£13,090 to £25,835	20%
£25,835 to £40,040	51%	40%	Over £25,835	40%
Over £40,040	41%	40%		

The figures used above are derived as follows:

£5,435	Earnings threshold for National Insurance
£6,800	Point at which age-related personal allowance starts to be withdrawn (i.e. £21,800, as per Section 10.3, less savings income)
£8,287/£8,387	Point at which the bonus or salary fully utilises the director's remaining personal allowance
£9,833/£9,933	Point at which salary or bonus has exhausted the 10% starting rate band (see below)
£12,790/£13,090	Point at which age-related personal allowance has been fully withdrawn (i.e. £27,790/£28,090, as per Section 10.6, less savings income)
£25,835	£40,835 less savings income
£40,040	Upper earnings limit for National Insurance

This third example demonstrates a further problem which arises where the director has a substantial amount of savings income and the payment of a bonus or salary causes a withdrawal of their age-related personal allowance at the same time that the bonus or salary is using up the 10% starting rate.

As we can see from the table above, this can cause an effective marginal tax rate of up to 56%!

This particular issue can only arise where the director has savings income of between £10,450 and £21,755 (or between £10,300 and £22,055 if aged over 75).

In this example, once the salary or bonus payment exceeds £6,800, the director's higher age-related personal allowance begins to be withdrawn at the rate of £1 for every £2 of additional income.

When the payment reaches £8,287/£8,387, it will have fully utilised the director's remaining personal allowance.

We then enter a band of income where the director's higher age-related personal allowance is still being withdrawn at the rate of £1 for every £2 of additional income at the same time that the salary or bonus is using up the 10% starting rate band.

This means that for every £2 of additional income there is £3 less of the starting rate band available for the director's savings income. This adds an additional 15% to the effective marginal tax rate until the salary or bonus income increases by a further £1,546 (£2,320 x 2/3) and the starting rate band is fully exhausted by salary or bonus payments.

Women aged 60 to 64

As we know, women who are over state retirement age, but under 65 at the end of the tax year, are exempt from primary National Insurance but are not eligible for higher age-related personal allowances.

Directors falling into this category may suffer some higher effective marginal tax rates when they also have some savings income but will not be prone to the additional problems caused by the withdrawal of age-related personal allowances. (I am again ignoring the impact of any married couples allowance which may be available.)

I will give you two more examples to demonstrate the position for these directors.

The effective marginal tax rates arising on the payment of salary or bonus to a woman over state retirement age, but not yet aged 65 at the end of the tax year, who has £1,000 of savings income, are as follows:

Up to £5,035:	0%	(£5,035 = £6,035 - £1,000)
£5,035 to £6,035:	10%	
£6,035 to £7,355:	20%	(£7,355 = £8,355 - £1,000)
£7,355 to £8,355:	30%	
£8,355 to £39,835:	20%	(£39,835 = £40,835 - £1,000)
Over £39,835:	40%	

The effective marginal tax rates arising on the payment of salary or bonus to a woman over state retirement age, but not yet aged 65 at the end of the tax year, who has £10,000 of savings income, are as follows:

Up to £6,035:	20%	
£6,035 to £8,355:	30%	
£8,355 to £30,835:	20%	(£30,835 = £40,835 - £10,000)
Over £30,835:	40%	

10.11 OLDER DIRECTORS WITH OTHER DIVIDEND INCOME

In Section 2.18, we saw the effect of paying bonuses or salary to directors under state retirement age who have dividend income from other sources.

Directors over state retirement age with other dividend income may also suffer a higher effective marginal tax rate on some salary or bonus payments.

This higher rate will arise whenever:

i) The director's total taxable income, excluding dividends, before payment of the bonus or salary is less than £40,835, and

ii) The director's total taxable income, including dividends, after payment of the bonus or salary is more than £40,835.

Remember, as explained in Section 2.8, that, in most cases, every £9 of dividends represents £10 of taxable income.

The effective marginal rate applying in these cases is generally 42.5% and it applies to the band of income which begins when the director's total taxable income <u>including</u> dividends reaches £40,835 and ends when the director's total taxable income <u>excluding</u> dividends reaches £40,835.

For example, where a director has £10,000 of dividend income and no other existing income, the effective marginal rate of 42.5% will apply to payments of salary or bonus of between £29,724 and £40,835. (£29,724 = £40,835 - £10,000 x 10/9)

Other Potential Marginal Tax Rates

Where the director's total income excluding dividends is less than £6,035, the effective marginal rate where criteria (i) and (ii) set out above apply is 22.5%.

Effective marginal rates of 32.5% or 52.5% can also arise where the director also has savings income: i.e. where the salary or bonus pushes the savings income into, or out of, the 10% starting rate band, respectively.

10.12   MARGINAL RATES ON DIVIDENDS FOR OLDER DIRECTORS

The marginal rates for dividends given in Section 2.7 may also sometimes be affected by the withdrawal of the additional age-related allowances described in Section 10.3. In this case, the only classes of directors who may be affected are:

- Those aged 65 or more at the end of the tax year, and
- Those with a spouse born before 6th April 1935.

Furthermore, the effective marginal Income Tax rate applying to dividends received by these directors is only affected when they have already utilised their personal allowance and/or their married couples allowance against other types of income.

In all cases, the marginal Income Tax rates on any dividends eligible for tax credits (see Section 2.8) received by directors whose total income lies in the following brackets, remains unchanged, as shown below:

Total annual income:
Up to £21,800:   0%
From £36,260 to £40,835:   0%
Over £40,835:   25%

As before, these rates are applied to the net dividend received, excluding tax credit (see Section 2.8).

Remember, however, that when considering the above limits, the dividends must be 'grossed up' by a factor of 10/9 to account for the notional (i.e. non-refundable) tax credit attached to them.

The marginal Income Tax rate scenarios set out below deal with the situation where the director has total annual income between £21,800 and £40,835 and has sufficient 'other' (i.e. non-dividend) income to utilise all of their available allowances.

Note that a £100 dividend is 'grossed up' by a factor of 10/9, so that, if the recipient taxpayer is in the relevant income bracket, this will result in the loss of £56 of their available age-related allowances (£100 x 10/9 x ½). This is reflected in the marginal rates set out below.

The effective tax rates arising in the £21,800 to £40,835 income bracket do not actually represent tax on the dividends themselves. What is happening, however, is that the receipt of the dividends is causing a withdrawal of allowances which, in turn, means that more of the director's non-dividend income will be exposed to tax.

The marginal tax rates set out below therefore represent the effective tax cost of receiving a dividend.

In this section, the 65 and 75 age limits refer always to the taxpayer's age at the end of the tax year.

The comments regarding the meaning of the headings given below and the meaning of the term 'unmarried', as set out in Section 10.5 above, also apply equally here.

i) Unmarried People Aged 65 to 74, Married People Aged 65 to 72

For a taxpayer aged between 65 and 74 who is:
- a) unmarried,
- b) married but both spouses were born after 5th April 1935, or
- c) married but not personally claiming any part of the married couples allowance,

the effective marginal tax rate on a dividend would be as follows:

Income from £21,800 to £27,790:	11.1%
Income from £27,790 to £40,835:	0%

ii) Unmarried People Aged 75 Or More

For a taxpayer aged 75 or over who is either:
- a) unmarried, or
- b) not personally claiming any part of the married couples allowance,

the effective marginal tax rates on a dividend are as follows:

Income from £21,800 to £28,090:	11.1%
Income from £28,090 to £40,835:	0%

iii) Married People aged 73 or 74

For a person aged between 65 and 74, where:
- a) either they or their spouse were born before 6th April 1935,
- b) their spouse is under 75 years of age, and
- c) they personally are claiming the full married couples allowance available to the couple,

the effective marginal tax rate on a dividend would be as follows:

Income from £21,800 to £27,790:	11.1%
Income from £27,790 to £35,780:	5.6%
Income from £35,780 to £40,835:	0%

iv) People aged 65 to 74 With Spouses Aged 75 or More

For a person aged between 65 and 74, whose spouse is aged 75 or more, and who personally is claiming the full married couples allowance available to the couple, the effective marginal tax rate on a dividend would be as follows:

Income from £21,800 to £27,790:	11.1%
Income from £27,790 to £35,960:	5.6%
Income from £35,960 to £40,835:	0%

v) Married People Aged 75 & Over

For a married person aged 75 or over, who personally is claiming the full married couples allowance available to the couple, the effective marginal tax rates on a dividend are as follows:

Income from £21,800 to £28,090:	11.1%
Income from £28,090 to £36,260:	5.6%
Income from £36,260 to £40,835:	0%

vi) People Under 65 With Spouses Aged 73 or 74

For a person aged under 65 at the end of the tax year, whose spouse is aged under 75, but born before 6th April 1935, and who personally is claiming the full married couples allowance available to the couple, the marginal tax rates applying to a dividend are as follows:

Income from £21,800 to £29,790:	5.6%
Income from £29,790 to £40,835:	0%

vii) People Under 65 With Spouses Aged 75 Or More

For a person aged under 65 at the end of the tax year, whose spouse is aged 75 or more, and who personally is claiming the full married couples allowance available to the couple, the marginal tax rates applying to a dividend are as follows:

Income from £21,800 to £29,970:	5.6%
Income from £29,970 to £40,835:	0%

Impact of Savings Income

When the director has some savings income, the 10% starting rate band may affect the marginal tax rates set out above in one of two possible ways.

Firstly, where the withdrawal of allowances only causes savings income to be taxed at 10% within the starting rate band, the 11.1% effective marginal rate in scenarios (i) to (v) above will be reduced to 5.6%.

This can only apply where the director has total taxable income, excluding savings income and dividends, of less than £9,030 (or £9,180 for a director aged over 75).

Conversely, in some cases, the withdrawal of allowances may cause the loss of availability of the 10% starting rate band for the director's savings income. Where this situation arises, the 11.1% effective marginal rate in scenarios (i) to (v) above will be increased to 16.7%.

This less favourable situation may occur where the director has total taxable income, excluding savings income and dividends, of between £6,035 and £11,500.

Each of these alternative effective rates can apply to a band of dividend income of up to a maximum of £4,176 in size.

10.13   THE TAXCAFE COMPUTER MODEL FOR OLDER DIRECTORS 2008/2009

Having worked out all (well, most) of the different marginal tax rate scenarios applying to 'older directors', we must now revisit the Taxcafe computer model to see how this impacts on the 'Salary or Dividend' question.

In this case, we will approach it slightly differently, owing to the fact that there are some thirteen different marginal rate scenarios for salaries and bonuses and seven for dividends (plus some variations thereon in each case).

To use the table set out below, therefore, you must first establish what marginal rate would apply to a bonus in your case by referring to Sections 10.6 to 10.11. Where your marginal rate on a bonus would be 30%, you will also need to check your marginal rate on a dividend in Section 10.12.

Exceptions

If you are below state retirement age and already have salary or bonus income of £40,040 or more, you should stick with the results given in Table D, rather than the ones set out below.

Older Directors 2008/2009: Salary v Dividend?

Our model's recommendations for making payments to older directors are summarised below.

Remember that, just as in Section 3.6, these recommendations simply represent a 'snapshot' at the current level of director's income and company profit.

Where the payment itself has the potential to alter either the director's or the company's marginal tax rate, a more detailed analysis will be required, along similar lines to those set out in Chapter 4.

The recommendations below apply for payments made, or deemed to be made, to directors during 2008/9. As explained in Section 3.1, we must therefore consider the position for company accounting periods ending anywhere between July 2007 and March 2010.

Our model's recommendations for payments to older directors during 2008/2009 are as follows:

Director's Marginal Rate on a Bonus	Director's Marginal Rate on a Dividend	Company Profit		
		Up to £300,000	£300,000 to £1.5M	Over £1.5M
0%	0%	Bonus	Bonus	Bonus
10%	0%	Dividend for APs ending by 31/5/2008	Bonus	Bonus
11%	0%	Dividend for APs ending by 30/4/2009	Bonus	Bonus
20%	0%	Dividend	Bonus	Bonus for APs ending by 31/8/2008
21%	0%	Dividend	Bonus for APs ending by 28/2/2009	Bonus for APs ending by 31/3/2008
22.5%	25%	Bonus	Bonus	Bonus
25%	5.6%	Dividend	Bonus for APs ending by 31/10/2009	Bonus for APs ending by 31/5/2008
30%	0% or 5.6% (See Section 10.12)	Dividend	Dividend	Dividend
30%	11.1% (See Section 10.12)	Dividend	Bonus for APs ending by 31/1/2009	Dividend

31%	0%	Dividend	Dividend	Dividend
32.5%	25%	Dividend for APs ending by 31/5/2008	Bonus	Bonus
36%	5.6%	Dividend	Dividend	Dividend
40%	25%	Dividend	Bonus	Bonus for APs ending by 31/8/2008
41%	0%, 5.6% or 11.1%	Dividend	Dividend	Dividend
42.5%	25%	Dividend	Bonus for APs ending by 31/5/2008	Dividend
45%	16.7%	Dividend	Dividend	Dividend
51%	25%	Dividend	Dividend	Dividend
52.5%	25%	Dividend	Dividend	Dividend
56%	16.7%	Dividend	Dividend	Dividend

AP = Accounting Period

Where a date is given above, the recommendation will switch to the other payment method for any accounting periods ending on a later date.

10.14   PLANNING   PAYMENTS   TO   OLDER DIRECTORS

The table in the previous section allows us to produce the following guidelines for the payment of salary, bonus or dividends to older directors. Owing to the many complexities which we have encountered, these are only guidelines and detailed analysis will often be required to produce the optimum result in practice.

The principles explained in Section 6.1 continue to apply when considering which accounting period the payments are deemed to be taken out of.

Companies with Profits Up To £300,000

These companies should pay salary up to the limit of the director's own personal 0% band as per Sections 10.6 to 10.11. Salary should also be paid when the director's marginal tax rate is 22.5% (see Section 10.11).

For accounting periods ending after 31st May 2008, salary should be paid when the director's marginal tax rate is 10% or 32.5% and for periods ending after 30th April 2009, salary should be paid when the director's marginal tax rate is 11%.

Generally this means paying a salary of at least £5,435 to all directors and up to the personal allowance for those over state retirement age. For accounting periods ending after 31st May 2008, payments of salary to directors over state retirement age should also cover any available married couples allowance.

For accounting periods ending after 30th April 2009, directors under state retirement age should also generally be paid a salary up to their personal allowance.

Any further payments beyond these amounts should generally be made by way of dividend.

The position may be altered where the director has savings income or dividends from other sources (see Sections 10.10 and 10.11).

Companies with Profits between £300,000 and £1,500,000

These companies should always pay salary or bonus when the director's marginal tax rate is 20% or less, 22.5%, 32.5% or 40%.

Salary or bonus may also be preferable when the director's marginal rate is 21%, 25%, 30% or 42.5%, depending on the accounting period.

What this generally means in practice is that salary should usually be paid until the director's total income reaches at least £21,800 where the director is over state retirement age.

Furthermore, for accounting periods ending on or before 31st January 2009, it will generally be preferable to pay salary to directors over state retirement age at any level of income.

For women aged 60 to 64, it will generally be worth paying salary at any level of income (except in some cases where the married couples allowance is available and the accounting period ends after 31st October 2009).

In other cases, salary should usually be paid up to the amount of the director's personal allowance (plus the married couples allowance for accounting periods ending on or before 28th February 2009).

Salaries or bonus will often also be better in the case of directors paying higher rate Income Tax at 40%. (For all accounting periods in the case of directors over state retirement age and for accounting periods ending on or before 31st December 2008 for younger directors.)

All of the above is subject to the fact that the position will often be altered where the director has savings income or dividends from other sources giving rise to effective marginal rates of 30% or more (see Sections 10.10 and 10.11).

'Step by Step' planning, as explained in Chapter 4, will therefore be needed to achieve the optimum result in many cases.

Companies with Profits over £1,500,000

These companies should always pay salary or bonus when the director's marginal tax rate is 11% or less, 22.5% or 32.5%.

Salary or bonus may also be preferable when the director's marginal rate is 20%, 21%, 25% or 40%, depending on the accounting period.

In practice, this means that salary or bonus should generally be paid up to the level of the director's personal allowance plus any available married couples allowance (but only up to the personal allowance for directors under state retirement age where the accounting period ends after 31st March 2008).

For accounting periods ending on or before 31st August 2008, salary or bonus should also generally be paid to directors over state retirement age until their income reaches £21,800; or £40,835 in the case of women aged 60 to 64 unless the accounting period ends after 31st May 2008 and they are eligible for married couples allowance.

Salaries or bonus are also generally better for accounting periods ending on or before 31st August 2008 where the director is over state retirement age and is paying higher rate Income Tax at 40%.

As usual, the position may be altered where the director has savings income or dividends from other sources which give rise to effective marginal rates of 30% or more (see Sections 10.10 and 10.11).

'Step by Step' planning, as explained in Chapter 4, will therefore again be the best way to achieve the optimum result in many cases.

10.15 PENSIONS

Most of the 'older directors' discussed in this chapter will be receiving pension income.

For those below state retirement age, the impact of pension income on the director's effective marginal tax rates on salary or bonus payments can be quite detrimental, as we have already seen in Section 2.18.

Men Aged 64 (Section 10.8)

For men currently aged 64, who will be aged 65 at the end of the tax year, there is the risk that an effective marginal tax rate of 51% may arise on salary or bonus payments where they will also receive pension income of more than £795 in total during the tax year.

If at all possible, these directors should restrict bonus or salary payments before their 65th birthday to a maximum amount equal to £40,835 less the amount of their pension income. In fact, as discussed in Section 10.8, they should ideally avoid any payments over £5,435. (But see Section 10.4 regarding payments normally falling due before state retirement age.)

Younger Directors with Older Spouses (Section 10.9)

Younger directors under state retirement age who are entitled to married couples allowance and also receiving pension income may also suffer the higher effective marginal tax rates set out in Section 2.18.

In these cases, the rates set out in Section 2.18 simply need to be adapted as set out below.

Where the director's spouse was born before 6th April 1935 but is aged under 75 at the end of the tax year:

  i) Reduce the rate by 10% where <u>total</u> income lies between £6,035 and £12,570
  ii) Increase the rate by 5% where <u>total</u> income lies between £21,800 and £29,790

Where the director's spouse is aged 75 or more at the end of the tax year:

  i) Reduce the rate by 10% where <u>total</u> income lies between £6,035 and £12,660
  ii) Increase the rate by 5% where <u>total</u> income lies between £21,800 and £29,970

Directors over State Retirement Age (Sections 10.6 and 10.7)

These directors are not subject to primary National Insurance and that makes life a lot simpler.

For directors over state retirement age, our tax band 'pecking order' (see Section 2.18) can be simplified as follows:

  i)   Any income not under (ii) or (iii) below
  ii) Savings income (including interest)
  iii) Dividends

Pension income and salary or bonus payments therefore both fall into heading (i).

This makes life really simple. When considering all of the advice given in this chapter, the director's pension income can be regarded as being exactly the same as an existing salary from their company.

Hence, for example, a director aged at least 65 now, but under 75 at the end of the tax year, who has a pension of £8,000 for 2008/9, can pay themselves a tax-free bonus or salary of just £1,030 (£9,030 - £8,000).

Thereafter, all of the bands set out in Section 10.6 apply in exactly the same way to the director's total income under heading (i) above, including their pension.

When it comes to the extra complexities discussed in Sections 10.10 and 10.11, the pension is simply part of the director's 'other' income.

The pension must also be taken into account before following the guidelines given in Section 10.14.

Pensions and Dividends

The impact of pensions on dividends is even simpler.

As usual, the marginal rate bands given in Section 10.12 apply to the director's total income and this, of course, includes their pension.

Chapter 11

Directors with Children

11.1 THE IMPACT OF TAX CREDITS

Another group of people facing a different set of marginal tax rates are directors with minor children.

These directors may be entitled to claim tax credits. However, just like older directors' higher personal allowances, tax credits are progressively withdrawn once income exceeds a certain limit. Once again, this creates another different set of effective marginal tax rates for the director.

The difficulty with any attempt to integrate tax credits into the rest of our 'Salary or Dividend' planning strategy is the fact that the withdrawal of tax credits is based on total household income and not on the director's own personal income alone. For anyone in a 'co-habiting' relationship we therefore need to include their spouse or partner's income when considering the impact of tax credits on our planning.

The tax credits themselves also come in two main varieties:

- Working tax credits, and
- Child tax credits

Before we proceed any further, it is worth mentioning that the current level of the 'income disregard', £25,000, will mean that much of what follows will be irrelevant in many cases.

We will return to the importance of the 'income disregard' in Section 11.6.

11.2 WORKING TAX CREDITS

Conceivably, a taxpayer could be claiming over £35,000 a year in tax credits.

However, in the absence of any qualifying 'children', most people working over 30 hours per week would be limited to a maximum claim of £4,305 for 2008/9.

Well, even that sounds worth having, but the catch is that Working Tax Credits are withdrawn at the rate of 39p per £1 of extra income once household income begins to exceed £6,420.

But, in the absence of any qualifying 'children', you need to be working at least 30 hours per week to get these credits and the Government will naturally expect you to get paid at least as much as the National Minimum Wage.

The National Minimum Wage for workers aged 22 or over is currently £5.52 per hour.

Hence, in the Government's view, anyone over 22 who is working 30 hours per week throughout the 2008/9 tax year ought to be getting at least £8,611 in salary for the year. This would reduce their Working Tax Credit claim by £854 (£8,611 - £6,420 x 39%).

This leaves a maximum Working Tax Credit claim of £3,451 (£4,305 - £854) in the absence of any qualifying children in most cases. (We will, however, return to the issue of the application of the national minimum wage to directors in Section 12.7.)

Nevertheless, it remains important to bear in mind that an additional 39% may need to be added to the marginal tax rate applying to Working Tax Credit claimants when household income exceeds £6,420.

In most cases, where there are no qualifying 'children', this additional 39% tax rate will disappear by the time total household income reaches £17,458.

11.3 CHILD TAX CREDITS

Far more possibilities open up when the household includes at least one qualifying 'child'.

For tax credit purposes, a child qualifies if they are:

- Under 16 years of age, or
- Between 16 and 18 years old and in full-time education.

'Full-time education' means attending a school or college for at least 12 hours per week. The child must also be studying for qualifications which are at (or below) the following levels:

- National Vocational Qualification Level 3 (NVQ 3)
- 'A' levels
- Scottish Higher levels.

To claim, you have to be the person responsible for the child. HM Revenue & Customs usually consider this to be the case if you receive Child Benefit for that child.

Space does not permit a full examination of every possible combination of child tax credit claims. In the absence of any eligible childcare costs, however, the likely claim for most households would be £2,085 per child plus the 'family element' of £545. This will be in addition to the Working Tax Credits of £4,305 which we saw in the last section.

The 'family element' is subject to different rules and is not withdrawn until household income exceeds £50,000. We will come back to the 'family element' in Section 11.5.

Leaving the 'family element' to one side for the moment, we can now begin to get a picture of the band of household income likely to be affected by the additional 39% effective marginal rate, as follows:

No. of Children	Total Claim*	Fully Withdrawn At:
0	£4,305	£17,458
1	£6,390	£22,805
2	£8,475	£28,151
3	£10,560	£33,497
4	£12,645	£38,843
5	£14,730	£44,189

* - The claim figures here exclude the family element.

The figures in the 'Total Claim' column are obtained by simply adding £2,085 per child to the £4,305 of Working Tax Credits which we saw in Section 11.2.

The figures in the 'Fully Withdrawn At' column show the income levels at which tax credits are taken away completely. We know that tax credits are taken away at the rate of 39p per £1 of income over £6,420. Hence, for example, where household income is £28,151 and there are two children:

£28,151 - £6,420 = £21,731 x 39% = £8,475

This equals the initial amount of the tax credit claim, so the claim is therefore completely eliminated by the withdrawal.

11.4 CHILDCARE COSTS

In addition to the claims covered already, parents may also claim up to 80% of eligible childcare costs. To be eligible, the childcare arrangements must meet a number of qualifying conditions. Eligible costs are also subject to a maximum of £175 per week (£9,100 per year, 80% of which is £7,280) for one qualifying child or £300 per week (£15,600 per year, 80% of which is £12,480) where the claimant has two or more qualifying children.

Building the maximum possible eligible childcare costs into our hypothetical 'average' family's claim, gives us a new set of maximum claims and bands of household income subject to the additional 39% marginal tax rate, as follows:

No. of Children	Maximum Claim*	Fully Withdrawn At:
1	£13,670	£41,471
2	£20,955	£60,151
3	£23,040	£65,497
4	£25,125	£70,843
5	£27,210	£76,189

* - Again, this excludes the 'family element'.

The 'Maximum Claim' column is obtained simply by taking the 'Total Claim' column from the table in the previous section and adding the maximum eligible childcare costs.

The figures in the 'Fully Withdrawn At' column show the income levels at which tax credits are taken away completely. For example, where household income is £60,151 and there are two children:

£60,151 - £6,420 = £53,731 x 39% = £20,955

As before, this equals the initial amount of the tax credit claim, so the claim is again completely eliminated by the withdrawal.

Hence, for example, in the case of a family with two children, paying the maximum eligible childcare costs, we can conclude that an additional 39% must be added to the marginal tax rate of either parent when the total household income for 2008/9 already lies in the range £6,420 to £60,151.

Except That

All of this is subject to the 'income disregard' (see Section 11.6).

11.5 FAMILY ELEMENT

As explained in Section 11.3, households with at least one qualifying child are also entitled to the 'family element'.

For 2008/9, the 'family element' is normally £545, but it is increased to £1,090 when there is a qualifying child under the age of one in the household. The higher figure is sometimes called 'Baby Tax Credit'.

The family element is only withdrawn when household income exceeds £50,000. It is then withdrawn at the rate of £1 for every £15 of household income over this limit. This will generally create an additional marginal tax rate of 6.67% for household income in the following bands:

- Families with a child under one: £50,000 to £66,350
- Other families: £50,000 to £58,175

Where the main tax credit withdrawal rate of 39% extends beyond £50,000, however, the family element does not begin to be withdrawn until after the other tax credits have been exhausted.

Adapting the table in the previous section to take this into account we can see how the two withdrawal rates fit together:

No. of Children	Maximum Total Claim**	Limit of 39% Rate:	6.67% Rate Applies	
			From	To
1	£14,215	£41,471	£50,000	£58,175
2	£21,500	£60,151	£60,151	£68,326
3	£23,585	£65,497	£65,497	£73,672
4	£25,670	£70,843	£70,843	£79,018
5	£27,755	£76,189	£76,189	£84,364

** - Now including the 'family element' of £545.

The 6.67% rate band would be doubled in size if the family included a qualifying child under one.

11.6 THE INCOME DISREGARD

At this point, it is worth expanding on my opening comments in this chapter concerning the income disregard.

Tax credits are initially claimed on the basis of the household's, taxable income for the *previous* tax year.

The claim is then adjusted upwards if the actual income for the claim year turns out to be less than that of the previous year.

The claim is only adjusted downwards, however, to the extent that the household's income increases by more than the level of the income disregard.

For 2008/9, the income disregard is £25,000.

This means that your household income can increase by anything up to £25,000 without affecting your tax credit claim.

This provides tremendous opportunities for director/shareholders to plan payments of bonuses or dividends which will not affect their tax credit claims.

Example

Arthur and Harriet have five children under 16, including a pair of eighteen month old twins attending a daycare centre.

The couple have claimed child tax credits of £14,114 for 2008/9 (including the childcare and family elements) on the basis of their combined taxable income for 2007/8 of £40,000.

For 2008/9 they have, once again, each taken a salary of £20,000 from their company, Waterloo Limited.

In March 2009, they also each take a bonus of £12,500.

The bonuses increase their household income to £65,000 but the 'income disregard' means that this does not affect their tax credit claim, so the additional effective 39% tax rate does not apply in 2008/9.

Arthur and Harriet's initial tax credit claim for 2009/10 will, of course, be reduced, due to the higher level of their household income in 2008/9. However, if they stick to their regular salaries of £20,000 each for 2009/10 and do not take any extra bonus or dividend that year, their claim will eventually be adjusted back to the higher level of £14,114 again (at 2008/9 rates).

Then, in 2010/11, they can pay themselves a tax credit friendly bonus again!

By paying themselves a bonus bi-annually, Arthur and Harriet can continue to claim tax credits on the basis of their modest regular salaries alone.

Unfortunately, the beneficial use of the income disregard suggested by the above example is not entirely beyond the range of a challenge by HM Revenue & Customs.

Under the tax credit regulations, any claimant who deliberately deprives themselves of income for the purposes of increasing a tax credit claim is treated as if they had received that income for tax credit purposes.

Clearly, this means that a director/shareholder who foregoes their normal regular salary without any commercial justification for doing so would be unable to exclude that salary when making a tax credit claim.

In the case of bonuses or dividends, however, the director/shareholder has surely not deprived themselves of any income, since these payments are not actually part of their regular income?

Hence, my view is that where a reasonable regular salary is already being taken from the company, director/shareholders should be able to use bi-annual bonus payments of up to £25,000 per household to avoid any further withdrawal of tax credits.

Bi-annual dividends could also be used for the same purpose but these will need to be kept to £22,500 due to the effect of the dividend tax credit of one ninth discussed in Section 2.8. (See Section 11.8 for a further explanation of the effect of dividends on tax credit claims.)

Furthermore, where a director has to reduce or even forego their regular salary for sound commercial reasons (e.g. to keep the company solvent), the resultant increase in their tax credit claim should also be safe from any attack.

Does all this mean that the effective additional marginal tax rates of 39% and 6.67% are completely irrelevant?

Absolutely not!

Where total household income is already at least £25,000 more than in the previous year, or is any less than in the previous year, the extra marginal rates will come into force.

For example, any further bonus paid to Arthur or Harriet in 2008/9 after the first £12,500 each would have an effective 39% cost for tax credit purposes.

Any bonus paid to them in 2009/10 would also have an effective 39% additional cost in lost tax credits except for amounts falling between £25,000 and £50,000, when the 'income disregard' would come into play again.

11.7 TAX CREDITS AND SALARY OR BONUS

Where the additional marginal rates of 39% or 6.67% do apply, the effective marginal tax rate for a director receiving salary or bonus will be increased and could be as much as 95% in a few rare instances!

More commonly, the total effective rates applying will usually be as follows:

Marginal rates on director's own salary or bonus where household income falls within 39% Tax Credit Withdrawal Band:

Income up to £5,435:	39%
Income from £5,435 to £6,035:	50%
Income from £6,035 to £40,040:	70%
Income from £40,040 to £40,835:	60%
Income over £40,835:	80%

Yes, it really is that bad!

Marginal rates on director's own salary or bonus where household income falls within 6.67% Tax Credit Withdrawal Band:

Income up to £5,435:	6.67%
Income from £5,435 to £6,035:	17.67%
Income from £6,035 to £40,040:	37.67%
Income from £40,040 to £40,835:	27.67%
Income over £40,835:	47.67%

If the director is also an 'older director', as defined in Chapter 10, the 39% or 6.67% rate will also need to be added to the effective marginal rates applying there.

11.8 TAX CREDITS AND DIVIDENDS

I've got good news and bad news.

The good news is that dividends are classed as 'investment' income and the first £300 of investment income received by the household is ignored for tax credit purposes.

Any director/shareholders suffering the additional tax rates described above should therefore certainly give serious thought to ensuring that their household does receive at least £300 in investment income for a start.

Well, actually, as far as dividends are concerned, it's only £270, which, I'm afraid, brings me to the bad news.

The bad news is that, for tax credit purposes, the amount of dividend income received includes the one ninth dividend tax credit. In other words, receiving a net dividend of £100 counts as taxable income of £111.11 for tax credit purposes and could therefore lose you up to £43.33 in tax credits (if you already have household investment income over £300).

So, assuming the household already has its £300 of investment income, the total effective rates applying to dividends received by a shareholder whose household is eligible for tax credits will be as follows:

Marginal rates on director's own dividend income where household income falls within 39% Tax Credit Withdrawal Band:

Income up to £40,835:   43.3%
Income over £40,835:   68.3%

Marginal rates on director's own dividend income where household income falls within 6.67% Tax Credit Withdrawal Band:

Income up to £40,835:   7.4%
Income over £40,835:   32.4%

These rates apply to the net dividend received, excluding the one ninth dividend tax credit. Don't forget, however, that, in applying the £40,835 limit, dividends must be 'grossed up' by a factor of 10/9 (see Section 2.8).

If the director is also an 'older director', as defined in Chapter 10, the rate of 43.3% or 7.4%, as per the above tables, will also need to be added to the effective marginal rates applying there.

11.9 THE TAXCAFE COMPUTER MODEL FOR DIRECTORS WITH CHILDREN

We can now look at the impact of the higher effective marginal tax rates described above on our main computer model. We will look at the results in two parts, based on the two tax credit withdrawal rates already discussed.

As in Section 3.2, the position for salary or bonus payments depends on the company accounting period which the payment is taken out of. Subject to meeting the criteria set out in Section 6.1, a payment to a director made, or deemed to be made, during the 2008/9 tax year may be taken out of an accounting period ending any time between July 2007 and March 2010.

As usual, therefore, the amounts given in the 'From' column in the tables in this section represent the costs for a bonus paid out of an accounting period ending on 31st July 2007 and the amounts given in the 'To' column represent the costs for a bonus paid out of an accounting period ending on 31st March 2010. The costs for all intermediate accounting periods will lie somewhere between the 'From' figure and the 'To' figure.

Effective Cost of Salary Or Dividends Where 39% Withdrawal Rate Applies

The total net tax suffered on an additional net £100 of bonus or dividend at different levels of company profit and director's income where household income lies within the 39% tax credit withdrawal band is as follows:

Company Profits up to £300,000

Director's Income	Total Tax on £100 (net) of:		
	Bonus		Dividend
	From	To	
Up to £5,435	£32.24	£27.87	£76.47
£5,435 to £6,035	£81.98	£75.97	£76.47
£6,035 to £40,040	£203.30	£193.28	£76.47
£40,040 to £40,835	£127.48	£119.96	£76.47
Over £40,835	£354.95	£339.92	£215.79

Company Profits between £300,000 and £1,500,000

Director's Income	Total Tax on £100 (net) of:		
	Bonus		Dividend
	From	To	
Up to £5,435	£10.38	£15.57	£76.47
£5,435 to £6,035	£51.90	£59.05	£76.47
£6,035 to £40,040	£153.17	£165.08	£76.47
£40,040 to £40,835	£89.88	£98.81	£76.47
Over £40,835	£279.76	£297.62	£215.79

Company Profits over £1,500,000

Director's Income	Total Tax on £100 (net) of:		
	Bonus		Dividend
	From	To	
Up to £5,435	£14.75	£18.03	£76.47
£5,435 to £6,035	£57.92	£62.43	£76.47
£6,035 to £40,040	£163.20	£170.72	£76.47
£40,040 to £40,835	£97.40	£103.04	£76.47
Over £40,835	£294.80	£306.08	£215.79

Effective Cost of Salary Or Dividends Where 6.67% Withdrawal Rate Applies

The total net tax suffered on an additional net £100 of bonus or dividend at different levels of company profit and director's income where household income lies within the 6.67% tax credit withdrawal band is as follows:

Company Profits up to £300,000

Director's Income	Total Tax on £100 (net) of:		Dividend
	Bonus		
	From	**To**	
	-	-	
Up to £5,435	£13.57	£16.43	£8.00
£5,435 to £6,035	£10.52	£6.86	£8.00
£6,035 to £40,040	£45.97	£41.15	£8.00
£40,040 to £40,835	£25.79	£21.64	£8.00
Over £40,835	£73.87	£68.12	£47.95

Company Profits between £300,000 and £1,500,000

Director's Income	Total Tax on £100 (net) of:		Dividend
	Bonus		
	From	**To**	
	-	-	
Up to £5,435	£27.86	£24.46	£8.00
£5,435 to £6,035	-£7.75	-£3.41	£8.00
£6,035 to £40,040	£21.85	£27.58	£8.00
£40,040 to £40,835	£5.00	£9.94	£8.00
Over £40,835	£45.13	£51.96	£47.95

Company Profits over £1,500,000

Director's Income	Total Tax on £100 (net) of:		Dividend
	Bonus		
	From	**To**	
	-	-	
Up to £5,435	£25.00	£22.86	£8.00
£5,435 to £6,035	-£4.10	-£1.36	£8.00
£6,035 to £40,040	£26.67	£30.29	£8.00
£40,040 to £40,835	£9.16	£12.28	£8.00
Over £40,835	£50.88	£55.19	£47.95

'Total Tax' means total Income Tax, National Insurance and Tax Credit Withdrawal suffered by both the company and the director, less the Corporation Tax relief obtained.

In each case, the £100 referred to in the above tables is the net sum in the director/shareholder's hands after all applicable taxes and tax credit withdrawals.

11.10 MODEL CONCLUSIONS FOR DIRECTORS WITH CHILDREN

39% Withdrawal Rate

Where the 39% withdrawal rate applies, one is tempted to suggest that it would be best not to take anything at all out of the company!

This may be difficult in practice, but the benefits of keeping increases under the level of the income disregard should certainly be considered.

Where household investment income is not yet in excess of £300, the first step must be to take sufficient dividends to bring it to that level (remembering to include the one ninth tax credit).

Where further income must be taken from the company, the next £5,435 should be taken as salary. Where company profits exceed £306,112 or the accounting period ends after December 2009, the salary should be increased to £6,035. Any further sums required should be taken as dividends.

6.67% Withdrawal Rate

When the 6.67% withdrawal rate is in operation, payment of a salary of £5,435 always remains beneficial as it produces a net tax saving overall. For companies with profits in excess of £306,112, the salary should be increased to £6,035.

Where further sums are required, the position depends, as usual, on the level of the company's taxable profits and, in some cases, on the company accounting period from which the payment is to be taken.

Company Profits not exceeding £306,112

For accounting periods ending on or before 31st May 2009, any further payments should be made by way of dividend.

For later accounting periods payments should be made as follows:

i)   First, where household investment income is not yet in excess of £300, take sufficient dividends to bring it to that level (remembering to include the one ninth tax credit).
ii)   Next, increase the director's salary to £6,035.
iii) Any further sums required should be paid by way of dividend.

Company Profits between £306,112 and £1,506,112

For accounting periods ending after 31st October 2008, the position is simply that any further sums required in excess of the amount yielded by a salary of £6,035 (see below) should be taken by way of dividend.

In other cases, where household investment income is not yet in excess of £300, the first step should usually be to pay sufficient dividends to bring it to that level (remembering to include the one ninth tax credit).

Thereafter, the position depends on the existing level of the director's income and sometimes also on the total amount of net income which they wish to withdraw.

For accounting periods ending on or before 31st July 2008, bonus or salary payments will be preferable whenever the director's income is over £40,040.

For accounting periods ending between August and October 2008, salary or bonus payments will only be preferable where the director's income is between £40,040 and £40,835.

Further detailed analysis along similar lines to Section 4.11 will therefore often be required in order to determine the optimum payment strategy for accounting periods ending on or before 31st October 2008.

If we are looking at 'bottom-up' planning, however, the table given in Section 5.6 will continue to apply (since by that point any tax credit claim will be exhausted anyway).

Company Profits over £1,506,112

For companies with profits in excess of £1,506,112, any further payments to the director after their salary of £6,035 should be made by way of dividend.

All of the above is, as usual, subject to the point that where the payment is large enough to have the potential to change the company's marginal Corporation Tax rate, further analysis will be required along the lines set out in Chapter 4. The comments set out in Section 9.6 should also be considered where the desired payment might potentially create a loss in the company.

Note 1: Net Income from Salaries of £6,035

As explained in Section 5.2, a salary of £6,035 paid to a director under state retirement age will yield a net sum of £5,969 after taking account of National Insurance.

The tax credit withdrawal rates of 39% or 6.67% will reduce this further to £3,615 or £5,567 respectively.

Note 2: Company Profits between £305,435 and £306,112

In this section, whenever an increase in salary to £6,035 is recommended for companies with profits in excess of £306,112 then, for companies with profits between £305,435 and £306,112, a salary equal to the amount which (including employer's National Insurance) reduces the company's profit to £300,000 should be paid.

Chapter 12

Making Payments to Directors/Shareholders in Practice

12.1 WELCOME TO THE REAL WORLD

We have now spent eleven chapters looking at when a dividend is preferable, when extra salary or a bonus is preferable, when interest or loan repayments might be a better idea, when payments make sense even if you don't need them and when it's really best to try not to take any money out of your company if you can possibly avoid it.

Everything we have said and done so far has been based purely on taxation considerations. In practice, of course, there are a great many other things to be taken into account.

There are also formalities to be observed in order to make sure that your payments are treated in the desired manner.

At this stage, therefore, it will probably be useful if we take a look at some of the practical aspects of paying dividends, interest, salaries or bonuses, as well as some of the additional taxation issues arising in practice which we have not yet covered.

We will also be able to dispel a few myths too.

Please do not, however, imagine for a moment that the matters covered in this chapter represent an exhaustive list. That would take a whole book of its own!

12.2 COMMERCIAL CONSIDERATIONS

Making any payments from a company will naturally have commercial implications for the company and its business. The director/shareholder ignores these at their peril!

The first, and generally most important, consideration will be cashflow. As a company owner, it would be irresponsible to take more money out of the company than it can realistically afford.

Furthermore, there may be severe repercussions when any payments are made when the company is insolvent, or which themselves actually render the company insolvent. Directors knowingly making payments under these circumstances can become personally liable for the company's outstanding debts and may also be guilty of fraud.

As we saw in Chapter 7, however, salaries, bonuses, dividends or interest may sometimes be deemed 'paid' even though the net funds are actually left in the company. Nevertheless, even then, allowance still needs to be made for the impact on the company's cashflow of any PAYE, National Insurance or other tax liabilities arising.

In addition to cashflow considerations, the inclusion of high levels of director's salary or large bonuses in the company's accounts will depress its reported profits. This could lead to difficulties in raising finance, poor credit ratings, etc, and may also reduce the company's value on a sale.

The pattern, and magnitude, of dividend payments made by the company will also affect how that company is perceived by the outside world.

A company which continually pays out most of its profits as dividends will be seen as a mere 'lifestyle' company existing only to support its owner.

On the other hand, a company which retains a substantial element of its annual profits may be seen as a more serious contender by potential trading partners.

As we saw in Chapter 8, dividends generally have to be paid to all shareholders of the same class, so the existence of any minority shareholders may cause difficulties.

Dividend waivers may sometimes be used as a mechanism to get around the problem of minority shareholders. Personally, however, I am not generally in favour of dividend waivers as a tax planning tool and see them as something which should only be used on a very occasional basis where exceptional circumstances dictate their use.

A better way to handle the differing requirements of two or more shareholders on a long-term basis is to issue different classes of shares and thus create a so-called 'ABC Company'.

Both dividend waivers and 'ABC Companies' are complex issues and space does not permit me to explore them here. These mechanisms may also be at risk of attack under the proposed 'income shifting' legislation due to come into force on 6th April 2009 (see Section 16.2).

12.3 IMPACT OF DIVIDENDS ON SHARE VALUE

The payment of dividends may have an impact on the theoretical value of the company's shares.

A regular pattern of dividend payments will often enhance the value of the company's shares, not so much in the event of a genuine 'arm's length' sale, but more in the case of any hypothetical valuation, such as for probate purposes or on the purchase of a minority shareholding.

Shares in most private trading companies are currently fully exempt from Inheritance Tax but, in the case of an investment company, the regular payment of dividends could result in an increased value for Inheritance Tax purposes.

This, in turn, could result in an increased Inheritance Tax liability on the death of the director/shareholder.

Failing to maintain a previous pattern of dividends can also have an impact on the value of the company's shares.

12.4 JUSTIFYING SALARIES OR BONUSES

Throughout the first eleven chapters of this guide, we assumed that the payment of any salary or bonus would attract Corporation Tax relief.

This, however, is not an automatic right and Corporation Tax relief will only be available when salaries or bonuses have been paid for the benefit of the company's trade or business.

For most employees, of course, there is no doubt over this, since there is no other reason why the company's owner would have paid them.

In the case of the director/shareholder themselves, however, the payment of a salary or bonus needs to be justified as a business expense. The same is true of any payments to the spouse or partner of a shareholder or to any of the shareholder's other close relatives.

Some or all of the following factors may be considered in establishing what level of salary or bonus payments to the director/shareholder, or to members of their family, might reasonably constitute a justifiable business expense:

- The number of hours per week which the recipient typically works in the company's business.
- The rate of pay offered to other employees in the company, particularly those in management roles.
- The level of responsibility undertaken by the recipient.
- The amount of experience which the recipient has in the company's industry and any relevant qualifications which they hold.
- The usual rate of pay for a person performing a similar role in other comparable companies.
- The salary level which would be required to recruit a manager to take over the duties currently performed by the director/shareholder.
- The company's overall financial performance and ability to pay the salary or bonus in question.

In general, there should not usually be any difficulty in obtaining Corporation Tax relief for salary or bonus payments where the above criteria support the rate of pay being used.

Extra care is, however, warranted when we are looking at large, 'one-off', bonus payments.

Where a bonus is paid as part of a bonus scheme applying to all of the company's employees, or even just all of the management, then the payment to the director/shareholder should be accepted as a business expense.

However, in the case of a large, isolated, 'one-off' payment to director/shareholders only, it will be sensible to document the commercial reasoning behind the additional payment in order to demonstrate that the recipient has justified this additional reward.

The best way to do this would be to record the rationale behind the bonus in the minutes of a directors' board meeting. This also provides an opportunity to reinforce the timing of the Corporation Tax relief for the payment by specifying the accounting period to which the bonus relates. (But see Section 6.1 above regarding the further criteria which may need to be met.)

An example of such a board minute might be as follows:

The directors noted the company's excellent trading results for the year ended 31st December 2008 with satisfaction. In view of these excellent results and pursuant to the company's memorandum of 24th December 2008, the board resolved to pay a bonus of £100,000 to Mr Eric Bloodaxe out of the profits for the year ended 31st December 2008.

It would also be wise for such a bonus to be ratified by the company's members (i.e. shareholders) in general meeting. The minutes of the meeting would thus include the following:

The members approved the payment of a bonus of £100,000 to Mr Eric Bloodaxe on 31st March 2009 out of the profits for the year ended 31st December 2008.

Samples of meeting minutes which might perhaps be suitable for these purposes are given in Appendix B. Readers are reminded that these are only illustrative samples and, in practice, this documentation should be drawn up by someone who is fully aware of the company's precise circumstances.

Unlike dividends (as we shall see in the next section), salaries and bonuses may be paid regardless of whether the company has any distributable profits. The issues explored previously in Section 12.2 regarding insolvent companies, as well as the points above regarding justification of the payment as a business expense will need to be borne in mind however.

Wealth Warning: Quasi-Dividends

Where salary or bonus payments are made to several directors in proportion to the recipients' shareholdings there is a risk that HM Revenue & Customs might argue that these should, instead, be regarded as dividends.

They will only do this if it gets them more tax, of course!

12.5 PAYING A DIVIDEND

Under company law, a dividend may only be paid where the company has sufficient distributable profits available.

HM Revenue & Customs may look to see if the company was able to prove that it had adequate distributable profits at the time of every dividend payment.

Unless the company has substantial distributable reserves brought forward from the previous accounting period, it will therefore be necessary to prepare regular management accounts in support of the payment of dividends.

If dividends are paid without there being adequate evidence available to show that the company had sufficient distributable profits (**after tax**) at that time, they are illegal under company law. 'Illegal' dividends may then be treated as salary, resulting in Income Tax and National Insurance liabilities.

Meeting these exacting requirements in practice may be very difficult if trying to pay out the maximum possible amount of dividend from current profits. In reality, it is usually better to be slightly less ambitious and take a lower level of dividends.

Documentation, recording the payment of a dividend, is also important in order to clarify the correct nature of the payment that has been made.

This documentation will include the minutes of a director's board meeting recommending the dividend payment and a general meeting of the company's members (i.e. shareholders) approving it.

A dividend voucher should also be issued to each recipient of the dividend.

Samples of suitable directors' board minutes and minutes of a general meeting of the members are included in Appendix B. A sample dividend voucher is also included. Readers are again reminded that these are only illustrative samples. In practice, this documentation should be drawn up by someone who is fully aware of the company's precise circumstances.

As with bonuses, a dividend may only be included as a liability in the company's accounts when an obligation to pay the dividend already existed at the relevant accounting date.

The dividend declared by our sample documentation in Appendix B would therefore probably not be included in the company's accounts to 31st December 2008.

As far as any tax planning is concerned, however, this point will usually be fairly academic as it is the date that the dividend is deemed to be <u>received</u> for Income Tax purposes which will usually concern us. In the case of our Appendix B sample documentation this would be 1st April 2009, thus ensuring that it is included in the director's income for 2008/9.

12.6 FREQUENCY AND AMOUNT OF PAYMENTS

There are no special requirements governing the frequency or amount of dividend, salary or bonus payments.

Custom dictates that salary is usually paid monthly, but it's just that: custom.

Bonuses can be paid whenever you like. They're really just extra amounts of salary paid in lump sums.

However, when wishing to relate a bonus back to the previous accounting period for Corporation Tax purposes, it will generally be advisable to pay this bonus in one single payment.

Contrary to popular belief, dividends may be paid in any amounts and with any frequency that the director/shareholders desire, subject to the important points made in the previous section of course.

12.7 THE NATIONAL MINIMUM WAGE

In Section 12.4, we looked at the need to justify salary or bonus payments. Under the National Minimum Wage, however, some directors may, in fact, be <u>required</u> to pay themselves a salary.

Does the National Minimum Wage Apply to a Director?

A director is not subject to the National Minimum Wage for the performance of their duties **as a director**. Where the director does not also have a contract of employment with the company, it is therefore possible to exempt them from the national minimum wage.

This will enable the director/shareholder to continue paying themselves the theoretical optimum level of salary, often just £5,435 or £6,035, even when this is less than the rate required by the national minimum wage.

Where, however, the director does have a contract of employment, they will only be exempt from the national minimum wage for the hours spent on their duties as a director (or as company secretary if applicable). If they also fulfil some other role in the company, then the national minimum wage will apply to the time spent on those other duties.

Many director/shareholders are, of course, also actively involved in the management of their company and hence, where they have a contract of employment, a large proportion of their duties will be subject to the national minimum wage.

What if the National Minimum Wage Does Apply?

On 1st October 2007, the national minimum wage for workers aged 22 or over was increased to £5.52 per hour.

In the previous chapters of this guide, we often concluded that a salary of just £5,435 or £6,035 represented the ideal pay structure for a director. Applying the National Minimum Wage, these salary levels would equate to around 19 or 21 hours per week of non-exempt management time respectively.

In some cases, where the director only works part-time, we may be able to stick with the ideal salary level despite the National Minimum Wage.

In many other cases, however, where the National Minimum Wage applies, it will mean that a higher salary level is required.

As a rough guideline, we might argue that a full-time working director works 35 hours per week and that, of these, say five are spent on his or her duties as a director.

This leaves 30 hours per week to which the National Minimum Wage will apply where the director has a contract of employment.

The total salary due under the National Minimum Wage of £5.52 per hour would thus be:

30 x 52 x £5.52 =   £8,611

From a tax perspective this would not be too bad, as it only exceeds our 'ideal' salary level by £3,176 or £2,576 (for an 'ideal' salary level of £5,435 or £6,035 respectively).

Each case will, of course, be different and many directors will be able to argue that their actual non-exempt working hours are not over the 19 or 21 hours per week which equates to an 'ideal' salary of £5,435 or £6,035 respectively.

Having read this section, you may be tempted into thinking that the best strategy is simply to avoid having a contract of employment with the company. However, I would not always advocate this approach in practice, as there are many other important factors to be considered.

Other Owner/Employees

As discussed in Section 2.17, for a variety of reasons, some company owners, or part owners, are employees, but not directors, of their company.

These non-director owner/employees will generally be fully subject to the national minimum wage on all of their working hours. Nevertheless, if they only work part-time, then their salary may often still be kept to the 'ideal' level of £5,435 or £6,035, as discussed above.

For a full-time 35 hour working week, however, the national minimum wage would necessitate a minimum salary of:

35 x 52 x £5.52 = £10,046

(Many company owners will, of course, scoff at the idea of 35 hours being 'full-time'.)

Note, however, that an owner/employee who is appointed as company secretary will be exempt from the national minimum wage in respect of the time spent performing their company secretarial duties.

12.8 STATE PENSION ENTITLEMENT

In order to maintain full entitlement to the state retirement pension, directors should always pay themselves a salary of at least the amount of the 'lower earnings limit' for National Insurance purposes.

For 2008/9, the lower earnings limit is £90 per week, which equates to an annual salary of £4,680.

Generally, where other factors are equally balanced between a dividend or salary, this will mean that salary should therefore take precedence.

12.9 UNCLASSIFIED WITHDRAWALS

The extraction of additional funds from the company without any declaration of bonus or dividend may result in an adverse balance on the director's loan account. Whilst this does often occur, care needs to be taken, as such balances:

- May be illegal under company law unless approved by the company's members (shareholders) in advance,

- Will give rise to Income Tax and National Insurance charges on a deemed benefit in kind equal to the notional interest (at an official HM Revenue and Customs rate) on the outstanding balance, and

- May also give rise to a temporary tax charge equal to 25% of the adverse balance (repayable when the adverse balance is repaid to the company by the director).

12.10 INTEREST CHARGES

In Chapter 7, we looked at the potential benefits of charging interest on a director's loan account in order to extract funds more tax efficiently than by using a bonus or a dividend in many cases.

This strategy is, of course, only beneficial if the company obtains Corporation Tax relief for the interest charges. In Chapter 7, we covered the fact that this means that the interest must be charged at no more than a reasonable commercial rate and must also be paid, or deemed to be paid, to the director within twelve months of the end of the accounting period in which it is charged.

There is one further potential snag.

To obtain Corporation Tax relief, the interest charged must actually be due to the director. In other words, the company must have an obligation to pay the interest. This is rather similar to the requirement for a bonus paid after the end of the accounting period which we discussed in Section 6.1.

In practice, therefore, the company and the director should draw up an agreement governing the terms of the director's loan account. The agreement should state that the director may charge interest for any accounting period during which the loan is outstanding at any rate up to a certain percentage.

The maximum percentage applying to the interest charges could be a fixed rate or could be set using a suitable formula (e.g. a certain percentage above LIBOR), as long as it is no more than a reasonable commercial rate.

A 'reasonable commercial rate' can be fairly high in these circumstances, as we are looking at an unsecured loan to a private company with no fixed repayment terms.

Chapter 13

Pension Contributions

13.1 THE NEW PENSIONS REGIME

On 'A Day', 6th April 2006, the entire UK pensions regime underwent a radical transformation. The two main tenets of the new system which came into force in April 2006 are the annual allowance and the lifetime allowance.

The annual allowance represents the maximum amount which may be added to an individual's total pension funds during the tax year ended on 5th April. For 2008/9, the annual allowance has been set at £235,000.

The lifetime allowance represents the maximum permitted value for all of an individual's qualifying pension funds. This allowance has been set at £1,650,000 for 2008/9.

It is important to remember that both the annual allowance and the lifetime allowance must be applied to each individual's *total* qualifying pension funds. This will include any defined benefit or 'final salary' schemes.

Penalties apply if either the annual allowance or the lifetime allowance are exceeded.

13.2 COMPANY CONTRIBUTIONS

So, can every director/shareholder get their company to contribute £235,000 to their pension fund in 2008/9 and get up to £75,846 in Corporation Tax relief?

Sadly, No!

HM Revenue & Customs have issued instructions to tax offices to be on the look-out for Corporation Tax relief claims for 'excessive' pension contributions.

They will judge what's excessive using similar criteria to those which we looked at in Section 12.4 for justifying salary or bonus payments.

They will look at the director/shareholder's total remuneration package, including salary, bonuses, pension contributions and any other benefits in kind, to see if the total value of this package can be justified commercially.

The good news, however, is that if you follow the strategy frequently recommended by our model and only pay yourself a minimal salary (plus a larger sum as dividends), you will often still have plenty of commercial justification to pay yourself further remuneration in the form of company pension contributions.

Where Corporation Tax relief is available, it will, of course, be given at the company's marginal Corporation Tax rate of up to 32.275% (see Section 2.3), making pension contributions a very attractive alternative to bonus or dividend payments.

This is a complex subject, however, and it is essential to get professional advice before making any company pension contributions.

13.3 PERSONAL PENSION CONTRIBUTIONS

Personal pension contributions continue to attract Income Tax relief at the investor's highest marginal rate of Income Tax, often 40%.

Here, there is no danger of contributions being regarded as 'excessive', as long as they do not exceed the annual allowance or cause the taxpayer's total fund value to exceed the lifetime allowance.

There is one fly in the ointment though.

From 6th April 2006, tax relief is only available on the greater of:

- £3,600, or
- The taxpayer's 'earnings' for the year.

And dividends do not count as 'earnings' for this purpose.

This presents us with a dilemma.

If the director only takes a small salary of, say, £5,435, he or she will only be able to get tax relief on that same level of pension contributions.

But if they take more earnings, i.e. salary or bonus, they will be able to get tax relief on a larger level of pension contributions.

So, what if they take salary purely to fund pension contributions?

Their tax relief will wipe out the Income Tax bill, so they'll just be left with National Insurance to worry about.

Meantime, the company will be getting Corporation Tax relief on the full amount of salary paid (plus the employer's National Insurance).

This creates an entirely new set of tax costs on the payment of salary or bonus to fund personal pension contributions.

Before we proceed, I must quickly point out that personal pension contributions are always made net of basic rate tax at 20%. Hence, to enable the director to make a gross pension contribution of £100, we only need to get a net sum of £80 into their hands.

This net pension contribution of £80 has been used as the basis for calculating the table below.

The Taxcafe Computer Model for Pension Contributions

Set out below is the total net tax suffered on an additional gross £100 personal pension contribution by the director funded by the payment of additional salary or bonus.

As usual, the position depends on the company's accounting period out of which the payment is made. We have therefore covered the range of answers arising for payments made out of accounting periods ending between July 2007 and March 2010.

The criteria set out in Section 6.1 continue to govern the question of which accounting period the company will obtain Corporation

236

Tax relief in and we also still need to be mindful of the need to justify the bonus payment as discussed in Section 12.4.

The 'From' column in the tables below gives the cost of funding the pension contribution with a bonus payment made out of an accounting period ending on 31st July 2007 and the 'To' column provides the same cost when the bonus is paid out of an accounting period ending on 31st March 2010. The cost arising for any intermediate accounting period will lie somewhere between the 'From' figure and the 'To' figure.

Company Profits up to £300,000

Director's Income	Total Tax on £100 Bonus	
	From	To
Up to £5,435	-£35.47	-£37.60
£5,435 to £6,035	-£18.21	-£20.91
£6,035 to £40,040	£5.50	£2.01
£40,040 to £40,835	-£7.86	-£10.90
Over £40,835	£3.38	-£0.70

Company Profits between £300,000 and £1,500,000

Director's Income	Total Tax on £100 Bonus	
	From	To
Up to £5,435	-£46.13	-£43.60
£5,435 to £6,035	-£31.73	-£28.52
£6,035 to £40,040	-£11.94	-£7.80
£40,040 to £40,835	-£23.09	-£19.47
Over £40,835	-£17.01	-£12.17

Company Profits over £1,500,000

Director's Income	Total Tax on £100 Bonus	
	From	To
Up to £5,435	-£44.00	-£42.40
£5,435 to £6,035	-£29.02	-£27.00
£6,035 to £40,040	-£8.45	-£5.84
£40,040 to £40,835	-£20.04	-£17.76
Over £40,835	-£12.94	-£9.88

'Total Tax' means total Income Tax and National Insurance suffered by both the company and the director, less Corporation Tax relief obtained on the bonus and Income Tax relief obtained on the pension contribution.

In each case, the £100 referred to above is the gross pension contribution made to the director/shareholder's pension fund, including the £20 tax relief given at source.

These results do look pretty impressive, but remember that all of the savings shown (and the few incidences of a net cost) include the £20 of tax relief given at source.

Hence, for example, the first figure in the first table is telling us that there is an overall net cost of £64.53 (£100 - £35.47) to get a net sum of £80 into the director's hands and thereby fund a gross pension contribution of £100.

Chapter 14

Non-Cash Payments

14.1 PAYMENT IN KIND

There is nothing, in principle, to stop a director/shareholder being paid by their company in a form other than cash.

A few years ago, such payments were often made in order to avoid National Insurance. Directors were paid variously in gold bullion, diamonds and platinum sponge.

Sadly, these bizarre ruses no longer work and I haven't seen anyone paid a bonus in platinum sponge for ages.

Leaving all that aside, both bonuses and dividends can still be paid in a non-cash form and these 'payments' are known, respectively, as a 'dividend-in-specie' or a 'bonus-in-specie'.

There is nothing particularly clever about a dividend in specie as the taxpayer is generally still taxed on the value of such a dividend in the same way as if it was the same sum in cash.

14.2 BONUS IN SPECIE

A bonus in specie, however, remains a useful tax planning tool since it remains possible to avoid employee's National Insurance.

However, to be exempt from employee's National Insurance, the asset which is the subject of the 'bonus-in-specie' must not be readily marketable or convertible into cash. This does away with all the platinum sponges!

Furthermore, a bonus-in-specie continues to be subject to employer's National Insurance.

So what does that leave?

14.3 THE CAR BONUS

Since the demise of the platinum sponge-type schemes, the best use of the bonus-in-specie route must now be the 'car bonus'.

We all know that company cars are now very highly taxed. We also know that a director who buys a car privately will usually need to take funds out of the company to fund the purchase, thus creating effective tax costs, as we have seen throughout this guide.

The answer to this dilemma comes in the shape of the car bonus. I will show you how it works with an example.

Example

Florence takes a modest salary of £20,000 per annum from her company, Balaclava Limited, which makes annual profits of £400,000.

In July 2008, Balaclava Limited buys a new company car for Florence at a cost of £36,000.

Just before the company's accounting year end on 30th September 2008, however, the car is transferred to Florence as a bonus in specie, when its market value is £24,000. (We all know how quickly cars lose their value once they've been used!)

To get a net sum of £36,000 into Florence's hands in order to enable her to buy the car would have cost as follows:

Tax-free dividend (using Table E):
£40,835 - £20,000 = £20,835 x £100/£111.11 = £18,751.50

Further net sum required:
£36,000 - £18,751.50 = £17,248.50

Further dividend required:
£17,248.50 x 100/75 = £22,998

Tax thereon:
£22,998 x 25% = **£5,750**

I won't repeat the calculation here, but to get this sum to Florence as a bonus would have cost £8,556. Refer to Section 4.11 for an explanation of the principles involved.

Instead of creating a tax cost of £5,750, however, Florence will pay tax on a bonus in specie of £24,000 and a benefit in kind of £2,100 (35% of £36,000 for just two months), total £26,100.

Her Income Tax bill is thus:

£40,835 - £20,000 =	£20,835 x 20% =	£4,167
£26,100 - £20,835 =	£5,265 x 40% =	£2,106
Total due:		£6,273

No employee's National Insurance is due and the Income Tax arising on Florence's 'benefits' will be collected though Self-Assessment rather than PAYE and hence will not be due until 31st January 2010.

Nevertheless, in the interests of fairness, we should take account of the cost involved in getting an extra net sum of £6,273 to Florence in order to enable her to pay this tax bill (but see the 'Tax Tip' below).

Florence is now a higher rate taxpayer, so to get a net sum of £6,273, requires a dividend of:

£6,273 x 100/75 = £8,364

The tax arising on this dividend will be:

£8,364 x 25% = £2,091

(If you are wondering whether it might have been better to pay Florence a further bonus instead of a dividend, refer to Section 2.18. Because the bonus in specie is exempt from employee's National Insurance, it is effectively like pension or rental income. Paying a cash bonus or further salary to Florence at this point would therefore have given her a most undesirable marginal tax rate of 51%!)

The company will have Class 1A National Insurance of £3,341 to pay on Florence's 'benefits' (£26,100 x 12.8%). This is also not due until July 2009.

However (here's the clever part), the company will get Corporation Tax relief on the **whole** cost of Florence's car, as a 'balancing allowance', as well as on the National Insurance it has paid. The total value of this relief at 31.125% (see Section 2.3) amounts to £12,245 (£36,000 + £3,341 = £39,341 x 31.125%).

This produces an overall **net saving** for the whole exercise of £540 (£12,245 - £6,273 - £2,091 - £3,341), which leaves Florence and Balaclava Limited £6,290 better off than if she had just taken a dividend to enable her to buy the car!

Similar savings might be achieved using other depreciating assets which have some element of business use, such as computers or mobile phones.

Tax Tip – Timing Dividend Payments

In the above analysis, as throughout this guide, we have grossed up payments to the director in order to account for the tax arising on those payments themselves and leave the director with the appropriate net sum after tax.

This is the right principle to use in order to carry out all of the comparisons we need for the 'Salary versus Dividends' question in all of the previous chapters.

However, in a case like Florence above, it may make more sense to only pay the dividend which is actually required at the time. Why? Because if she sticks to her modest salary of just £20,000 again next year, there will be scope to pay out around £19,000 of tax free dividends in 2009/10. These tax free dividends would then provide ample funds to pay the Income Tax due on 31st January 2010 without the need for any grossing up.

Using this method, the Income Tax arising on a £36,000 dividend paid to fund her car purchase would be just £4,312 (£17,248.50 x 25%).

Better still, however, when using the car bonus, there would be no need to pay any dividend in 2008/9 at all. The £6,273 required to pay Florence's Income Tax bill could be funded by way of a tax free dividend in 2009/10.

On this basis, the car bonus would produce an overall **net saving** of £2,631 (£12,245 - £6,273 - £3,341) which would then leave Florence and Balaclava Limited £6,943 (£2,631 + £4,312) better off than if she had simply taken a dividend to fund her car purchase.

Directors with Independent Resources

The analysis set out above is based on the premise that the director needs to extract the necessary funds to purchase the car.

It is worth noting, however, that a significant net saving can sometimes still be achieved (e.g. £2,631 in Florence's case), even if the director could have afforded to buy the car anyway.

Closing Down Sale – Offer Must End 1st April 2009!

Sadly, the technique described above will not work so well when the car is transferred to the director on or after 1st April 2009.

From that date, expenditure on company cars is to be 'pooled' for capital allowances purposes meaning that the £36,000 balancing allowance in our example would not arise.

Instead, the company would only obtain a 'writing down allowance' on the car. For more expensive cars, these allowances will usually be at just 10% per annum on the remaining unrelieved balance of expenditure. Hence, in our example, Balaclava Limited would obtain an allowance of just £3,600 on Florence's car in the year of purchase, followed by allowances of £3,240 in the next year, £2,916 in the third year, and so on.

Anyone wishing to use the 'car bonus' technique should therefore be sure to transfer the car to the director by 31st March 2009.

The Double Deduction Myth

A few years ago there was a school of thought that a 'car bonus' could be used to obtain a double deduction for Corporation Tax purposes – the balancing allowance described above **AND** a deduction as director's remuneration for the market value of the car at the date of the transfer to the director.

This is not the case and HM Revenue and Customs' own manual confirms that the company may claim **either** a balancing allowance **or** a deduction for director's remuneration in respect of the car's value at the date of transfer, but **not both**.

What is not yet clear is whether a deduction for director's remuneration will still be available on a 'car bonus' after 31st March 2009 when the balancing allowance is no longer available.

Chapter 15

The Third Way - Capital Growth

15.1 MAXIMISING CAPITAL GROWTH

As we know from previous chapters, extracting profits from the company usually (though not always) has a tax cost.

It is worth bearing in mind that, with a flat rate of Capital Gains Tax at just 18%, it may often be a lot more tax efficient to sell the company rather than extract the profits and pay Income Tax and possibly National Insurance too.

Furthermore, where entrepreneur's relief is available (see Section 15.3), the shares in a small private trading company can usually be sold at an effective Capital Gains Tax rate of just 10% after being held for a mere one year or more.

Hence, it is well worth considering retaining as much profit as possible within the company, rather than extracting it, so that this highly beneficial tax rate may ultimately be obtained.

Naturally, however, as discussed in Chapter 7, the situations where there is an apparent *negative* cost involved in paying a salary, or a *nil* cost in paying a dividend, should be exploited first.

Example

To illustrate the potential benefits of the capital growth route we will look at two individuals, Greedy and Happy and their companies, coincidentally called Greedy Limited and Happy Limited.

Both companies are trading companies (for entrepreneur's relief purposes) and were set up and commenced trading on 1st April 2008 with an issued share capital of only £100.

Both companies perform extremely well and generate profits before tax of £200,000 in each of the years ending 31st March 2009 and 2010 before being sold on 1st April 2010.

Greedy (living up to his name) wishes to extract all available profits from Greedy Limited each year.

Having reviewed Table D, he concludes that he should do this as follows:

i)   *Firstly, he pays himself a salary of £5,435. This has no cost for Income Tax or National Insurance purposes and is fully deductible for Corporation Tax purposes (thus reducing the company's taxable profit to £194,565).*

ii)   *Secondly, he pays himself a dividend equal to the remaining net profits after Corporation Tax.*

(Greedy decides to ignore the fact that a salary of £6,035 would be slightly more beneficial for the year ending 31st March 2010. Although this would yield a net saving of £6.10, he can't be bothered with the paperwork.)

For the year ending 31st March 2009, Greedy Limited will pay Corporation Tax at 21% (see Section 2.3), i.e. £40,859, thus leaving a profit after tax of £153,706 to be paid to Greedy as a dividend.

From Section 2.9, we know that Greedy is exempt from Income Tax on the first £31,860 of his dividend, leaving £121,846 exposed to a 25% tax charge, equating to £30,462.

For the year ending 31st March 2010, Greedy Limited will pay Corporation Tax at 22% (see Section 2.3), i.e. £42,804, thus leaving a profit after tax of £151,761 to be paid to Greedy as a dividend.

Sticking with the 2008/9 tax bands for the sake of illustration, £119,901 (£151,761 - £31,860) of this dividend will be exposed to Income Tax at 25%, thus giving rise to a charge of £29,975.

Combining all this, we see that Greedy has so far received a total sum of £255,900 (£5,435 + £5,435 + £153,706 - £30,462 + £151,761 - £29,975).

Happy, on the other hand, is content to withdraw only a modest level of income from Happy Limited and to re-invest the remainder within the company.

Happy has seen both Table D and Section 2.9, so he decides to pay himself a salary of £5,435 and a dividend of £31,860 each year (he also ignores the minor saving of £6.10 for a salary of £6,035 in the second year).

These sums, as we know, are tax free, leaving Happy Limited to reinvest the remainder of its after tax profits in growing the business.

The amounts retained by Happy Limited are therefore equal to Greedy's taxable dividends, i.e. £121,846 for the year ending 31st March 2009 and £119,901 for the year ending 31st March 2010; or £241,747 in total.

Selling Up

After two years, Greedy and Happy both decide to sell their companies.

For the sake of illustration, we will make the very simplistic assumption that the value of each company equates to the original £100 invested plus the amounts reinvested in the business.

Naturally, this is simplistic but not without some justification since funds reinvested would tend to enhance the company's value.

Greedy therefore simply gets back his original £100 (rather like cashing in a premium bond). No gain, no Capital Gains Tax and his overall net profit after tax remains the £255,900 of net proceeds withdrawn over the last two years.

Happy, on the other hand, will receive proceeds of £241,847 (his original £100 plus retained profits of £241,747). This gives him a capital gain of £241,747, which is reduced by four ninths to £134,304 by entrepreneur's relief (see Section 15.3).

After deducting his annual Capital Gains Tax exemption (assumed to remain at the 2008/9 level of £9,600), Happy is left with a taxable gain of £124,704. His Capital Gains Tax liability at 18% is therefore £22,447.

This leaves Happy with a net gain after tax from his sale of £219,300. Adding this to two year's worth of annual salaries at £5,435 and dividends of £31,860, gives Happy an overall total profit from Happy Limited of £293,890.

Analysis of the Greedy-Happy Example

- The first, and most important, point to note is that Happy's more prudent reinvestment approach has left him some £37,990 (£293,890 - £255,900) better off after a two year period. To put that into context, that amounts to a 15% improvement in the overall return achieved.

- As we saw in Chapter 7, if Happy had not wished to extract quite so much from the company each year, he could have achieved the same result by reinvesting part of his dividends into the company in the form of a loan account.

- Naturally, this example relies, as many examples do, on a great many assumptions. However, in reality, the reinvestment of profit in the company will generally lead to even greater rates of capital growth, thus improving the 'Happy' scenario still further.

15.2 INVESTMENT COMPANIES

Even without the availability of entrepreneur's relief, the new 18% flat rate of Capital Gains Tax still represents a saving on the tax paid on either bonuses or dividends by higher rate taxpayers.

This can be demonstrated by returning to our example.

Example Revisited

Let us now assume that everything is exactly the same as in the example in the previous section except that Happy Limited and Greedy Limited are both investment companies and Happy is not therefore eligible for entrepreneur's relief on the sale of his shares.

Happy can still deduct his annual exemption of £9,600 from his capital gain of £241,747 to leave him with a taxable gain of £232,147. His Capital Gains Tax liability at 18% will therefore now be £41,786.

This still leaves Happy with a net gain after tax from his sale of £199,961. Adding this to two year's worth of annual salaries at £5,435 and dividends of £31,860, now gives Happy an overall total profit of £274,551.

Greedy's position is unchanged since he did not have a capital gain and he therefore still has the same net profit of £255,900.

The revised example shows that the capital reinvestment strategy still produces a saving when entrepreneur's relief is not available. In this case, Happy is still £18,651 (£274,551 - £255,900), or 7.3%, better off than Greedy.

The position described in the revised example above might apply to a property investment company or any other company which is not a qualifying company for entrepreneur's relief purposes but which, nevertheless, is still not a close investment holding company (see Section 9.7).

Using the same approach for a close investment holding company, based on the example above, would yield total net profits of £236,930 for Greedy and £253,810 for Happy. Hence, the capital reinvestment strategy remains worthwhile for almost any type of company.

15.3 ENTREPRENEURS' RELIEF

Entrepreneurs' relief was introduced with effect from 6th April 2008. Where a capital gain qualifies for entrepreneurs' relief, four ninths of the gain arising is exempted, thus reducing the effective rate of Capital Gains Tax from 18% to 10%.

Entrepreneurs' relief is available on the disposal of shares or securities in a 'personal company'.

The definition of a 'personal company' for the purposes of entrepreneurs' relief is broadly as follows:

    i)   The individual holds at least 5% of the ordinary share capital

    ii) The holding under (i) provides at least 5% of the voting rights

    iii) The company is a trading company (see below)

    iv) The individual is an officer or employee of the company (an 'officer' includes a director or company secretary)

Each of these rules must be satisfied for the period of at least one year prior to the disposal in question or, where the company has ceased trading, for at least one year prior to the cessation. In the latter case, the disposal must take place within three years after cessation.

Each individual may only claim entrepreneurs' relief on a maximum cumulative lifetime total of £1m of capital gains. Thereafter, the Capital Gains Tax rate on all further capital gains will revert to 18%.

Safeguarding Entrepreneurs' Relief

For a director/shareholder to qualify for entrepreneur's relief on a sale of shares in their company, the company must qualify as a trading company for entrepreneur's relief purposes.

The retention of excessive cash funds within the company, well beyond its trading requirements, could jeopardise that trading status.

This is a new, complex and still evolving area of tax law, so it is difficult to be too definitive about all of the situations which could result in a deemed loss of trading status.

It is, however, possible that the retention of surplus funds, beyond normal working capital requirements, in excess of 20% of the company's net assets, would result in the loss of entrepreneur's relief.

This is not to say that a company with surplus funds equal to 19% of its net assets is completely safe from attack, as there are other tests which might apply.

For this purpose, 'surplus funds' includes not only surplus cash, but also any other non-trading assets or investments held by the company.

Hence, in order to safeguard the company's trading status, and thus also the director/shareholder's entrepreneur's relief, it may sometimes be necessary to extract surplus funds out of the company, even when this gives rise to a short-term tax cost.

On the other hand, however, even without entrepreneur's relief, the reinvestment of surplus funds within the company may still be more beneficial, as we saw in Section 15.2.

These situations will therefore each need to be considered individually and the conflicting factors weighed up in each case. It is a question of whether extracting some funds at a cost of 25% is worthwhile in order to prevent the effective Capital Gains Tax rate on the remaining value in the company increasing from 10% to 18%.

The benefit of retaining funds within the company *for trading purposes* is more clear-cut and should usually result in quite substantial long-term tax savings.

15.4 GUIDING PRINCIPLES

Having analysed all of the factors involved, and also worked through a few examples, what guiding principles have emerged when we look at the three-way choice of salary, dividend or capital growth?

Firstly, it is clear that any funds which can be extracted from the company with an overall negative tax cost should be 'extracted'. Remember always that 'extracted' might mean a deemed payment of funds which can then be left outstanding on a director's loan account.

Typically, this will be salaries equal to the National Insurance earnings threshold or the director's personal allowance, although sometimes extending a little further.

Secondly, extracting profits by way of dividend at zero tax cost will usually achieve further savings in the long run. The opportunity to pay zero cost dividends usually applies when the director/shareholder is not yet into higher rate Income Tax.

Having exhausted the negative and zero cost profit extraction options, it then becomes preferable, from a purely tax perspective, to retain funds within the company and reinvest them for capital growth.

This, of course, is reliant on four key (and perhaps slightly flawed) assumptions:

a) The director/shareholder does not need to extract further funds from the company.
b) A sale of the company is in prospect within the foreseeable future.
c) The retention of additional funds does not alter the company's trading status.
d) The position will not be altered by future changes to the tax system.

In most cases, therefore, more detailed analysis will become necessary. Even so, it nevertheless remains worthwhile to bear in mind the additional benefits of capital growth within the company.

Chapter 16

Other Important Points

16.1 PERSONAL SERVICE COMPANIES

Those who are unfortunate enough to have a company classed as a 'personal service company' must operate the infamous 'IR35' regime.

Broadly speaking, a 'personal service company' derives its profits wholly or mainly from the provision of professional services by the company's director/shareholder. Typically, this will tend to apply to companies run by I.T. consultants, public relations consultants and others where the personal skills of one individual are really the main asset of the company's business.

When 'IR35' applies, the company must pay tax, in broadly the same way as under the PAYE system (including National Insurance), as if the director had been paid a notional salary equal to the excess of the company's 'relevant income' over any actual salary paid to the director.

'Relevant income' for this purpose means any of the company's trading receipts from any contracts with third party customers which HM Revenue & Customs deem to be merely disguised employment contracts. A small, and not very generous, notional deduction is allowed in respect of the company's own running expenses (not the **actual** running expenses).

The company still pays Corporation Tax on its remaining profits as normal, leading to a severe danger of punitive double taxation charges on the same income.

The practical effect of all this is that anyone whose company is caught by 'IR35' would be unable to fully benefit from following the advice contained in this guide, as the actual or potential impact of any deemed 'notional salary' would have to be taken into account.

The best way to safeguard against 'IR35' is to ensure that all customer contracts are clearly not disguised employment contracts.

This is an extremely complex subject in its own right, but I will just briefly mention two of the best defences against an accusation of 'disguised employment'. These are to ensure that:

i) The contract carries a 'right of substitution', i.e. the right to send another person to do the work in place of the director/shareholder, **and** this right is **actually exercised** from time to time.

ii) There is no 'mutuality of obligation', i.e. you should avoid allowing a situation to develop where there is an expectation that the customer will always provide you with work and you will always be available to carry out work for them.

16.2 INCOME SHIFTING: THE GATHERING STORM

A severe problem looms just ahead in the near future for many director/shareholders attempting to extract funds from their company tax efficiently.

In yet another attack on the UK's small and medium-sized business sector, the proposed 'income shifting' legislation, now expected to come into force on 6th April 2009, may potentially affect almost everyone with a business set up as a company or a partnership.

Family businesses and couples in business are the most likely targets of the new legislation, although, at present, it appears that no-one is really safe from attack except for sole traders and other 'one man bands' (and the Government has found other ways to attack them!).

In this guide we are, of course, concerned only with companies but the proposed new legislation may affect almost any company paying dividends.

The proposed new legislation is the latest, and perhaps final, episode of a long-running saga called 'Arctic Systems' which all sprang from an attack on some basic tax planning for a 'husband and wife' company.

Before we look at the wider implications of the new legislation, therefore, let's take a look at that original attack which sparked it all off.

Dividends to Spouses or Partners

Many companies are owned by couples. Since the introduction of 'separate taxation' in 1990, these 'husband and wife' companies have often provided a useful mechanism for doubling the amount of tax-free income that could be paid out as dividends. Each spouse or partner is entitled to their own personal allowance and basic rate tax band which, when combined, are available to shelter up to a total of £73,503 in dividends from Income Tax (at 2008/9 tax rates).

For many couples, be they married, unmarried, or in a civil partnership, owning and managing their own company, this strategy has worked well for many years and continues to work well today.

A few years ago, however, HM Revenue & Customs started attacking small 'husband and wife' companies.

In essence, they took a dislike to any tax planning which utilised the payment of dividends to a non-working spouse.

At first, HM Revenue & Customs' attack seemed to focus on any arrangements involving complex share structures which effectively enabled the husband or wife of the main controlling shareholder to receive dividend income without having any real involvement in the company or its business.

At one stage, it had therefore been thought that keeping the share structure to a single class of ordinary shares would avoid these problems.

Since the emergence of the 'Arctic Systems' case in September 2004, however, this strategy has been under the threat of attack by HM Revenue & Customs whenever the company is owned by a couple and one spouse or partner does not carry out a fully active role in the company's business.

In this infamous case, HM Revenue & Customs argued that, by not taking a full commercial rate of salary out of the company, a taxpayer was making a settlement in favour of his partner who held shares in the company. Where a person makes a settlement in favour of another person, the income received by that other person can, under certain circumstances, be treated for tax purposes as belonging to the person who made the settlement.

The case involved a married couple, Mr and Mrs Jones, who held perfectly normal ordinary shares in their own company. However, because Mr Jones performed all the work that gave the company its profits, but did not receive a commercial rate of salary for that work, HM Revenue & Customs attempted to deem all of the dividend income to belong to him.

HM Revenue & Customs originally won the 'Arctic Systems' case in the High Court. Thankfully, however, the High Court decision was later overturned by both the Court of Appeal and the House of Lords.

Why then, is there still a risk?

Firstly, whilst the decision which was finally handed down in the House of Lords in July 2007 was a well deserved victory for the taxpayers (and all our thanks must go to Mr & Mrs Jones for 'sticking it out' all the way to the Lords), sadly it was not quite a complete victory.

The Lords actually decided that the structure used in the Arctic Systems case *did* represent a settlement. The taxpayers only won due to a technical argument based on an exemption available to married couples and civil partners.

So, here's the quandary: so far, HM Revenue & Customs have been attacking married couples. Ultimately, they have lost, but, in doing so, part of their argument has been vindicated; they only lost because their intended victims were a married couple. What then, is there to stop them from now attacking unmarried couples, families and other people in business together?

Secondly, in the immediate aftermath of this landmark decision by the highest Court in the land, our new Darling Chancellor announced, almost before the ink was dry at the House of Lords, that new legislation would be introduced to reverse this decision.

One has to ask what on Earth the point was of a long, protracted and expensive legal case if the Government's intention all along was to change the law anyway. It's rather like a World Cup final going all the way to a penalty shoot-out only for FIFA to announce they were changing the rules so that the losers could win anyway. Talk about 'moving the goalposts'!

The Government's behaviour in this matter is truly diabolical. It seems that, if they don't get their way in court, they'll make sure that they get it some other way.

So, I am sorry dear reader, but despite the House of Lords' decision, the 'Arctic Systems' saga continues. HM Revenue & Customs clearly have a strong objection to couples using companies to mitigate their tax bills through dividend payments to a non-working spouse and they intend to have their way at whatever price.

I just wonder how many poor couples HM Revenue & Customs will need to persecute before they've paid the legal fees for the 'Arctic Systems' case?

The Proposed Income Shifting Legislation

It now seems that HM Revenue & Customs are ultimately likely to get their way, with new legislation enabling them to deem all of the dividends paid by a company owned by a couple to belong, for Income Tax purposes, to the one spouse or partner who is the main contributor to the day-to-day running of the business.

In fact, draft legislation published in December 2007 went much further than the Arctic Systems case and, if enacted, would have enabled HM Revenue and Customs to attack dividends received by **any person**.

The draft legislation would have empowered HM Revenue and Customs to deem dividends received by one person to belong, for Income Tax purposes, to another person whenever they perceived that dividends were being allocated in a 'non-commercial' way in order to reduce the total tax burden of the company owners.

The greatest problem with the draft legislation was that HM Revenue and Customs would have had the right to decide what a commercial payment was. This was truly preposterous since, as anyone in business knows, measuring the value of each person's input into the business is an extremely complex matter depending on a whole host of different factors, many of which are impossible to measure objectively.

In short, the proposed legislation was truly unworkable and in danger of creating some ludicrously unfair and unreasonable results.

On top of all this, the very fact that the Government is trying to suggest that dividends need to be 'earned' is ridiculous in itself.

It seems that, in the Government's eyes, an investor in a company can only receive dividends if they actually work in the business!

In my view, this stance runs contrary to basic principles of UK law which have stood for over a century. What the Government is effectively saying is that a dividend is not, as it should be, a reward for investment but, instead, a reward for effort, like a salary.

For some reason, however, this peculiar attitude only seems to apply to private companies. There does not appear to be any suggestion that all of the dividends paid by quoted companies need to be allocated to their executive directors, for example. Under this Government, there seems to be one rule for 'The City' and another rule for the poor hard-working small and medium-sized businessman and businesswoman!

Thankfully, the proposed legislation has now been postponed to permit a further period of consultation. (In other words, they got the first draft spectacularly wrong!) It would therefore now appear that the new 'income shifting' legislation is not likely to come into force until 6th April 2009.

258

When the new rules do come into force, however, they could cost some company owners almost £10,000 per year in extra Income Tax for **each** so-called non-working shareholder.

Example

Homer is the managing director of Iliad Trading Limited, a successful trading company making profits of over £200,000 per annum after paying Homer's salary of £50,000.

Homer owns 20% of the shares in the company. His wife Helen and his three sons Hector, Paris and Troy also own 20% of the shares each and each of them has no other income of their own.

In 2009/10, the company pays a total dividend of £200,000, i.e. £40,000 to each shareholder.

Homer will have an Income Tax bill of £10,000 on his dividend but each of the other shareholders will have a bill of just £812 (using 2008/9 tax rates for the sake of illustration).

Let us suppose, however, that HM Revenue and Customs deem the dividends paid to Helen, Hector, Paris and Troy to belong to Homer for Income Tax purposes under new income-shifting legislation coming into force with effect from 6th April 2009.

Homer will now have to pay Income Tax at an effective rate of 25% on the whole £200,000 dividend paid by the company, i.e. £40,000.

The additional cost to the family will therefore be a total of £36,752 (£40,000 – 4 x £812).

Will This Really Happen?

Given that the Government's first attempt at this legislation has been abandoned, we cannot be sure what form the final version will take, although it does appear that HM Revenue and Customs are out to cast their net pretty wide and will be hoping to catch married and unmarried couples alike, as well as many family companies and anyone else who catches their eye too!

Personally, I would tend to argue that most trading businesses, which carry a far higher degree of commercial risk than the sort of personal service company used by Mr & Mrs Jones in the Arctic Systems case, should not be subject to any income-shifting rules.

Sadly, that's just my opinion and time will tell just how widely the new rules will be drawn and, more importantly, how they will be applied in practice.

In the meantime, at least we have a bit of 'breathing space' during 2008/9 before any new rules come into force.

What Should We Do In the Meantime?

For the time being, married couples and civil partnerships might wish to 'make hay while the sun shines' and ensure that they make the most of the current position this year, safe in the knowledge that HM Revenue and Customs' attack in the Arctic Systems case has failed.

A little more caution is warranted for unmarried couples, family companies and others with their own company, as there remain significant doubts over whether they are safe from attack under the current law.

Nevertheless, in all cases, it does look like 2008/9 may be the last year that many company owners are free to plan their affairs as tax efficiently as possible without interference from HM Revenue and Customs. Hence, even those who are not protected by the Arctic Systems decision may well be better to make the most of things this year before the new legislation comes into force.

Planning for the New Legislation

In the longer-term, all company owners will need to take precautions to avoid problems under whatever 'income shifting' rules we end up with after April 2009.

The position is likely to depend on how much each shareholder is involved in the company's business.

Couples and families are likely to be exposed to the greatest risks.

Looking forward, therefore, the main tax-planning point for everyone with their own company is to make sure that each shareholder is actively involved in the company's business.

Bear in mind here that Mrs Jones, the wife in the 'Arctic Systems' case, did work in the company's business in an administrative capacity and HM Revenue & Customs still chose to attack Mr Jones.

To be as safe as possible from attack, therefore, each shareholder really needs to be working 'at the coal face' in the actual operation of the company's business.

It is also worth considering that we already have other legislation which deems a business partner to be 'non-active' when they work an average of less than ten hours per week in the partnership's business.

It is quite possible, therefore, that the final version of the income-shifting legislation coming into force in April 2009 may also deem shareholders to be 'non-active' when they work less than ten hours per week in the company's business.

Another potential safeguard from attack is therefore to ensure that each shareholder is working an average of at least ten hours per week in the company's business.

16.3 BUSINESS PROPERTY HELD BY DIRECTORS

Many director/shareholders own their company's trading premises personally, outside the company.

This provides another potential profit extraction method: rent.

Subject to the wealth warning set out below, rent is generally an efficient method of profit extraction.

As with most other payments, however, this is dependent on the availability of Corporation Tax relief and this, in turn, means that the rent must not exceed a normal market rate.

For directors under state retirement age, the effect of charging their company rent is much the same as charging interest (see

Chapter 7), except that there is no need for the company to deduct Income Tax at source from the payment (unless the director is non-UK resident) and the 10% starting rate band will not be available.

For directors over state retirement age, the effect of any rent received will be exactly the same as additional salary (see Chapter 10). In view of the wealth warning below, therefore, it will generally be preferable for these directors to be paid in other ways.

Wealth Warning

Charging rent after 5th April 2008 on business premises used by your own company may result in the restriction, or loss, of entrepreneur's relief on the property in the event of a sale.

16.4 DIRECTORS WITH OTHER INCOME

In Section 2.18, we saw the impact of other sources of income on the effective marginal tax rates suffered by a director on salary or bonus payments.

In this last section, it therefore just remains for us to look at the resultant cost of paying bonuses or additional salary to a director where one of the 'abnormal' effective marginal tax rates seen in Section 2.18 applies.

The results in this section apply only to directors under state retirement age. The position for directors over state retirement age who have other sources of income was covered in detail in Chapter 10.

The Taxcafe Computer Model for Directors with Other Income

As usual, the amounts given in the 'From' column in the tables in this section represent the costs for a bonus paid out of an accounting period ending on 31st July 2007 and the amounts given in the 'To' column represent the costs for a bonus paid out of an accounting period ending on 31st March 2010. The costs for all intermediate accounting periods will lie somewhere between the 'From' figure and the 'To' figure.

These tables only apply where one of the 'abnormal' effective marginal tax rates seen in Section 2.18 arises. In other cases, tables A, B and C in Appendix A continue to apply.

Company Profits up to £300,000

Director's Marginal Tax Rate	Total Tax on £100 (net) of: Bonus		Dividend
	From	To	
10%	£10.37	£13.33	£0.00
20%	£0.83	-£2.50	£0.00
41%*	£54.22	£49.13	£0.00
43.5%	£61.05	£55.72	£33.33
51%	£85.70	£79.56	£33.33
53.5%	£95.68	£89.21	£33.33

Company Profits between £300,000 and £1,500,000

Director's Marginal Tax Rate	Total Tax on £100 (net) of: Bonus		Dividend
	From	To	
10%	-£25.18	-£21.67	£0.00
20%	-£15.83	-£11.88	£0.00
41%*	£28.73	£34.79	£0.00
43.5%	£34.43	£40.75	£33.33
51%	£55.00	£62.29	£33.33
53.5%	£63.34	£71.02	£33.33

Company Profits over £1,500,000

Director's Marginal Tax Rate	Total Tax on £100 (net) of: Bonus		Dividend
	From	To	
	-	-	
10%	£22.22	£20.00	£0.00
	-	-	
20%	£12.50	£10.00	£0.00
41%*	£33.83	£37.65	£0.00
43.5%	£39.75	£43.75	£33.33
51%	£61.14	£65.75	£33.33
53.5%	£69.81	£74.66	£33.33

* - The 41% rate used here refers to the situation where the director has savings income and this rate arises on salary or bonuses between £6,035 and £8,355 (see Section 2.18). It does not refer to the usual 41% rate normally applying where the director's income exceeds £40,835.

'Total Tax' means total Income Tax and National Insurance suffered by both the company and the director, less the Corporation Tax relief obtained.

In each case, the £100 referred to in the above tables is the net sum in the director/shareholder's hands after all applicable taxes.

Conclusions

Referring back to Section 2.18, we can see that, despite the presence of other income, the above tables generally tell us to continue paying the director a salary of at least £5,435 (i.e. where the 10% and 20% rates apply).

There is one minor exception. For companies with profits under £300,000, the model tells us to restrict any bonus or salary payments in order to avoid the effective 20% marginal tax rate where the payment would come out of an accounting period ended on or before 31st March 2008. Simple answer: charge it in the next accounting period!

As we saw in Section 2.18, salary or bonus payments between £5,435 and £6,035 may be subject to marginal tax rates of 11%, 21% or 31% where other income is present.

Each of these coincides with one of the 'normal' marginal tax rates and the question of whether to increase the director's salary to £6,035 (or to £6,035 less the amount of other income, where this is less than £600) can therefore be answered by referring to our old friend Table D in Appendix A (with suitable adaptation: the 11% rate equates to income between £5,435 and £6,035; the 21% rate to income between £40,040 and £40,835 and the 31% rate to income between £6,035 and £40,040).

Where any of the 'abnormal' rates listed above which are greater than 20% apply, the above tables tell us to pay dividends.

As usual, more detailed analysis will be required in any case where the payment itself may potentially cause a change in the director's or the company's effective marginal tax rate.

In addition to the marginal rates set out above, it is possible for a director with more than £35,400 of other taxable income (including dividend tax credits where applicable) to suffer effective marginal tax rates of 40% or even 42.5% on the first £5,435 of salary or bonus payments (see Section 10.11 if you want to see how the 42.5% rate arises).

Where the 40% rate arises, a salary of £5,435 is still beneficial unless the company has profits of less than £300,000 and the salary is charged in an accounting period ended on or before 31st March 2008. The same simple answer as above can be used here!

Where the 42.5% rate arises, a salary of £5,435 only remains beneficial if the company has profits of more than £300,000. (It may be worth bearing the points made in Section 12.8 in mind though.)

Appendix A

Tax Planning Tables

Our main tax planning tables are reproduced again here for ease of reference.

Table A

Total net tax suffered on an additional *net* £100 of bonus or dividend: company profits up to £300,000

Director's Income	Total Tax on £100 (net) of:		
	Bonus		**Dividend**
	From	**To**	
Up to £5,435	£19.33	£22.00	£0.00
£5,435 to £6,035	£2.24	-£1.14	£0.00
£6,035 to £40,040	£31.87	£27.51	£0.00
£40,040 to £40,835	£15.18	£11.37	£0.00
Over £40,835	£54.22	£49.13	£33.33

Table B

Total net tax suffered on an additional *net* £100 of bonus or dividend: company profits between £300,000 and £1,500,000

Director's Income	Total Tax on £100 (net) of:		
	Bonus		**Dividend**
	From	**To**	
Up to £5,435	£32.67	£29.50	£0.00
£5,435 to £6,035	£14.66	£10.65	£0.00
£6,035 to £40,040	£10.08	£15.25	£0.00
£40,040 to £40,835	-£3.86	£0.66	£0.00
Over £40,835	£28.73	£34.79	£33.33

Table C

Total net tax suffered on an additional *net* £100 of bonus or dividend: company profits over £1,500,000

Director's Income	Total Tax on £100 (net) of:		Dividend
	Bonus		
	From	**To**	
Up to £5,435	£30.00	£28.00	£0.00
£5,435 to £6,035	£11.28	-£8.75	£0.00
£6,035 to £40,040	£14.43	£17.70	£0.00
£40,040 to £40,835	-£0.05	£2.81	£0.00
Over £40,835	£33.83	£37.65	£33.33

Table D

Overview of Model Results 2008/2009

Director's Income	Company Profit		
	Up to £300,000	**£300,000 to £1.5M**	**Over £1.5M**
Up to £5,435	Bonus	Bonus	Bonus
£5,435 to £6,035	Dividend for APs ending by 30/4/2009	Bonus	Bonus
£6,035 to £40,040	Dividend	Dividend	Dividend
£40,040 to £40,835	Dividend	Bonus for APs ending by 28/2/2009	Dividend*
Over £40,835	Dividend	Bonus for APs ending by 31/12/2008	Dividend

'AP' = Accounting Period

* - see note in Section 3.4

Table E

Increase in Director's Taxable Income

Director's Income	Increase caused by £100 net Bonus	Increase caused by £100 net Dividend
Up to £5,435	£100.00	£111.11
£5,435 to £6,035	£112.36	£111.11
£6,035 to £40,040	£144.93	£111.11
£40,040 to £40,835	£126.58	£111.11
Over £40,835	£169.49	£148.15

Table F

Reduction in Company's Taxable Profit (or cost to company)

Director's Income	Reduction in profit caused by £100 net Bonus
Up to £5,435	£100.00
£5,435 to £6,035	£126.74
£6,035 to £40,040	£163.48
£40,040 to £40,835	£142.78
Over £40,835	£191.19

Sample Documentation

1. Company Memorandum

MEMORANDUM

Memorandum issued by Standard Ltd, 100 London Road, London, ZZ10 1AA.

Date: 24th December 2008.

To: All directors of Standard Ltd.

Bonuses in respect of the accounting period ended 31st December 2008 will be determined in accordance with the formula set out in the company memorandum dated 1st November 2008 as soon as the company's final trading results for the period have been established and will be paid to eligible directors as soon as practicable thereafter.

Signed

H. Godwinson,
Company Secretary
24th December 2008

2. Director's Board Meeting Minute

BOARD MINUTE

Minutes of a Meeting of Directors of Standard Ltd held at 100 London Road, London, ZZ10 1AA on 31st March 2009.

Present: Mr A B Crown – Director
             Mrs A B Crown – Director
             Mr E F Bloodaxe - Director

             Mr H Godwinson – Company Secretary

Motions:

1) It was recommended that the company pay a dividend of £2.50 per Ordinary share out of the profits for the year ended 31st December 2008, to be paid on 1st April 2009.

2) The directors noted the company's excellent trading results for the year ended 31st December 2008 with satisfaction. In view of these excellent results and pursuant to the company's memorandum of 24th December 2008, the board resolved to pay a bonus of £100,000 to Mr Eric Bloodaxe out of the profits for the year ended 31st December 2008.

3) No other motions.

Signed _____   Date _____
         (Mr A B Crown)

Notes (Not Part of the Minute)

The minutes of a directors' board meeting should:

a) *Indicate the persons present.*
b) *Include sufficient information to describe how directors reasonably came to reasonable decisions.*
c) *Include details of any conflicts of interest or abstainment from voting.*
d) *Be signed by a director present at the meeting.*
e) *Be retained with the company's statutory records.*

Regarding point (a) above, a quorum may need to be present for the meeting to be valid. This depends on the company's own constitution as set out in its Articles of Association.

3. Member's General Meeting Minute

GENERAL MEETING OF MEMBERS

Minutes of an Extraordinary General Meeting of the Ordinary Shareholders of Standard Ltd held at 100 London Road, London, ZZ10 1AA on 31st March 2009.

Present: Mr A B Crown – Ordinary shareholder
              Mrs A B Crown – Ordinary Shareholder
              Mr E F Bloodaxe - Ordinary Shareholder

              Mr H Godwinson – Company Secretary

Motions:
1) The members, all being present, agreed to accept the short notice period for the meeting.
2) The members approved the recommendation of the directors that the company pay a dividend of £2.50 per Ordinary share for the year ended 31st December 2008. Payment to be made on 1st April 2009.
3) The members approved the payment of a bonus of £100,000 to Mr Eric Bloodaxe on 31st March 2009 out of the profits for the year ended 31st December 2008.
4) No other motions.

Signed _____   Date _____
       (Mr A B Crown)

4. Dividend Voucher

Tax Voucher

Standard Limited
100 London Road, London, ZZ10 1AA

Ordinary shares of £1 each

Mr A B Crown   1st April 2009
1 Viking Crescent
York
Y1 1AA

Payment of the final dividend in respect of the year ended 31st December 2008, at the rate of £2.50 per share on the Ordinary Shares registered in your name on 31st March 2009 is enclosed herewith.

H. Godwinson, Company Secretary

Shareholding	Tax Credit	Dividend Payable	Payment Number
10,000	£2,777.78	£25,000.00	1

This voucher should be kept. It will be accepted by HM Revenue & Customs as evidence of a Tax Credit.

Appendix C

Tax Rates and Allowances: 2006/2007 to 2008/2009

	Rates	Bands, allowances, etc.		
		2006/7	2007/8	2008/9
		£	£	£
Income Tax				
Personal allowance		5,035	5,225	6,035
Starting rate band	10%	2,150	2,230	(1)
Basic rate band (2)	20%	31,150	32,370	34,800
Higher rate:	40%			
Normal higher rate threshold:		38,335	39,825	40,835

National Insurance Contributions

Class 1 – Primary	11%	) On earnings between earnings threshold and		
Class 4	8%	) upper earnings limit		
Earnings threshold		5,035	5,225	5,435
Upper earnings limit		33,540	34,840	40,040
Class 1 – Secondary	12.8%	- On earnings above earnings threshold		
Class 1 & Class 4	1%	- On earnings above upper earnings limit		
Class 2 – per week		2.10	2.20	2.30
Small earnings exception		4,465	4,635	4,825
Class 3 – per week		7.55	7.80	8.10

Pension Contributions

	2006/7	2007/8	2008/9
Annual allowance	215,000	225,000	235,000
Lifetime allowance	1.5M	1.6M	1.65M

Capital Gains Tax

Annual exemption:	2006/7	2007/8	2008/9
Individuals	8,800	9,200	9,600
Trusts	4,400	4,600	4,800

Inheritance Tax

	2006/7	2007/8	2008/9
Nil Rate Band	285,000	300,000	312,000
Annual Exemption	3,000	3,000	3,000

Pensioners, etc.

	2006/7	2007/8	2008/9
Age allowance: 65-74	7,280	7,550	9,030
Age allowance: 75 and over	7,420	7,690	9,180
MCA: born before 6/4/1935	6,065	6,285	6,535
MCA: 75 and over	6,135	6,365	6,625
MCA minimum (3)	2,350	2,440	2,540
Income limit	20,100	20,900	21,800
Blind Person's Allowance	1,660	1,730	1,800

Notes

1. For 2008/9, a 10% starting rate band of £2,320 applies to interest and other savings income only.
2. Basic rate on income other than interest, dividends and other savings income is 22% until 5 April 2008. The rate applying to dividends is 10%.
3. The Married Couples Allowance, 'MCA', is given at a rate of 10%.
4. The personal allowance and basic rate band for 2008/9 were initially set at £5,435 and £36,000 respectively but were revised to the above figures in a subsequent announcement on 13 May 2008. The initial figures will be used for PAYE purposes until September 2008, at which point all employed earners and pensioners will be subject to a tax adjustment to bring the figures given above into force. The new figures will be used for Self Assessment purposes in the normal way.

Need Affordable & Expert Tax Planning Help?

Try Taxcafe's Unique Question & Answer Service

The purpose of Taxcafe guides is to provide you with detailed guidance, giving you all the information you need to make informed decisions.

Ultimately, you may want to take further action or obtain guidance personal to your circumstances.

Taxcafe.co.uk has a unique online tax help service that provides access to highly qualified tax professionals at an affordable rate.

For more information or to take advantage of this service please visit:

www.taxcafe.co.uk/questions

Pay Less Tax!

...with help from Taxcafe's unique tax guides and software

Using a Property Company to Save Tax
By Carl Bayley

Currently a 'hot topic' for the serious property investor, this guide shows how you can significantly boost your after-tax returns by setting up your own property company and explains ALL the tax consequences of property company ownership.

"An excellent tax resource....informative and clearly written" **The Letting Update Journal**

Keeping It Simple
By James Smith BSc ACA

This plain-English guide tells you everything you need to know about small business bookkeeping, accounting, tax returns and VAT.

Property Capital Gains Tax Calculator
By Carl Bayley

This powerful piece of software will calculate in seconds the capital gains tax payable when you sell a property and help you cut the tax bill. It provides tax planning tips based on your personal circumstances and a concise summary and detailed breakdown of all calculations.

Non-Resident & Offshore Tax Planning
By Lee Hadnum LLB ACA CTA

By becoming non-resident or moving your assets offshore it is possible to cut your tax bill to zero. This guide explains what you have to do and all the traps to avoid. Also contains detailed info on using offshore trusts and companies.

"The ultimate guide to legal tax avoidance" **Shelter Offshore**

The World's Best Tax Havens
By Lee Hadnum

This book provides a fascinating insight into the glamorous world of tax havens and how you can use them to cut your taxes to zero and safeguard your financial freedom.

How to Avoid Inheritance Tax
By Carl Bayley

Making sure you adequately plan for inheritance tax could save you literally hundreds of thousands of pounds. *How to Avoid Inheritance Tax* is a unique guide which will tell you all you need to know about sheltering your family's money from the taxman. This guide is essential reading for parents, grandparents and adult children.

"Useful source of Inheritance Tax information" **What Investment Magazine**

Using a Company to Save Tax
By Lee Hadnum

By running your business through a limited company you stand to save tens of thousands of pounds in tax and national insurance every year. This tax guide tells you everything you need to know about the tax benefits of incorporation.

Salary versus Dividends
By Carl Bayley

This unique guide is essential reading for anyone running their business as a limited company. After reading it, you will know the most tax efficient way in which to extract funds from your company, and save thousands in tax!

Selling Your Business
By Lee Hadnum

This guide tells you everything you need to know about paying less tax and maximizing your profits when you sell your business. It is essential reading for anyone selling a company or sole trader business.

How to Avoid Tax on Stock Market Profits
By Lee Hadnum

This tax guide can only be described as THE definitive tax-saving resource for stock market investors and traders. Anyone who owns shares, unit trusts, ISAs, corporate bonds or other financial assets should read it as it contains a huge amount of unique tax planning information.

How to Profit from Off-Plan Property
By Alyssa and David Savage

This property investment guide tells you everything you need to know about investing in off-plan and new-build property. It contains a fascinating insight into how you can make big money from off-plan property... and avoid all the pitfalls along the way.

How to Build a £4 Million Property Portfolio: Lifetime Lessons of a Student Landlord
By Tony Bayliss

Tony Bayliss is one of the UK's most successful student property investors. In *How to Build a £4 Million Property Portfolio* he reveals all his secrets – how he picks the best and most profitable student properties; how he markets his properties and how he enjoys capital growth of 12% pa, year in year out.

280

Disclaimer

1. Please note that this Tax Guide is intended as general guidance only for individual readers and does NOT constitute accountancy, tax, investment or other professional advice. Neither Taxcafe UK Limited nor the author can accept any responsibility or liability for loss which may arise from reliance on information contained in this Tax Guide.

2. Please note that tax legislation, the law and practices by government and regulatory authorities (e.g. HM Revenue and Customs) are constantly changing. We therefore recommend that for accountancy, tax, investment or other professional advice, you consult a suitably qualified accountant, tax specialist, independent financial adviser, or other professional adviser. Please also note that your personal circumstances may vary from the general examples given in this Tax Guide and your professional adviser will be able to give specific advice based on your personal circumstances.

3. This Tax Guide covers UK taxation only and any references to 'tax' or 'taxation' in this Tax Guide, unless the contrary is expressly stated, refer to UK taxation only. Please note that references to the 'UK' do not include the Channel Islands or the Isle of Man. Foreign tax implications are beyond the scope of this Tax Guide.

4. Whilst in an effort to be helpful, this Tax Guide may refer to general guidance on matters other than UK taxation, Taxcafe UK Limited and the author are not expert in these matters and do not accept any responsibility or liability for loss which may arise from reliance on such information contained in this Tax Guide.

5. Please note that Taxcafe UK Limited has relied wholly on the expertise of the author in the preparation of the content of this Tax Guide. The author is not an employee of Taxcafe UK Limited but has been selected by Taxcafe UK Limited using reasonable care and skill to write the content of this Tax Guide.

Printed in the United Kingdom
by Lightning Source UK Ltd.
133803UK00001B/73-117/P